Tony Pastor:

DEAN OF THE VAUDEVILLE STAGE

Parker Zellers

TO

Mother and Dad

ACKNOWLEDGMENTS

This book would never have been written had it not been for the invaluable help and guidance I received from the late George Freedley, former Curator of the Theatre Collection at the New York Public Library; Helen D. Willard, Curator of the Theatre Collection at Harvard University; May Davenport Seymour, Curator of the Theatre Collection of the Museum of the City of New York; Marguerite McAneny, Custodian of the William Seymour Theatre Collection at Princeton University; and W. H. Crain, of the Hoblitzelle Theatre Arts Library of the University of Texas at Austin. I am also indebted to those many individuals who in person or by correspondence were willing to share with me their knowledge—sometimes even their personal memories—of "the good old days." My thanks also go to those colleagues who supplied encouraging words and valuable criticism along the way. And a special round of thanks to Brooks McNamara who was responsible for putting me on the Pastor trail in the first place.

P. Z.

Contents

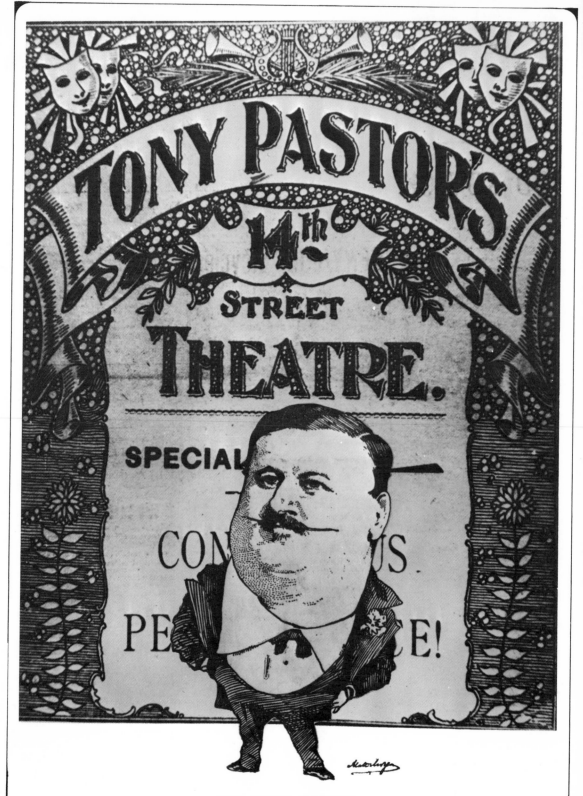

MR. TONY PASTOR.

(Caricature: courtesy of the Hoblitzelle Theatre Arts Library, The University of Texas at Austin)

Tony Pastor:

DEAN OF THE VAUDEVILLE STAGE

PARKER ZELLERS

EASTERN MICHIGAN UNIVERSITY PRESS

Ypsilanti, Michigan   1971

Foreword

Vaudeville was a crazy-quilt form of family entertainment that loomed large upon the American scene in the days when the 20th century was still young and movies had not yet become the national pastime. Millions of Americans, young and old, found delight, enchantment and escape in a kaleidoscopic stage world of singers, dancers, comics, jugglers, acrobats, magicians, hat spinners, ventriloquists, knife-throwers, trained chimpanzees and what have you, a tinseled world dedicated to the sentiment that variety is indeed the spice of life. Almost every sizable town had a Bijou or Gaiety Theatre featuring "Count them—12 Big Acts—Count Them," and booking offices routed thousands of performers over a network of circuits that covered the country from coast to coast and border to border. It was big entertainment. It was also big business.

The giants of the vaudeville industry were men like Benjamin F. Keith, Edward F. Albee, F. F. Proctor, and Percy C. Williams. In many ways, however, these men built their edifice on a foundation laid years earlier by a short, rotund entertainer and manager named Tony Pastor. The labels "Father of Vaudeville," "Dean of Vaudeville," and the like were applied to Pastor during his final years in obvious recognition of his pioneer efforts to shape, popularize, and refine this genre of entertainment in the 1860's and 1870's when it was called "variety" and was little more than saloon fare.

Pastor was just what early variety needed—an astute showman and a pugnacious reformer. He sought and won first class patronage for his shows by making them the best and the cleanest in town. His efforts to assemble and mount diverse and top-grade bills, his attention to detail, his eye for talent, and his ability to gauge accurately the tastes of the public were exceptional in variety circles. So was his crusade to free variety entertainment from the saloon trappings of drink, smoke, and coarseness. Earlier managers had attempted reforms of one kind or another, but Pastor was indisputably the first to launch a persistent, continuous, and finally successful campaign to remove variety from the saloon altogether and fashion it into respectable family fare in a theatre of its own.

Pastor's career and his influence on the evolution of the variety stage in this country have never been the subject of a comprehensive study. This present work hopes to replace the existing brief, romanticized, and frequently contradictory sketches of the showman with a more detailed, accurate, and documented study derived as far as possible from contemporary evidence. We wish that the past could have been more generous, that it could have furnished us, for example, with a Pastor diary or scrapbook or business records of his various theatres. Unfortunately, however, these have not been uncovered. As far as the business records are concerned there is good reason to believe that all his office files were dutifully destroyed according to the instructions of his will, dated January 21, 1899. But the periodicals of his day had much to say about him; several libraries have files of pertinent clippings, photographs, programs and postbills as well as articles and even letters on and by the showman. There are also many autobiographies and reminiscences by those who knew him and wrote about him. These sources have furnished most of the raw material for the present work. Commentary on Pastor by modern writers also has been utilized and measured against contemporary findings.

The titles of several key newspapers have been shortened in the following pages: The *New York Clipper* is referred to simply as the *Clipper*, the *New York Dramatic News* as the *Dramatic News*, the *New York (Dramatic) Mirror* as the *Mirror*, and *Wilkes' Spirit of the Times* as the *Spirit of the Times*. Each special library file, furthermore, has been given an appropriate symbol:

THE HOBLITZELLE THEATRE ARTS LIBRARY, THE UNIVERSITY OF TEXAS AT AUSTIN:

Tony Pastor File (T.P. file, Hoblitzelle)

THEATRE COLLECTION AT THE HARVARD UNIVERSITY LIBRARY:

Tony Pastor File (T.P. file, Harv.)
New York City Vaudeville File (N.Y.C. Vaud. file, Harv.)
Vaudeville and Variety File (V.V. file, Harv.)

THEATRE COLLECTION AT THE MUSEUM OF THE CITY OF NEW YORK:

Tony Pastor File (T.P. file, Museum, CNY)

THEATRE COLLECTION AT THE NEW YORK PUBLIC LIBRARY:

American Vaudeville File, MWEZ n.c. #4547 (American Vaud. file, NYPubl.)
Robinson Locke File, Series 11 (Robinson Locke, NYPubl.)
Tony Pastor File, MWEZ n.c. #11, 143 (T.P. file, NYPubl.)
Townsend Walsh File of Miscellaneous Programs, MWEZ n.c. #5181 (Townsend Walsh, NYPubl.)

THEATRE COLLECTION AT THE PRINCETON UNIVERSITY LIBRARY:

Tony Pastor File (T.P. file, Princeton)

P.Z.

Introduction[1]

The type of American entertainment that became known as "variety," and later as "vaudeville," developed its peculiar form during the early 1850's in conjunction with the appearance of special amusement resorts commonly referred to as "concert saloons." The proprietors of these places sought to offer their patrons the opportunity to enjoy a glass of lager or a good smoke and watch a show at the same time. The show was nothing more than an inducement for patronage and the sale of "refreshments." Light, amusing, and especially varied fare was desired to keep the customers in a happy and drinking mood, and the result was an "olio" or melange of specialty acts and skits drawn from blackface minstrelsy and the circus. This was not commonly referred to as "variety" until the 1860's; at the outset it was called simply an "entertainment" or "concert," and the establishments offering such a show were popularly branded "concert saloons."

Many proprietors tried to escape the saloon association by classifying their places as "concert rooms," "concert gardens," "music halls," etc., and by adopting fancy names like The Melodeon and The Alhambra. But regardless of their size and fancy nomenclature, these places remained essentially saloons. A proprietor of one such place summed it all up when he said: "A concert saloon is a gin mill on an improved plan, that's all, my friend."[2] Operating on "an improved plan," a saloon owner might boast of impressive decor, a variety of gambling opportunities, or a bevy of waitresses, but he always boasted of a show.

The American concert saloon may well have taken its cue from the English music hall, a tavern-annex affair that began to come into popularity in England in the late 1840's.[3] Exactly when and where the first concert saloon was founded in this country is not known, but this type of resort certainly gained its earliest foothold in New York in the early 1850's. Legend has it that a man named William Valentine opened the first such place in the city in 1848 or 1849 and that he was also the first to label his program a "variety show" because "I'm going to have a variety of things in my entertainment."[4] What establishment Valentine might have been operating at this time, however, has never been determined, and I have found no record of the man himself before 1859. In that year, according to one source, a William P. Valentine was proprietor of Vauxhall Garden, a concert saloon in the Bowery.[5]

By 1859, however, Vauxhall Garden was but one of dozens of concert saloons that dotted the lower part of the city. One of the largest and most popular of these was White's Varieties, which opened in the Bowery on September 13, 1852. Similar resorts began to appear in increasing numbers during the next few years, and by the season of 1856-57, concert saloons were common in the city, especially in the thickly settled business districts in the Bowery and along Broadway. As their number increased, so did the demand for "variety" performers, and, as Odell states, "this was the season [1856-57] of the rise in variety entertainment—a type of amusement that was to grow formidably with the years."[6]

Most of these early resorts were modest affairs, occupying small halls or sites of former small stores. There was the Broadway Free Concert Saloon, for example, and the Bowery Concert Hall, the Arcade Concert Rooms, E. Klein's Concert Saloon, and the Santa Claus Concert Hall, to name but a few. The success of these small ventures encouraged men of capital to open during the next few years such pretentious establishments as the Gaieties, the Canterbury, the American Concert Hall, and the Broadway Music Hall. As the new decade of the 1860's got underway, public excitement for variety entertainment in the concert saloons of New York was indeed intense. "The field was a springing bed of mushroom concert halls," says Odell. "Variety was in possession."[7]

The popularity of the concert saloon was by no means limited to New York. These establishments spread the idea of variety entertainment throughout the country in the late 1850's, and the new decade was not very old before there were variety resorts in most of the principal cities from coast to coast. By the mid-1860's, saloons operating on "an improved plan" began appearing in smaller communities like Lafayette, Indiana; Saginaw, Michigan; and Petersburg, Virginia. On May 13, 1865, for example, a resort operating at Mechanic's Hall in Petersburg advertised in the *Clipper:* "Talent always acceptable in this CHIEF D'OUVRE of amusement."[8] As the west opened up, almost every frontier town had its variety hall where customers could quench their thirst, gamble, and frequently brawl to the accompaniment of some type of entertainment.

The shows in the smaller resorts were generally presented on a stage erected at one end of the room. Sometimes the stage was no more than a crude platform standing unadorned against the wall. Some of these places charged a general admission fee of from 6¢ to 12¢. Others charged no admission at all, making their profit strictly on the sale of drinks, smokes, food, and the operation of gambling tables. These were often nicknamed "free concert saloons," "honky tonks," or "free-and-easies." The larger establishments were generally equipped with a regular auditorium and stage, and the admission fee depended on where a customer wanted to do his drinking. He could stand in the vicinity of the bar for one fee or have his drinks served to him in the auditorium for another.

The typical auditorium was divided into a parquette, or parquet, as the lower floor was commonly called at this time, and a gallery. Each was furnished with rows of benches, the backs of each bench fitted with a sort of wooden gutter to hold the drinking utensils. Some auditoriums were ringed with private boxes, generally enclosed in such a manner that their occupants could view the stage without being observed by the rest of the house — a perfect spot for those who, for one reason or another, wanted privacy!

The concert saloons were essentially haunts for men, and the atmosphere of even the most pretentious place was usually coarse and boisterous. The *New York Evening Post*, for example, noted in 1862 that the Broadway Music Hall was "extensively patronized by the public, especially on Saturday nights, when all parts of the house are crowded by male visitors . . .[who] wear their hats and caps at pleasure, smoke cigars and pipes, and conduct themselves generally in accordance with the popular song of 'We'll be free and easy still.' "[9] In the main, concert saloon patrons were laborers, soldiers, adventurers, idlers, ruffians, and, so we are told, "very young men who wanted to 'see life.'"[10] But occasionally "gentlemen" from reputable circles attended certain of these places in search of diversion, thrills, and feminine company.

Harry Hill's concert saloon and dance hall on Houston Street in New York was one such place. It was a honky tonk, drab and dismal, but, for some reason or other, it was noted as a popular rendezvous spot for all classes. In his description of the "sunshine and shadows" of New York life in 1869, Matthew Hale Smith claimed that at Hill's one could see "men of all grades and all degrees— officers in uniform; sergeants and officers of police without uniform; judges of courts, and leading men of the bar; merchants, jewellers, book-men, and bankers; politicians, and candidates for the high honors in the state and nation; clerks, men, boys, with all classes and kinds."[11] Hill supplied about one hundred girls to dance with his customers, but, according to Lloyd Morris, he insisted that "whatever bargains were made, alliances formed, or traps set for the unwary male, no victim must be snared while at Harry Hill's; any crime to be committed must take place elsewhere. As a result, his place was distinguished as the only 'reputable vile house' in New York."[12]

Some concert saloons tried to improve their image by insisting on some degree of decorum from their patrons. But Morris assures us that all such places "were known to be in some degree dangerous," and at the worst resorts "pleasure was intensified by the thrilling possibilities of assault, robbery and the addition to liquid refreshments of knock-out drops."[13] The general rough-and-ready character of these resorts is perhaps illustrated by a story that is supposed to have originated in Volk's Garden, a concert saloon on Bowery street in New York. Douglas Gilbert, in *American Vaudeville*, tells the story: "During the course of the bill, so runs the yarn, the manager announced to his beer-sodden patrons, 'And now, gents, Miss Lillian McTwobucks will sing "Love Among the Roses." ' Where-upon a drunk arose and in stentorian tones replied, 'She is a whore.' The unabashed manager dismissed the interruption. 'Nevertheless,' he said. 'Miss Lillian McTwobucks will still sing "Love among the Roses." ' "[14] We can only guess at what kind of response she received.

Performers had to have strong constitutions to face concert saloon audiences. A favorite act was usually met with hearty approval, but a so-so turn was either totally ignored or, worse yet, bombarded off the stage by jeers, catcalls, and a shower of peanut shells.

Women were encouraged to attend the concert saloons as lures and play-mates for the men, but the women who obliged courted a damaged reputation if, indeed, they had any reputation in the first place. Such women are generally referred to in the records as "abandoned women" and "loose women," a good number of them undoubtedly outright prostitutes. It seems highly unlikely that "respectable" women would have willingly visited such establishments unless, perhaps, on a lark with a group of curious slummers.

Several of the more prominent concert saloons, however, hoping to put their idle daytime hours to profit, offered afternoon performances aimed at the family trade. The earliest record found of such a matinee appeared in the *Clipper* for May 5, 1860: an ad for Frank Rivers' Melodeon in Philadelphia announced a "GRAND MATINEE .... SATURDAY AFTERNOON, MAY 5th, for the accommodation of FAMILIES AND CHILDREN."[15] Similar afternoon performances were offered about the same time at such popular New York spots as the Canterbury, the Broadway Music Hall and the American Concert Hall. Most advertised that all drinking and smoking would be forbidden during the matinee. The Broadway Music Hall, for example, announced in the *Spirit of the Times* on June 8, 1861: "A Grand Matinee, every Saturday afternoon at 2 o'clock, for the accommodation of Ladies and Children, on which occasion the bars will be closed, and no liquor or cigars will be sold or permitted to be used in the theatre."[16] The only information uncovered about the nature of the matinee performance itself is an undated program for the Canterbury that announced a "Ladies Matinee Every Saturday when all choice Gems of the evening performance will be given."[17] Just how successful these matinees were in drawing women and families and what class of people were represented in the audience is problematical. Journalistic notes about the matinees are rare and relatively uninformative. For instance, the *Spirit of the Times* for July 20, 1861, noted only that "the Saturday matinees for ladies have proved a highly successful feature of the Broadway Music Hall."[18] The fact that the matinee idea became a regular feature at many places suggests that the afternoon shows were at least drawing satisfactory business, female or otherwise.

One group of females always on hand in concert saloons during the regular evening hours was the waitresses. These waitresses — who represented an innovation in saloon service and were called "waiter-girls" — were considered a lost and wretched sorority by the world of respectability. One writer of the period described them as "simply a collection of poor wretches who have gone down almost to the end of their fatal career. They may retain faint vestiges of their former beauty, but that is all. They are beastly, foul-mouthed brutal wretches."[19] The waiter-girls hustled drinks, flirted with the patrons, permitted certain familiarities, and often made assignations for after hours. Sometimes they even appeared in the show. At some places the girls were offered as essentially the main attraction. The *Clipper*, for example, complained on September 15, 1860, that "too many [concert saloons] neglect nearly altogether their performances, relying upon the 'prettiest waiter girls in the city' for a full house and the sale of liquors and cigars."[20]

One establishment that the paper may have had in mind was the Gaieties in New York. Here the waiter-girls were an institution in themselves. In an ad in the *New York Herald* in January, 1860, the Gaieties promised that "in addition to the performances the most fascinating and Prettiest Young Ladies are engaged to attend the wants of the visitors. Gentlemen can rest assured of being well repaid by visiting the Gaieties, 600 Broadway, where they will be amused by seeing the 'best singing and dancing' and at the same time pass an hour in the company of the most captivating and agreeable society of young ladies they ever experienced."[21] The waiter-girls were greatly responsible for causing polite society to brand concert saloons as scurrilous and indecent dens and to look upon all that transpired there, including the variety show, with a suspicious eye. As Odell says, "the female waitress was the serpent that made variety, in its early days, an evil thing."[22] But early variety was not entirely an innocent victim by association. It was essentially stag entertainment and usually well spiced to suit the male taste.

The early variety shows tended to be boisterous and unsophisticated; the comedy was low, robust, and often quite "blue." The shows were built primarily on the elements of blackface minstrelsy: comic and sentimental songs, jig and buck-and-wing dancing, instrumental solos, and comic skits. To these were soon added circus acts, such as acrobatics, juggling, and even trapeze and tight-rope displays. Some establishments — those that were evidently hopeful of support from cultured circles — often beefed up their usual light olio with musical and vocal selections from the classical repertoire. By the late 1850's, the larger establishments were embellishing their olios with "ballet" and topping off the bill with an afterpiece. The *corps de ballet* of the concert saloon was composed of from six to a dozen more or less shapely young ladies whose terpsichorean displays ranged from a veil-waving pastoral number to a saucy, high-kicking can-can. Frequently, the dancers donned abbreviated military dress and maneuvered themselves in a drill popularly called a "Grand March of the Amazons." Pulchritude was the rule — precision the exception.

The afterpiece was a "dramatic" concoction that ran about twenty minutes and featured a return appearance by a large portion, if not all, of the performers on the bill. It was virtually an enlargement of the comic skit. The skit, however, was usually composed by or for the performers themselves and carried about in their repertoire. The afterpiece was considered the sole responsibility of the management. Scenic spectacle, moreover, was a key ingredient in afterpieces while sketches might get by with the simplest of fittings.

Sometimes the afterpiece was a madcap farce or a hearty burlesque on a popular or classic play or on some current fashion. Pantomimes were also popular as afterpieces. These were often based on a familiar Mother Goose rhyme or some other popular story and revolved around the antics of Harlequin, Columbine, Clown, and other stock *commedia* characters. Much of the entertainment was performed in dumb show, but songs and dialog were introduced freely. Still other afterpieces were specifically designed to cater to the public's taste for melodrama. These were called "sensational dramas" and were always filled with thrills and excitement. All the afterpieces were built on the flimsiest of themes or stories — the important thing was that the performers be given ample opportunity to display their particular specialties. Most of the smaller resorts omitted the afterpiece because of the added expense. When "variety" became "vaudeville" in the mid-nineties, the afterpiece disappeared altogether and a straight olio of a dozen or so turns, sketches, and an occasional one-act play comprised the standard bill.

Concert saloons increased steadily in number and in notoriety throughout the country during the Civil War. Nowhere was this growth more apparent than in New York. Many people, including the numerous soldiers assigned or on furlough in the city, evidently found escape from the gloom of the war in the glitter and laughter of the concert saloon and its various attractions. As the glitter became more dazzling and the laughter more drunken, many persons of a different character came to see these resorts as constituting an infamous outrage on public morals. By the end of 1861 much of the New York press was beginning to launch an all-out attack against these dens.

Since all the concert saloons in the city were, or at least could be, licensed by the state as both saloons and places of amusement, there was no current law that could be used to suppress them. John A. Kennedy, Superintendent of Police, noted this fact in the *New York Times* on January 5, 1862, and urged the new State Legislature "to pass an act which will enable the authorities to effectually shut-up the concert saloons in the City."[23] Urged on by Kennedy and others, the legislature took the matter under consideration and passed, on April 17, 1862, an *Act to Regulate places of public amusement in the cities and incorporated villages of this State.*

The law had three stipulations: (1) All places of amusement had to be properly licensed, (2) no "wine, beer, or spiritous liquor" could be sold or furnished in these places of amusement, and (3) no "female" was to be employed to furnish "refreshments to the audiences or spectators or any of them, at any of the exhibitions or performances" at any place of amusement.[24] It was signed by the governor on April 19.

The New York police informed proprietors of the new law and warned them to comply with the stipulations set forth or close down operations. The immediate result, as noted by the *New York Times*, was "not exactly a general suppression of the business, but a general compliance in one way or another; in reality, or by pretense; in part, or altogether; fractional, if not total. Some stopped their customers' lager, but continued the performances; others shut up shop instantly, keeping open only for the accommodation of a few private friends; others had the waiter-girls present in street clothes, as part of the audience — not as connected with the establishment, but as spectators of the performances — who obligingly chatted with the male customers, and walked about leisurely, to see that the little boy waiters attended to their business; others stopped the theatricals, but continued the singing and dancing."[25]

These subterfuges continued into May, and some of the larger resorts made scalding attacks on the new law in their advertisements. The American Concert Hall, for example, cried out in the *New York Herald* on April 28 that "the Music Hall of the masses, the Institution of the People, Rises Superior to all attacks of Bigotry and Ignorance."[26] The Canterbury boasted in the same paper on May 4 that "the Great Canterbury Cannot be Crushed. So far from being closed by the machinations of fanatical legislators and biased theatrical managers, the Great Canterbury flourishes all the more."[27] But the Canterbury did not flourish long. It was closed down and the premises sold at auction on May 15. By the end of the month numerous others, especially the smaller ones, had closed their doors as well; still others, like the Gaieties and the American Concert Hall, managed to keep operating under one subterfuge or another. In June and July the situation was relatively quiet. Bitter words had ceased, police surveillance relaxed, and by the end of the summer the entire matter seemed forgotten.

By fall, however, the period of quiet had ended. The old concert saloons began returning to their old ways, and new resorts began appearing with all the old features. The police made no open attempt to interfere. Throughout 1863 the world of the concert saloon operated as it had before the legislative action; entertainment, refreshment, and pretty waiter-girls were all available to patrons. The police still did not interfere, nor did they interfere very often or with much effect in the years to follow. Perhaps, as the *Spirit of the Times* suggested in May, 1864, "the keepers of such places have sufficient influence with the bench and the bar of New York to evade or deny the execution of any law intended to restrain their devilish business."[28] In any event, the concert saloons of New York continued to operate by one means or another for the remainder of the century.

The situation was much the same throughout the country. Crusades against the concert saloons came and went, but the resorts themselves remained. They survived moral censure and police intervention to become the night clubs — big, small, respectable, and otherwise — of the twentieth century.

Long before this, however, variety entertainment had broken away from the concert saloon to win popularity in its own right. In the years immediately following the Civil War, variety moved into regular theatres freed in part or altogether from the saloon features of drink and smoke. It strove valiantly for three decades to escape its early stigma as saloon fare and to win the stamp of approval from family audiences. Astute managers scrubbed its complexion, tamed its coarse manners, added more and more quality and polish to its production, and finally gave it a new name, "vaudeville." The result was auspicious. Variety entertainment entered the new century as a giant industry destined to charm and captivate family audiences from coast to coast for more than thirty years.

CHAPTER ONE

Burnt Cork and Sawdust

In 1830 New York was a flat city of some 200,000 nestled in the lower tip of Manhattan Island. Her skyline was pierced here and there by church steeples and by the tall masts of vessels tied up in the slips and docks on the North and East Rivers. In the residential areas along Bowery Street, Greenwich Street and Broadway, and in the northern reaches of the city around Bond Street the pace of life was slow and leisurely. But along the waterfront and in the heart of the city below Canal Street the tempo was brisk, and the air was alive with the buzz of industry and the chatter of workers, shoppers, and pleasure-seekers moving along the docks and gas-lighted streets. And it was to this impelling tempo that New York marched into and through the new decade.

She was a city very much on the move, energized in great part by the opening in 1825 of the Erie Canal which linked her waterfront and commercial interests with Albany, Buffalo, and other inland communities. This was the tempo that would carry her into the final decades of the century as the nation's major commercial center and seaport, when visitors would call her "The Empire City" and be awed by her versatility and splendor. During the 1830's New York's population grew to over 300,000 and her city limits crawled northward. From the steeple of St. Paul's Church on Broadway one could watch the chang- ing scene — shops and businesses multiplying and encroaching on the residential areas; an occasional daring six-or-seven-story tenement building rising above its neighbors; sea traffic growing heavier as dock facilities expanded; and the farms, meadows, and apple orchards above Bond Street slowly giving way to fashionable homes.

Somewhere in New York during this restless decade Antonio (Tony) Pastor was born. Exactly when and where never has been firmly established. When asked about this later in life, Pastor, with a twinkle in his eye, replied, "I was not aware of my surroundings at the time, but my parents told me that I first saw the light in Greenwich Street opposite the old Pacific Hotel on May 28,

1

1837, and they surely ought to know."[1] Greenwich Street is on the west side of the city and runs northward from Battery Park to merge into Ninth Avenue just below 14th Street. The Pacific Hotel stood on the lower end of the street in the one-hundred block. Most writers agree with the showman as to the location, month and day of his birth, but three other years have been suggested: 1832, 1835, and 1840.[2] Pastor's headstone supplies what is probably the truth of the matter: "Antonio Pastor Died August 26, 1908, Age 76 years."[3]

Young Antonio, or Tony, as he was promptly dubbed, displayed an early interest in mimicry and in putting on a show. He was a precocious and spunky youngster and needed little encouragement to leave such boyish delights as marble-rolling or kite-flying to entertain family visitors with a song or recitation. Sometimes, when he was able to coerce his year-or-two-older sister, Caroline, to assist him, he even put on impromptu skits. His proud mother, who operated a modest perfumery at home, was always anxious to have him show off his talents, and his father, a violinist of Italian descent who supported the family by playing in orchestras at various New York theatres, occasionally would take out his fiddle to supply musical accompaniment. Tony later recalled that his youthful interest in "show business" was probably kindled to a great extent by the stories his father brought home from work.

"Often have I listened with wonder," he wrote, "at his narration of events that had come to his notice when he would relate to my mother the scenes at the theatre, with bits of chat and gossip of the society folk who attended, the popular actors, and the exciting plays."[4]

By the time he was seven or eight and a student at Thames Street School, Pastor was already recognized around the neighborhood as a showman of sorts. He put on penny circuses, mimicked local personalities, and could always be counted on to entertain at school functions. Upon at least one occasion, so he recalled, he organized a group of neighborhood chums to convert the family cellar into a miniature playhouse. A stage was built upon "upright barrels," seats were fashioned out of "neatly piled cordwood," and scenery was acquired by applying burnt cork figures to "one of my mother's best linen sheets." It seems that the entire project was undertaken without the knowledge of Pastor's father, who "would not relish the proceedings should they come to his notice." Rehearsals were conducted secretly, and the theatre was finally opened on a Saturday afternoon when the young showman knew his father would be away. Spectators paid their admission fee in "pins, marbles, and other bric-a-brac" to see a show in which "Richard III bore strange resemblance to Hamlet, Nick of the Woods, and Schnapps in the 'Naiad Queen,' while Ophelia danced a hornpipe with Macbeth or Falstaff."

The festivities came to a sudden halt, however, when the head of the household returned home and was drawn to the cellar by the commotion. Pastor remembered that "one of the boys... was shouting for a horse, the audience were shouting themselves hoarse, when with utter terror I recognized the familiar creak of my father's boots coming down the stairs. I gave the cue to run, and

2

without disrobing our mimic kings and queens tumbled over the audience in a mad race for the street. The wild scramble so amused my parent that he forgot to be angry and so I escaped punishment."[5]

Young Pastor made his formal debut as a public entertainer in 1843. His performance of a song and recitation in a school ceremony caught the attention of certain visitors affiliated with a temperance group called The Hand in Hand Society. They were quite taken with the young performer, especially his winning way with an audience, and they were sure he would be a big attraction for the Society's current temperance revival at Dey Street Hall. Pastor's parents apparently gave their approval to the venture, and "for the next two years he was kept busy singing at temperance meetings."[6] Whether he had other duties with the Society is not known. All he said about the experience was that "while with the Hand in Hand people I sang duets with Mr. Christian B. Woodruff, afterwards a prominent politician."[7] In any event, his success with the temperance group made performing all the more attractive to him. Nothing else seemed to give him as much fun and satisfaction. The bug had bitten him.

It was shortly after his stint as a crusader for teetotalism that he discovered and became enamoured of a spanking new type of entertainment — blackface minstrelsy. Comic performers who sang, danced, and presented skits in blackface had begun appearing in the circus and between the acts of plays in the theatre around the turn of the century. Apparently the idea of banding such performers together into a troupe did not take hold until the early 1840's. Some American theatre historians, like Richard Moody, believe that the first such troupe was formed late in 1842 or early in 1843 and was called the Virginia Minstrels.[8] The early blackface groups were composed of from four to six performers who sang, danced, joked, and supplied their own music on the banjo, violin, bone castanets, tambourine, and jawbone.

It was high-spirited and foot-stamping entertainment, and young Pastor was captivated by it. He would blacken his face with burnt cork and cavort for hours in front of a mirror, rolling his eyes and trying to imitate the rhythm of the bone castanets with two of his mother's table spoons. "One day," he wrote, "I had the good fortune to find on the street a two-dollar bill, which I invested in a tambourine and a negro wig."[9]

Soon afterward he attached himself to a minstrel troupe appearing at Croton Hall on the corner of Division and Chatham. "I was not employed," he explained, "but was rated a volunteer and used to carry water for Pony Moore, the comedian, who afterwards became my life-long friend . . . . At Croton Hall I got an occasional opportunity to display my talent, but my father now interfered."[10]

Pastor's father may have smiled away his son's earlier theatrical displays in the living room and cellar, but apparently he had little patience with the young man's growing interest in show business and especially his current fascination with Croton Hall and blackface minstrelsy. He decided sometime in the spring of 1846 to send his son to visit a farmer friend some miles north of the city limits,

3

hoping thereby to check the youngster's attraction to the stage. According to Pastor, the strategy did not work.

He went to the farm, he recalled, but "I was no sooner in the country than I was in full blast as an amateur entertainer, and the whole country grew to know Tony Pastor, 'the clever boy from New York.' On one occasion while traveling along a country road a young farmer stopped me and caused me to mount a hay wagon and do a song and dance for the amusement of his hay-makers, put a dollar in my hand and sent me on my way."[11] His visit to the country was short. He claimed that he "soon tired of country life" and returned voluntarily to New York.[12] But another story had it that "in a few weeks the boy came back, bringing a note from the farmer, who complained that Tony's impromptu performances had seriously interfered with work around the farm."[13]

At any rate, the budding young performer returned home, "and my parents, seeing that my inclination could not be diverted, gave up their opposition and I entered the services of P. T. Barnum at the famous Barnum's Museum, corner of Broadway and Anne Street, where I was regarded as sort of an infant prodigy."[14]

Barnum's Museum was a remarkable institution. There were few places in this country, or in the world for that matter, where 25¢ would buy a bigger package of amusement. Along with oddities like dwarfs, giants, mermaids, and albinoes, the public could see moral dramas, concerts, flower shows, poultry shows, living statuary, and performances by jugglers, educated dogs, ventriloquists, blackface minstrels, and the like. Pastor joined the Barnum enterprise in the fall of 1846 as part of a minstrel troupe which consisted at various times of such early burnt cork favorites as Charley White, Billy Whitlock, and Hall Robinson. His main job was to bang and rattle the tambourine and sing along with the group, but every now and then he got a chance to do a solo.

Asked in 1904 the name of the first song he remembered singing at the Museum, he replied: " 'Stop that Knocking.' Yes, it was a good song. One of the best minstrel songs ever written. It was the kind of song a man would sing to himself while he was brushing his hair or buttoning his collar. They don't write 'em nowadays. How much do you suppose I got for singing it and thumping the tambourine? Two dollars a week . . . . Yes, indeed, I'd have sung it for nothing. You know a boy, especially a boy with burnt cork on his face."[15]

Pastor remained at Barnum's until April 1, 1847, when he joined the Raymond and Waring Menagerie for a seven-month tour through the hinterlands.

Earlier in the century there had been a sharp distinction between a menagerie and a circus. The first had been simply a collection of "wild" animals, the second a troupe of equestrian performers and clowns. Eventually, however, as Chindahl points out in his history of the American circus, "it became usual for menageries to engage equestrians and clowns to present performances in a circus ring, the distinction between circuses and menageries thus gradually fading."[16] By 1847 the menagerie and circus were essentially one, although a greater variety

4

of acts was now featured. Along with the traditional displays of horsemanship and clowning, audiences now saw tumblers, jugglers, trapeze and wire artists, and novelty turns of various descriptions. Most of the larger troupes included a dramatic afterpiece in the show, especially one that afforded ample opportunity for the use of horses and other animals. Titles like *The Devil's Horse*, *Putnam*, and *The Taylor's Ride to Brentford* adorned the playbills of the day.

Traveling troupes generally performed outdoors in a ring enclosed by a fence or a canvas tent, but some appeared indoors in regular theatres or vacant buildings. In a few of the larger cities, like Boston, Chicago and New York, amphitheatres were built primarily for circus performances. Some of these structures were equipped with regular stages where a portion of the afterpiece was played. Still another big feature of the early circus was the "concert," an extra show offered after the main performance and usually for an additional fee. The concert consisted in the main of dancing and singing and often featured a blackface minstrel group. It was as part of such a group that Pastor was employed by the Raymond and Waring Menagerie.

Barnum's young graduate was enchanted by this colorful world of sawdust and tinsel, and when he was not singing and thumping on the tambourine, he usually could be found standing inside the main entrance watching the regular performers go through their turns. He was especially taken with the clowns, who in those one-ring days not only engaged in pantomimic tomfoolery, but sang, delivered monologs, and exchanged quips with the princely ringmaster. He memorized their jokes, songs, and comic routines and secretly nursed the hope that one day he would get the chance to join their merry ranks.

The Menagerie, like most touring groups of its kind, usually performed in the daytime because of the problem of installing temporary yet adequate illumination in most small communities. The free evenings often hung heavy on the troupe, and Pastor eventually hit upon a scheme to put these idle hours to advantage. He organized some of the younger circus performers into a concert troupe and offered shows in school houses, hotel dining rooms, or any other available quarters along the tour route. Here was his chance to play the clown. He probably made the most of it. He managed to have the shows announced from the ring in the afternoon, and apparently the response from the local gentry was gratifying.

"As the expense was at zero," he recalled, "the profits were considerable; but the managers of the menagerie did not relish the idea of my making too much money and they put a stop to my concerts."[17]

As the Menagerie was concluding its road season in Pittsburgh in November, 1847, Pastor was surprised one afternoon by a visit from an old family friend, John J. Nathans. Nathans was an equestrian and tumbler and at that time co-manager of the Welch, Delevan, and Nathans Circus then showing in Allegheny City, just across the river from Pittsburgh. Accompanying Nathans on the visit were Pastor's two younger brothers, Frank and William.[18] The records are obscure, but apparently Pastor's father had died sometime in 1846 or

5

1847,[19] and his mother, finding herself in a financial bind, had apprenticed Tony's brothers to Nathans. It was customary for most first-class artists to take apprentices for a certain number of years, during which time the charges were schooled in the particular specialties of their teacher. Nathans asked Tony if he too would like to become an apprentice and follow the circus life. The young entertainer was eager for the opportunity, and it was agreed that he would accompany the WDN company to New York to seek his mother's permission.

"Mr. Nathans got the consent of my mother," said Pastor, "and I was apprenticed to him. In reality, it was to learn to be an equestrian and acrobat, but as these things were not legally recognized, my apprentice papers read that I was to learn to be a farrier and veterinary man."[20]

Pastor made his sawdust debut late in 1847 with the WDN Circus in Welch's National Amphitheatre in Philadelphia. He and his brothers were considered "general performers." This meant that they served in whatever capacity the management and their own talents dictated. Nathans coached his three young pupils in the skills of riding and tumbling, but only Frank and William displayed any real talent in this direction. Frank became one of the most skilled circus riders of his day and one of the first to throw a back somersault through a hoop. William, on the other hand, earned an enviable reputation as a tumbler and vaulter. He became noted in particular for his ability to perform a rapid series of back hand springs, or flip flaps, and one writer pointed out that the performer was able to throw "fifty flip flaps on a pocket handkerchief."[21]

Tony learned to do simple tumbling tricks and to handle a horse well enough to ride and hold objects in the grand entree, but he was more interested in mimicry and showed himself to best advantage playing juvenile roles in the afterpieces. Some writers have suggested that he became a good enough rider to perform an act called "The Peasant's Frolic" or "Pete Jenkins."[22] In this, a tipsy rube in the audience began complaining aloud to the ringmaster about the poor quality of the riding in the show. Soon he was in the ring, stumbling around and bragging that he could do as well as any of the equestrians. The ringmaster called his bluff, a horse was brought out, and the rube climbed on. After a few misstarts and anxious moments — all of which were dependable laugh-getters — the rube suddenly stood up on the horse and proceeded to amaze everyone with a brilliant display of trick riding. Tony's skill as an equestrian, however, is doubtful. He later admitted that "I was never a great success as a rider."[23] If a Pastor did perform this turn, it was probably Frank.

The WDN Circus stayed at the Amphitheatre in Philadelphia until the spring of 1848; then it toured through the west and southwest, closing the season at Syracuse in the fall. The Pastor brothers accompanied Nathans to Boston for a winter equestrian season at the Federal Street Theatre, and in the spring of 1849 they journeyed back to Syracuse to rejoin the WDN company for a summer tour through the midwest. It was on this tour that Tony, following in the spirit of his earlier evening concerts with the Raymond and Waring show, introduced another independent speculation:

> *I purchased a number of illustrated periodicals and cutting out the pictures, mounted them on muslin strips in panorama style. I started a peep show. This consisted of a box wagon with small peep holes in sides and rear, with a tin reflector at the top to throw the light upon the muslin, which gave the pictures a transparent appearance, yet sharply defined. A team of horses, a base drum and plenty of red, white and blue calico completed the outfit, and with this I would take my stand in the market place or alongside the menagerie entrance, and with the beating of drum and clanging of the cymbals announce 'a grand panorama of the world, all to be seen for a sixpence.'[24]*

The young entrepreneur's venture had barely got off the ground, however, when a certain town council closed him down for doing business without a license: "They fined me $10 for the offense, $10 for obstructing the roadway, and if I had not kept quiet would have fined me $10 more for contempt of court. I pleaded inability to pay and they confiscated my wagon."[25]

The WDN forces were rolling through Ohio in July when a cholera epidemic brought the season to a sudden halt. "After losing several members of the company," said Pastor, "and finding the people too much frightened to go to the circus, we concluded to wind up business."[26] The company disbanded in Columbus, the Pastors traveled back to New York to visit their family, and young Tony managed to find summer minstrel work in and around the city.

The trio was back under Nathans' wing again in September when the WDN enterprise reorganized at Columbus for a continuous touring season that lasted until the end of summer in 1851. Pastor performed his variety of duties as before but something new and special was in the offing. The circus routine was upset midway on tour by the death of Neil Jamieson, ringmaster for the show. A replacement had to be found, and Nathans convinced his partners to let Pastor take over the position.

"This was a great honor for a stripling like me," he recalled. "The position was very prominent in those days when the clown was a big part of the show, and one had to play interlocutor to a merry fellow, who was likely to spring all sorts of unexpected gags on you."[27]

The chief "merry fellow" with the show was Bill Worrell, father of the three Worrell Sisters who later captivated New York with their songs and charms. Worrell was an old-timer at the business of being funny and a master at improvising gags and bits of horseplay, a challenge to even the most experienced ringmaster. Pastor apparently rose to the occasion with his natural wit and storehouse of comic material gathered over several years of clown-watching. "It was good mental training," he said, "and the necessity of meeting one gag with another just a bit better kept me primed to the situation."[28]

In addition to acting as a feeder and foil for the clowns, a ringmaster had to announce the various acts and Pastor seems to have cultivated an eloquence

7

well befitting his shiny boots, top hat and suit of broadcloth and gold lace. He even grew a bristly mustache that added to his dignity, and liked it so much that he kept it the rest of his life. His friendly manner and sharpness of wit soon won the confidence of the management and he filled the ringmaster position fairly regularly through the rest of the season.

Pastor also succeeded in winning the respect and friendship of Worrell. Many of his off-duty hours were spent in the clown's company, thrilling to his stories of circus life and picking up pointers on showmanship and comic banter. He told Worrell of his ambition to be a clown and it was mainly on the strength of the veteran's recommendation that Pastor was given an opportunity that same season to do a comic turn in the show.

Decked out in "calico pants, a red vest, a yellow coat, and a vermillion nose," he appeared just after the grand entree to sing a topical song entitled "Things I Don't Like to See."[29] The management must have been impressed, for he appeared in the same slot on several occasions during the season. When the circus played a week's engagement at the Bowery Amphitheatre in New York in April, 1851, he was awarded a benefit performance, one feature of which, according to Odell, "was a grand pedestrian match in the ring, with five competitors, for a silver cup."[30]

When the WDN Circus disbanded at the end of the summer of 1851, Pastor's apprenticeship was at an end but he did not break away immediately from his brothers and Nathans. The latter joined his forces and finances with those of Richard Sands for a winter season at the Bowery Amphitheatre and Pastor was in the ranks as a general performer. "As my apprenticeship was at an end," he wrote, "I enjoyed my first real engagement. I was given the big salary of six ($6.00) per week, which was a grand one in those days for a young chap like me."[31]

He worked hard for his pay. His main job was that of ringmaster, but somehow he managed to perform a variety of other duties as well and must have become adept at making quick changes. Along with thrusting and parrying with such clowns as John Gossin and Alexander Rockwell, he tumbled a bit, rode and held objects, sang comic songs whenever he got the chance, and appeared in most of the afterpieces. On one occasion he played the comic lover in a farcical piece called *A Shoemaker's Shop in an Uproar*, and on another he was said to have drawn praise for his portrayal of the Castelan in the famous horse piece, *Mazeppa*.[32] He stayed on as general performer with the Sands and Nathans troupe when it toured the east in the spring and summer of 1853 and after it again settled down in the Bowery Amphitheatre for another fall and winter season.

When the circus closed its indoor season in the spring of 1853, Pastor started out on his own. He had little trouble finding work. He was a general performer with Franconi's Traveling Hippodrome through the summer of 1853 and ringmaster as well as general factotum with the Mabie Brothers' Circus from spring to fall in 1854. When he was not working in the world of tanbark, he donned burnt cork again to work with minstrel troupes in the Bowery, at Croton Hall, and elsewhere in and around New York. As he himself put it, "I got to be proficient as a negro banjoist, and I got extra winter work when the circus was not going, doing negro business."[33]

His comic talent was strongly in evidence with the Franconi and Mabie forces; he sang comic songs and acted in almost every afterpiece. On one occasion, moreover, he was chosen to substitute for the Mabies' chief clown, Sol Lipman. The *Clipper*, a sporting and theatrical journal of the day, reported in September, 1864, that when Lipman was taken ill on tour in the spring of 1854, "Tony was called upon at a moment's notice to put on the dress of motley and play the Fool. He made a big hit, and promised to become one of the best clowns in the country."[34]

Although the young performer apparently proved himself funny, he did not get the chance to specialize in clown parts exclusively for another two years. When he signed on for a tenting season with the Levi J. North Circus in the spring of 1855, he once again served as ringmaster and general performer. He continued to perform these duties when the North troupe settled down for a fall and winter season at North's grandiose Amphitheatre in Chicago.

The North proprietors must have been duly impressed with Pastor's comic talents and perhaps sympathetic to his clowning ambition as well for, when the company was reorganized in the spring of 1856 for a season under canvas, they gave him his first regular clown engagement. He exchanged quips with William Kennedy, ringmaster on the tour, and played an assortment of comic roles in the afterpieces. But it was as a singing clown that he made his biggest hit. Dressed up in a baggy, one-piece outfit covered with colorful polka dots, he delighted audiences with humorous ditties like "Teetotal Society," "Wedlock is a Ticklish Thing," and "My Grandfather was a Wonderful Man." Thereafter, comedy was his province and comic singing his forte. His ringmaster and general performer days were over.

It is generally held that Pastor's voice, a sort of husky bathroom baritone, left much to be desired but it was his manner, not his voice, that put him over with the public. One writer attributed the performer's success to a "witchery of personality."[35] "It was the way he had that made him popular," said another, "and to his loyal patrons whatever he did was right."[36] Apparently, Pastor's clown was a Puck-like creature, sporting an impish twinkle in the eye and something like the telltale look of the little boy who has just put a frog in the teacher's desk. He was a bundle of energy, bouncing and strutting through his songs with mischievous glee, accompanying the words with winks and stares, nimble dance steps, twirls of the mustache. He often entered the circus ring at full gallop, took a tumble, made a quick somersault to his feet, then went right into his song as if nothing unusual had happened.

Pastor was a friendly, good-natured person and this carried over to his performance. His relationship with the audience was always warm and direct. He performed as if he were in the midst of old friends and was at his best perhaps

9

when he could work close to the spectators, addressing them individually, tapping heads, stroking chins, and kissing the ladies' hands with roguish delight. All in all, it seems that his appeal as a clown lay essentially in the happy blending of boyish enthusiasm with warm, homespun familiarity, a dominant characteristic of his stage personality until the end.

Pastor's popularity as a singing clown grew by leaps and bounds over the next few years. He was billed as "the great American clown" and "the clown prince of song" with such troupes as the Mabie Southern Circus, the Mabie and Crosby Eastern Circus, and the Nixon and Kemp Circus. He claimed that while with the Mabie and Crosby forces in the summer of 1858 he was "clowning at the big salary of $40.00 per week. I also got extra for appearing in the side show, and also sold my song books. I made fully $90.00 per week, which was big money in those days."[37]

His brothers, Frank and William, meanwhile, had completed their apprenticeship with Nathans and had set out on their own as well. Frank had sailed for England in November, 1856, to ply his equestrian skills abroad. William had been touring the circus routes as a "champion vaulter and carpet leaper." William and Tony worked under the same management on several occasions in the late 1850's. They were "added features" with the Nixon and Kemp Circus in November, 1858, at the Nixon Palace Gardens in New York, but moved on before the month was over to join the Sands and Nathans Circus for a brief season at the Old Broadway Theatre. They toured with this company during the summer of 1859, then signed on with the Nixon and Aymar Circus in the fall.

As the decade of the fifties neared its end, the growing tension between the North and South was beginning to hurt the circus road business. Attendance was falling off and some outfits were even running into open "anti-Yankee" opposition along the southern routes. Pastor wrote: "The mutterings of trouble that was soon to burst on us with all its awful carnage and woe appalled the proprietors of circuses and menageries."[38]

William suggested that they might be wise to seek greener pastures abroad with brother Frank, who was then in partnership with an English circus manager, Thomas Price. Tony was not too keen on making an ocean crossing. His reluctance was due in part at least to his great fear of deep water,[39] a phobia that first had begun to bother him years earlier when he had been part of a minstrel band entertaining summers on a steamboat shuttling between New York and Staten Island. He resolved the question by signing on for a tour with the Richard Sands Circus in the spring of 1860. William sailed off alone to rendezvous with Frank for a series of show dates in Spain.[40]

The Sands tour proved to be only moderately successful, but the manager was able to keep his company together and his wagons rolling until the season ended in September. Pastor then took careful stock of the situation. The "mutterings" of trouble were becoming louder; many companies were idle, their future plans indefinite. He decided that the immediate future offered little promise of steady work in the sawdust arena and that he should begin looking around for new opportunities. He was soon to find these opportunities in an institution and in a type of entertainment that had begun to grow vigorously in the late 1850's. The institution was the concert saloon, and the entertainment was "Variety."

CHAPTER TWO

Enter the Comic Singer

Tony Pastor made his variety debut in the early fall of 1860 at Frank Rivers' Melodeon on Callowhill Street in Philadelphia. Rivers' establishment was a fancy and extremely popular concert saloon with a barroom lined with gilded mirrors and an adjoining auditorium equipped with a stage, parquette, and two galleries. The manager presented big shows replete with ballet, afterpieces, and some of the best specialty performers of the day. "I was a comic singer," said Pastor, "and was the biggest salaried member of the company, getting $25 a week. I made a big hit with a war song called 'Brother Jonathan,' and wore a get-up to match the song."[1] He also played in the dramatic offerings, sharing honors with such long-since-forgotten artists as Joseph Wheelock and Kitty Blanchard. Variety's new recruit was an immediate hit in Philadelphia, and he stayed on at the Melodeon for several months.

Early in December he journeyed back to New York to play clown for a few weeks with the Spalding and Rogers Great New Orleans Circus at the Old Bowery Theatre. He sang comic songs and appeared in at least two major afterpieces. Beginning on December 24, he played a character called von Blunder in a spectacular comic pantomime entitled *The Monster of St. Michael; or, Harlequin and the Golden Sprite of the Sulphur Mine*. In late January he dressed in female attire to impersonate Judy Mahony, a camp follower, in an extravaganza called *Tippo Saib; or, The Storming of Seringapatam*, a piece based on the recent Anglo-Indian mutiny. He recalled an amusing incident that took place during the latter production:

> At that time there flourished in the Bowery a social coterie called 'The Side-pocket Club,' a number of young men, who, being always ready for fun, prevailed on the stage manager to let them go on as supers for one night only. In the action of the play was a battle between the Sepoys and the British troops, with cannon fired from the back of elephants and other East Indian realism. The

British, of course, were the victors, but the side pocket boys, led on by Dan Kerrigan, turned the tables and, as Indians, beat the British army of paid supers, putting them to rout and driving George Foster, the stage manager, distracted. The battle raged until the curtain was rung down.[2]

When the Spalding and Rogers company left for Boston early in February, Pastor returned to Rivers' Melodeon and remained one of the chief attractions there until spring.

Harry S. Sanderson, who became business manager for Pastor's Broadway house in 1877, caught the show at the Melodeon sometime in February, 1861.

"Beautiful women danced upon the stage," he wrote. "Amazing negro comedians created much laughter, and dexterous acrobats held me in breathless yet fearsome delight. After a while a movement in the audience presaged the coming of the principal attraction — Tony Pastor. Can I ever forget my sensations? I had read of Tony Pastor, had purchased his song books and essayed to sing his songs, and indeed had created an ideal. Fancy my surprise when a dapper little chap of about 110 pounds came on the stage dressed in the garb of a circus clown, and sang 'Everything is Lovely and the Goose Hangs High.' "

This particular number poked at current events and at the same time breathed the sentiment that the country would be in good hands once Lincoln was in the White House. "Inasmuch as we were on the verge of civil war," said Sanderson, "the sentiment was cordially endorsed and re-demanded. Tony obliged again and again."[3]

The bantam weight performer was a good entertainer, but a poor prophet, at least in this instance. Lincoln's inauguration on March 4 did not make "everything lovely"; indeed, the South became more restless than ever, and many were convinced that open conflict was inevitable.

Pastor was given a testimonial benefit on Thursday, April 11, to mark the end of his engagement. It was a gala affair. Many top-flight variety and minstrel artists took part, and the resort was extra thick with smoke and lager fumes as scores of people crowded in to salute the little performer. It was on the following day that the "inevitable" happened — Fort Sumter was shelled. The "mumblings" of war had found full voice. Pastor gave his last performance at the Melodeon on Saturday night, April 13, and a wild night it was. Patriotism was as thick as the cigar smoke, and if a Union army recruiter had been on hand he might have signed up a company. The young entertainer left the next day for New York to begin an engagement at the American Concert Hall on April 17.

The American Concert Hall was commonly referred to as simply "444," its address on Broadway. It was a long, narrow hall with a low ceiling and, except for a small area around the bar near the main entrance, it was fitted out as a theatre. The place had served many a minstrel troupe before being converted into a concert saloon on August 8, 1860, by Robert Butler. Butler promised his patrons "a variety of Ballet, Pantomime, Opera, interspersed with negro extravaganzas" at the following prices: "Parquet 20 cents, Gallery 10 cents, seats in Private Boxes 50 cents."[4] Waiter-girls, of course, were on hand to dispense drinks, smokes, and "good fellowship" throughout the house.

Gilbert claims that "444" was Pastor's "first independent venture as a manager."[5] But this view is not supported by contemporary evidence. For example, the *New York Times* for January 5, 1862, named the owners of all buildings occupied as concert saloons along with their lessees and sublessees. The performer's name was not mentioned. The "Estate of G. W. Miller" was cited as the owner of "444" and "Robt. Butler" as the proprietor.[6] All indications are that Butler was the sole proprietor and manager of the resort from its opening in August, 1860,[7] until its destruction by fire on February 12, 1866. We do not find the slightest hint in the newspaper ads and accounts of the day to suggest that Pastor was ever anything more at "444" than a hired entertainer.

When Pastor joined Butler's show on April 17, billed as "the greatest clown and Comic Singer of the age,"[8] the war fever was spreading fast. Lincoln had already issued his call for 75,000 troops. New York was aflame with patriotic spirit and recruiting stations were springing up in Battery Park. The music of martial bands filtered through the business districts, and windows, store fronts and carriages were decorated with flags and tri-colored bunting. Each day saw the streets filled with marching soldiers and cheering crowds. On Saturday afternoon, April 20, a mass patriotic meeting was held in Union Square, several blocks north of "444." Thousands of people wearing union cockades in their hats and bonnets filled the Square and spilled over into the side streets and avenues that emptied into it.

"There were several stands for orators," wrote diarist George Templeton Strong, "and scores of little speechifying ganglia besides, from carts, windows, and front stoops ... The crowd, or some of them, and the ladies and gentlemen who occupied the windows and lined the housetops all round Union Square, sang 'The Star Spangled Banner,' and the people generally hurrahed a voluntary after each verse."[9]

Butler's young comic singer attended the rally that afternoon and, so the story goes, was deeply moved by the great outpouring of patriotic emotion. "I mused on the situation," he said, "and somehow I did not feel like singing comic songs that night. I went to a music store and bought 'The Star Spangled Banner,' and I committed the words to memory, and that night asked the audience to join me in the chorus."[10]

An anonymous patron at "444" that evening recalled what happened: "That night Tony sang 'The Star Spangled Banner,' and I thought the roof of the building would fly off ... Tony sang the first verse amid the most intense silence. He then asked the audience to join in the chorus. It was tremendous, I tell you."[11]

This was supposedly the first time the number had been sung on the variety stage. Apparently recognizing a good thing when he saw it, Pastor used the song as the concluding feature of his act through the war years. It became his trademark, and audiences at "444" and elsewhere eagerly anticipated that moment in the program when the little showman would ask all assembled to join him in a glorious salute to the old stars and stripes.

Pastor's initial association with "444" was brief. The sawdust ring beckoned again, and he left the resort before the end of his second week to sign on with the Spalding and Rogers Great Railroad Circus then showing at the New York Military Garden. The circus managers were planning to risk a spring and summer road season following the New York date. Somehow or other they convinced Pastor that he was needed to help bolster the troupe's chances in the unpredictable hinterlands. The young entertainer joined the circus during its final week at the Garden and was billed as "the unrivalled clown and comic vocalist."[12]

The troupe enjoyed a brisk business in New York, but the subsequent tour, despite Pastor's contribution, drew only lukewarm response. The circus disbanded after two disappointing weeks and the young entertainer headed back to New York.

Meanwhile, the war fever was taking a heavy toll at the city's legitimate theatres. "The houses at the various places have only been tolerable," said the *Spirit of the Times* on May 4, "and the audiences have exhibited the utmost restlessness."[13] Several weeks later the same publication noted that people "won't visit the theatre, no matter what the inducement."[14]

But if the drama was being neglected in New York during these early months of the war, the light entertainment and boisterous congeniality of the concert saloons was drawing more attention than ever. New resorts were rising up everywhere throughout the city. "The more serious attractions of the drama," said Pastor, "did not suffice to dispel the gloom and sorrows of that conflict ... when men sought laughter and glitter rather than philosophy in their hours of relief."[15] They certainly could find plenty of both in the concert saloons.

Upon his return to New York, Pastor found Butler making preparations to open a second amusement resort. He had taken over Wallack's recently vacated theatre at 483-485 Broadway and was busy converting the place into the Broadway Music Hall. When the new resort opened its doors on May 22, the mustached comic singer was on the bill. He had returned to variety again, and this time he had returned to stay. His circus days were over. For the rest of his professional life he was to devote himself to the variety stage as either a performer or manager, most of the time as both.

Pastor held forth at the Broadway Music Hall through the rest of the year. The new resort did not measure up to Butler's expectations, however, and he closed it down in late January, 1862, preferring to concentrate full time on the going "444." With the closing of the Music Hall, Pastor joined the show at "444" and was performing there when the legislative axe fell on the New York concert saloons in late April. Apparently he was out of the city during the heat of the battle in May, but was back on the bill again by the first of June. An ad for the resort in the *New York Herald* on June 1 announced:

First week of the re-engagement of the
great unimitable Tony Pastor.
  The great Tony Pastor the talk of the town.
  The famed comic singer, wit, jester, and clown.
  Blue devils and all that to sorrow belongs
  Fly off at the sound of his glorious songs.[16]

He remained a more or less permanent fixture at "444" for the next three years, ballyhooing the Union cause and chasing away "blue devils" at every opportunity with his repertoire of "glorious songs." It was sometime during this period that he stopped singing long enough to get married. All we know about the event is that his wife's name was Anna and that she was a consumptive.

Pastor's repertoire at "444" covered a lot of ground. Night after night, for example, he demonstrated that "songs on some of the most commonplace themes will often entertain an audience such as a fellow's best girl, the old man's boot, the mother-in-law, the scolding wife, and so forth."[17] He bragged that "My Grandfather Was a Wonderful Man," complained of "Things I Don't Like to. See," and advised the girls that "If Your Foot is Pretty, Show it." He loved to sing of feminine charms and fashions and to recount his imaginary adventures or misadventures in matters of romance and chivalry. He told his audiences about "My Matilda Jane," "Sweet Kitty O'Neil," "The Girl with the Golden Hair," "Polly Perkins of Washington Square," and "Sarah's Young Man." But the majority of his songs dealt in one way or another with the war and the Union cause. He declared himself a fierce patriot, and the sound of marching feet was a sound he carried to the variety stage with fervor.

He had customers cheering and stamping with such songs as "March for the Union," "Freemen, Rally," "We are Marching to the War," "Hunky Boy is Yankee Doodle," and "Ye Sons of Columbia." He kept telling them that "Our army now is moving—they're pressing on their way;/ Of victory, on land and sea, we're hearing every day."[18] As the news of a victory, battle, deed of heroism, or of the death of a hero reached the north, he invariably turned it into a song. He sang of the sea fight between "The Monitor and Merrimac," of "The Peaceful Battle of Manassas," of "Sumter, the Shrine of the Nation." He remarked on "Old England's Position," saluted the exploits of "The Irish Volunteers" and "The New England Boys," and bemoaned "The Fall of Lander."

If his songs failed to swell the ranks of the northern volunteers, it certainly was not for want of effort on his part. In one after another he denounced the secessionists' cause, praised the courage of northern manhood, reminded Americans about their heritage of liberty, and exalted the glories of the stars and stripes. In "Freemen, Rally," for example, he called out:

17

> *Awake from your slumber, brave heroes,*
> *And hark to the bugle's deep tones,*
> *That call you to fight for your country,*
> *Swear vengeance on patriot's sons;*[19]

and in "The New England Boys" he summoned all "loyal sons of liberty" to be:

> *Away! Away! o'er ocean's spray—*
> *Our country on us calls!*
> *To where on flowers all beautiful*
> *The genial sunshine falls.*
> *True brothers all, we heard the call,*
> *To mingle in the fray.*
> *And when the brave McClellan leads,*
> *Oh, who would stay away?*[20]

Now and then he employed a stereopticon and flashed likenesses of McClellan, Grant, and other military and political figures on a screen while singing of their deeds.

He occasionally preached his patriotic messages in speech as well as song. He would mount a box or fake tree stump to deliver a "stump speech" on liberty and freedom. The idea of the stump speech seems to have originated in the minstrel show when a blackface orator delivered a burlesque panegyric. Pastor had given blackface stump speeches in the past, and he may have continued to don burnt cork for some of his patriotic sermons. More often, however, he mounted the "stump" in the person and dress of a "true-blue" Yankee eccentric. Such was the case, for example, in a monolog called "The Yankee's Escape from Secesh." He appeared as a Connecticut peddler describing his travels in the south just prior to the outbreak of the war. Part of the speech ran as follows:

> *Jerusalem! May I be goll darn'd ef I aint most superlatively happy to git back into a Christian white man community once more, whar that ere glorious old Star Spangled Banner waves triumphantly over the heads of a free and independent people that's sound on the goose, for the Constitution of '76 and the hull Union.*
>
> *I tell you what, folks, when I got north o'Mason and Dixon's line, and seen that ar flag a flying over Washington .., I felt all over as if I'd been indulgin in a dozen fourth of July and Thanksgiving bustifications all consolidated into one. I did, by Jehu! Talking of consolidation just puts me in mind how I've made out to get out o' that darned yellow, consumptive, cantakrious, piratical rattlesnake nest, Montgomery, presided over by old Satan's twin brother, Jeff Davis. He's as mean a dam'd skunk as wore hair. He is, by Jehu! Why, a decent Yankee dog wouldn't condescend tew bark at him no*

18

how. If he did, Jeff would only promise him' a licking, and then repudiate payment, by Jehu![21]

Referring to his Civil War songs in a later interview, Pastor admitted that "it would, I think, have been unsafe for me to have sung such songs south of Philadelphia."[22] And, no doubt, to have given such stump speeches as well!

Pastor did not have to go south of Philadelphia to get into trouble. One of his songs about conscription sparked a rumpus one evening in his own home territory. The government's adoption of a draft on March 3, 1863, was met with cries of protest from many circles. When he introduced a topical song praising the new policy and chiding its opponents, several anti-conscription toughs in the "444" audience became riled. The song was called "The Draft," and a portion of it ran as follows:

The draft, the draft, is the subject now
*   That causes agitation;*
You hear the which, the why, the how,
*   Discussed throughout the nation.*
We'll have, at length, the people's strength,
*   That rebels long have laughed at;*
Our land to save, no man that's brave
*   Objects to being drafted.*

Chorus

But some, the cowards, keeping shy,
*   Whose hearts with fear are grafted,*
The various dodges how they try
*   For to avoid being drafted.*

A dandy beau among the girls
*   Has passed for eight-and-twenty,*
With whiskers black and jetty curls,
*   From hair-dye used in plenty.*
But suddenly white locks appear,
*   Black hairs away are wafting;*
He owns at last he's fifty near,
*   For to avoid the drafting.*[23]

The toughs gave out with a continuous round of jeers and cat-calls. When the singer paid them little heed, they threw down their beer mugs and made for the stage. A number of hefty bartenders intercepted the crew and managed, with no small difficulty, to hustle them out of the hall. Pastor was unruffled by the demonstration. In the midst of it all, he cooly unfurled an American flag, held it aloft, and sang "The Star Spangled Banner."

Pastor did not originate the idea of singing about current events nor was he without his rivals in the field. The topical song had come to variety from the circus and minstrel show. Its exponents were legion on the variety stage during the war years. But none did more than Pastor to develop and popularize this musical idea. It remained one of the most popular features of his act until the very end of his long singing career. Programs and ads over the years announced "Tony Pastor's Local Items," "Tony Pastor and his Rhymes for the Times," and "Tony Pastor's Portfolio of Timely Topics."

Almost any current event served as grist for his song mill. In 1866, for example, he sang about "The Great Atlantic Cable," and when Boss Tweed went into hiding in 1875 Pastor offered a song entitled "Where Tweed is Gone," describing various places where the controversial politician might have been concealed. Later he commented on "The Alabama Claims" and "The Civil Service Reform." He sang about "The Waterfall" hair style of the ladies, of their faddish addiction to "The Grecian Bend," and he joked about "The Electric Shock," a magical belt that many believed offered a sure cure for lumbago. In 1885 he sang about Abraham S. Hewitt, the millionaire merchant who was running for mayor of New York. The song was called "What's the Matter with Hewitt?" and gave rise to a catch phrase still heard today — "What's the Matter with So-and-so? He's all right!" Incidentally, Hewitt won.

One of the most enduring of the thousand or more songs that Pastor sang during his lifetime was a "444" number entitled "Down In a Coal Mine." It was "a lugubrious ditty, begging cheap sentiment for the miner,"[24] but audiences loved it and were still requesting it during his final years. The song became a popular barroom ballad and, according to Gilbert, "a parlor chant in thousands of homes."[25] The chorus ran as follows:

Down in a coal mine, underneath the ground,
Where a gleam of sunshine never can be found,
Diggin' dusky diamonds all the season round;
Down in a coal mine, underneath the ground.[26]

Pastor seems to have had several sources for his songs. Some he purchased. "I generally pay $15 for a good song," he told a reporter. "Why, would you believe that I receive on an average one hundred songs a week from different persons, and out of each thousand I'll get only ten good songs?"[27] Among those who furnished him with numbers at "444" and are so credited in his song books were George Edeson, John F. Poole, George French, Jimmy Reynolds, William Carlton, T. Ramsay, and Eugene T. Johnston. Some songs he adapted from the London music halls and some he "borrowed" from fellow entertainers. A good many of them, however, he wrote himself, drawing his ideas primarily from the newspapers.

"I believe not only in the power of the public press," he explained, "but in its utility. It is the most valuable agent the vocalist has ever had for securing subjects for popular songs. The comic vocalist must be quick to perceive the peculiar topic or phase of human life which is liable to interest the amusement going public, and must be a little ahead of time."[28]

A few of his songs sported original melodies, but most were set to familiar airs of the day.

Although Pastor could turn almost any subject into a song, and frequently did, he never forgot the traditional appeal of patriotic sentiment and flag-waving. His fiery patriotism did not burn out with the end of the war in 1865. He offered his customers a new national song every week or so. Moreover, the national emblem always adorned his stage, and for many years after the war his house orchestra regularly opened each bill with "The Star Spangled Banner." When the rumblings of the Spanish-American War were heard in the spring of 1898, he dusted off some of his old Civil War songs, changed a few words here and there, and sang them again. He was not to be around for World War One, but a performer who had frequently appeared with his family at Pastor's 14th Street Theatre around the turn of the century was to carry on in the manager's flag-waving tradition — his name was George M. Cohan.

A "444" ad in the *Spirit of the Times* in December, 1863, announced the appearance of "Tony Pastor, the world renowned comic vocalist, in a variety of new and original songs on the topics of the day."[29] Although Pastor certainly had not achieved "world renown" by this time, his popularity in New York was indeed immense, and his frequent appearances outside of the city, along with the publication of several books of his favorite songs, was spreading his fame around the country. Whenever he ventured forth from "444" to play a date in another community, his reception was usually impressive. Nick Norton, an old-time variety performer, saw him at Chadwick's Varieties in Chicago sometime between 1862 and 1865 and recalled that "Mr. Pastor was at that time the largest salaried performer in America, and a tremendous favorite everywhere."[30]

With Pastor enjoying such popularity and acclaim in variety circles, it must have been a surprise to many when the *Clipper* for September 17, 1864, rumored that "Tony intends leaving the music hall business at the close of this season, and next season will return to the sawdust business, he having had several liberal offers to travel again and play clown."[31] It is uncertain whether Pastor had actually intended to return to the circus come spring of 1865 but, in any event, he did not. The *Clipper's* information proved to be wrong in fact, but it was at least right in spirit, for the popular entertainer did make a major move later in the 1864-65 season. It followed a two-week engagement at the Casino, a music hall in Philadelphia, in early March. The *Clipper* for March 25 contained the following item: "Casino, Philadelphia — Tony Pastor concluded his engagement here on the 18th inst., which has been immensely successful; it is with much regret both by the management and the public, that Mr. Pastor's previous arrangements compel him to leave."[32]

Previous arrangements!

They were not to join a circus, not even to return to "444." That ambition and leadership capacity that first had shown itself long ago in his father's cellar had surfaced again. He had decided to take a fling at variety management and was scheduled to begin a tour with his own troupe on March 22.

CHAPTER THREE

The Manager's Boots

On March 11, 1865, the following notice appeared in the *Clipper:* "A New Variety Troupe is at present organizing in this city, under the direction of Tony Pastor and a well-known minstrel manager, and is to be called 'Tony Pastor's Variety Show.' "[1]

This seems to have been the first public announcement of the comic singer's decision to try on the boots of management. The minstrel manager was Sam Sharpley, a well-heeled veteran of blackface minstrelsy. The general plan was to conduct a spring and summer tour through the northeastern states, then settle down in a more or less permanent home base somewhere in New York.

Variety companies had been venturing into the backwoods off and on for several years. One of the earliest was Frank Rivers' Melodeon troupe in the summers of 1861 and 1862. But such tours were still looked upon as experimental and, considering the likely competition from the many popular minstrel troupes on the road, highly risky. Apparently, Pastor and Sharpley were ready to take the risk.

The exact arrangements made between them are not known, but it seems that each invested a sum of money in the venture. We are told much later in an unidentified newspaper clipping that "Tony was to put up part of the capital and go shares in a variety show with Sharpley, but when the time came he could not get it. His disappointment was so keen that Sharpley put up all the cash required. And Tony paid him back in a few weeks."[2] In any event, the two men formed some kind of partnership during the early months of 1865 for the purpose of launching a new traveling variety troupe.

They were indeed fortunate in securing Charles B. Griste as advance agent for the company. Griste had been booking road dates for various minstrel groups for years and was well acquainted with the New England territory. His initial task was to find a house and date for the New York engagement so the tour could be planned accordingly. The search led eventually to the Bowery Minstrel Hall where arrangements were made with Richard M. Hooley, the lessee, to have the troupe take over the quarters on July 31. This done, Griste took to the road with his date book, leaving Pastor and Sharpley to assemble a company.

Joseph Braham was hired to lead an orchestra of from five to eight pieces, and, interestingly enough, Fernando (Dody) Pastor, Tony's youngest brother, was taken on as company treasurer and to help out in the sketches. Little is known about Fernando's earlier activities, except that he was born in New York on August 16, 1842, and had followed his brothers into apprenticeship with John J. Nathans without enjoying like success.[3] He was a fragile person whose efforts to build a reputation as a circus clown had been continually frustrated by illnesses of one kind or another. By 1865 he was already suffering from the early stages of consumption, a disease that was to take his life ten years later.

Most of the performers recruited for the troupe had shared bills regularly with Pastor at "444." There were James Gaynor, a singing comic who accompanied himself on the banjo; Ida Duval, a young serio-comic songstress and comedienne; Sheridan and Mack, who decked themselves out in green jackets and white breeches to sing Irish songs and perform double clog dances; Mlle. Marie Bertha, a versatile dancer who specialized in pastoral numbers with lots of flowing veils; and Blanche Stanley, another serio-comic songstress, and her husband, Johnny Wild, a blackface comic. Wild was one of the first performers to make the traditional slow-witted and shuffling stage Negro into a dapper and urbane figure. He later achieved great popularity with Harrigan and Hart at the Theatre Comique on Broadway.

Also on hand, of course, was Pastor himself. The enterprising young performer had no intention of trading in his "glorious songs" for booking contracts and payrolls; he would merely graft the one role onto the other. In truth, his own nature and the demands of his public would hardly have allowed any other course.

There is some question as to just how big the company payroll was at the outset. Three figures have been cited: $225, $250, and "less than $300."[4] It was Pastor's recollection that he paid Johnny Wild and Blanche Stanley $50 a week as a team.[5] This would have been excellent money for a team in those early days of variety; all but the most popular duos were fortunate to receive $50 a week well into the 1880's. The troupe, however, was beefed up with additional performers along the tour route, so the payroll was undoubtedly increased over the weeks to follow. Pastor was to become noted for his firm belief that variety should be served up in generous helpings and that the variety kaleidoscope should be shaken often and with vigor.

The tour was kicked off with performances on March 22 and 23 at Paterson, New Jersey, followed by a two-night stand in Newark. A printed program for one of the Newark dates reveals that the show consisted essentially of a series of olio turns and sketches topped off with an afterpiece, a pantomime in which Pastor appeared as Pierrot.[6] The company moved on to other New Jersey towns, including Trenton and Elizabeth, then up through New York State to New

England. They played in whatever quarters Griste was able to obtain — variety resorts, town halls, legitimate theatres, minstrel houses, etc. The papers gave frequent reports on the troupe's good fortune. The *Clipper* noted on April 1 that "the Tony Pastor Combination has been meeting with great success wherever they have appeared. We are pleased to chronicle the success of Tony Pastor in his new undertaking, for he is deserving in every respect."[7] Several weeks later the *Spirit of the Times* reported that the troupe "is meeting success in the New-England States."[8]

The company was traveling through the heart of Yankee country when news that the war had ended reached the north, only to be followed a few days later by the stunning report of Lincoln's assassination. Apparently, however, the tour was not disrupted by the turn of events nor did business fall off to any great degree. The *Bridgeport Farmer* said that the troupe enjoyed "an immense house" on April 17 in that city; and the *Clipper* noted that "the Tony Pastor Show did a good business in Music Hall, New Haven, Conn., April 18th and 19th, although the Assassination operated against them."[9] Pastor wore a black armband and saluted Lincoln's memory in word and song at every performance for two weeks following the assassination.

Griste had been able to obtain a four-week engagement for the troupe at the Morris Brothers Opera House (actually a minstrel hall) in Boston beginning on June 5. The *Clipper* reported that the company opened to a "crowded house" and that during the first week "the house was filled to repletion every night, and on Wednesday and Saturday the matinees were big."[10] The bill of fare was changed weekly, and business held up well during the run. The Opera House was to become a regular and profitable port of call for Pastor's traveling forces in the years to come. After closing there on July 8 with a benefit for Pastor, the company started working southward in anticipation of its New York opening. After a performance on July 29 at Stamford, Connecticut, the troupers arrived in Manhattan and, as the *Clipper* had forecast a week earlier, "on the 31st the party open[s] in the Bowery at the Minstrel Hall now occupied by the Iron-Clad Minstrels."[11]

The Iron-Clad Minstrels was Sharpley's own company, which had been on tour since the end of March and had moved into the Bowery house on June 12. Sharpley was not cited in the ads or newspaper commentary as having been on the road with the minstrel outfit, but he was listed as part of a troupe bearing his name that was coming to New York to settle down in the Bowery on June 12.[12] This raises the suspicion that the minstrel manager was not on tour with his partner after this date. It may well be that he had not gone on the road with Pastor at all. The papers never mentioned his name in their remarks about the variety troupe.

It is quite possible that arrangements called for the two partners to join forces once the variety company had reached New York. Meanwhile, each man would tour his own troupe and Sharpley would move his Iron-Clads into the Bowery Minstrel Hall in early June to await Pastor's arrival. Something like this arrangement was later implied in an article in *Variety:* "March 22, 1865, saw the birth of 'Tony Pastor's Own Company' at Paterson, N. J. whence he went on tour, winding up with a four-week engagement in Boston. Mr. Pastor then joined hands with Sam Sharpley, an old-time minstrel manager, and together they opened Tony Pastor's Opera House."[13] At any rate, the blackface crew moved out of the Bowery Minstrel Hall after its performance on Saturday evening, July 29, the Pastor comapny moved in over the weekend, and the two managers opened the establishment on Monday, July 31, as "Tony Pastor's Opera House." The Bowery booking was auspicious. "Tony Pastor's Opera House" remained a permanent institution on New York's east side for ten years.

The Bowery Minstrel Hall was located at 201 Bowery opposite Spring Street and had been built originally by Otto Von Hoyme in 1858 as a place of amusement for the growing German population of the area.[14] Bowery Street ran parallel with Broadway and was the city's second principal thoroughfare. The area in and around the street was referred to simply as "The Bowery." It had been a fashionable residential area in the 1830's, especially the real estate around 4th, Great Jones, Bond, and Bleecker Streets. Southward toward the East River, commercial establishments of a cheaper sort had led rapidly into the slums of Five Points. As the city expanded up the island of Manhattan, the Bowery area had begun to lose caste. In the late 1840's and early 1850's many fashionable families had begun to migrate northward to Union Square and beyond. The erection of the Academy of Music on 14th Street in 1854 was a clear sign that the world of fashion was on a northward trek to escape the multiplying slums and mercantile interests to the south.

By the time Pastor and Sharpley arrived on the scene, saloons, tenements, warehouses and cheap shops of one kind or another lined Bowery Street, and the poorer classes were everywhere. The Bowery was now a popular spot for cheap milliners and small traders and a favorite shopping ground for bargain hunters. Waves of immigrants had been reaching these shores in the 1850's. The Bowery had become a haven for many national groups. The air was filled with the chatter of mixed tongues. As one contemporary New Yorker put it, the Bowery "presents all nationalities, men from all quarters of the globe, nearly all retaining their native manner and habits, all very little Americanized. They are all 'of the people.' There is no aristocracy in the Bowery."[15] The Irish and Germans were particularly numerous in the area.

While the Bowery was a colorful bazaar for shoppers by day, darkness turned it into a sinister and dangerous playground for revelers and adventurers. One writer of the period advised his readers that "respectable people avoid the Bowery, as far as possible, at night."[16] It certainly furnished an exotic setting for Tony Pastor's Opera House — a patchwork milieu for an establishment that had for sale a patchwork commodity, Variety.

Pastor and Sharpley had chosen a good time to introduce their motley-garbed wares to the Bowery. There was very little formal entertainment to be had in the area during late July and early August. Over on Broadway, Niblo's

Garden was in the middle of the successful summer run of Boucicault's popular *Arrah-na-Pogue*, and the San Francisco Minstrels were holding forth nightly in their minstrel hall just across the street. In the Bowery itself, however, the Old Bowery Theatre was not scheduled to open until August 12 and the Varieties at 37-39 Bowery, the most popular variety emporium in the neighborhood, not until August 19. There were many cheap saloons providing some kind of entertainment for their bibulous customers and German beer gardens offering concerts as an accompaniment to the flow of lager but the only big competition at the outset of the Opera House venture was the New Bowery Theatre. It had opened a dramatic season on July 29 with a triple-header: *Kathleen Mavourneen, The Wandering Minstrel,* and *The King and Freebooter.*

The comparative lack of attractions in the area, Pastor's own reputation as a comic singer, and perhaps a normal curiosity on the part of many Boweryites to take in a new place of amusement seem to have more than compensated for sticky weather. The *Clipper* reported that the new management was greeted on opening night with "an immense house, and the performers were received with the greatest enthusiasm."[17]

Opening night patrons filed down a long corridor to the Opera House box office where Fernando Pastor and Sharpley sold tickets — 25¢ for a seat in the gallery or family circle, 35¢ for one in the parquette. Just beyond the box office were the doors to the auditorium itself. The auditorium was wider than it was long and was illuminated by gas lamps suspended from a domed ceiling. Long benches accommodated customers throughout the house, and several windows lined each wall. During the summer when the weather was clear these windows were opened wide to let in any cool air that happened to be around.

Of course, open windows let out the noise within, and apparently this caused some difficulty now and then in the neighborhood. In April, 1867, for example, a Methodist meeting next door found itself in competition with the Pastor show. "The evening being pleasant," said the *Clipper,* "the windows of both establishments were thrown open, so that while Tony was singing about the ballet girls, the preacher man was praying; and while Johnny Allen was singing 'Nicodemus Johnson,' the brethren and sisters next door were trying to drown 'Nicodemus' with 'New Jerusalem.' "[18]

The capacity of the Opera House in 1865 is uncertain, but Pastor renovated the premises frequently over the years, and the *Clipper* noted in March, 1869, that the house then had a "crowded" seating capacity of 1,194.[19]

The auditorium doors were opened for the first-nighters at 7:00. At 7:45 a stagehand lighted the gas footlights with a long wax taper, and Joseph Braham and his musicians took their places to play the overture — "The Star Spangled Banner," what else? Then, after a few words of welcome from Pastor, the show got under way.

And a big show it was! The audience was entertained for nearly three hours with dances and ballads by Ernestine DeFaiber, exotic capers by Mlle. Marie Bertha, a Zouave drill in complete uniform by Carrie Austin, more dances by Ellen Collene, comic songs by Amelia Wells, funny business with the banjo by James Gaynor, Irish jigs and ditties by Doty Duly, and various other musical and comic specialities by the likes of Johnny Wild, Willis Armstrong, and Sheridan and Mack. There was a comic named Robert Butler, but whether or not this was the Butler of "444" fame is not known. Pastor, of course, was on hand with "New Comic Songs, Humorous Ballads, and Admirable Adaptations."[20] There were also several sketches, an afterpiece, and possibly a ballet.[21]

The hot weather of late July continued into August, but attendance remained good. The *Clipper* reported in mid-month that "no more seats has been the cry every night at Tony Pastor's Opera House. We 'dropped in' three nights last week and found it a difficult matter to obtain even standing room, every seat being occupied and extra seats placed in all the aisles. Opening this place with a first-class variety troupe has proved to be the thing that the east-siders wanted, and they are turning out in full force."[22] Even after the Old Bowery and the Varieties opened for business in mid-August, the east-siders continued their hearty support. According to the *Clipper*, August receipts totalled $9,348.50.[23] If we consider 30¢ as an average admission, such receipts represent an attendance for the month of around 31,000.

Pastor and Sharpley must have been pleased with the way things were going and buoyantly confident that the future held more of the same, for sometime in late August or early September they managed to purchase Hooley's five-year lease on the hall. The *Clipper* noted on September 16 that the two "are now showing in their own hall."[24]

The new lessees marked the occasion with several innovations. Up to this time the Opera House had been identified by bold letters painted across its face. Now, a long gas-light sign was added. It read "Tony Pastor's" and projected out across the sidewalk to advertise the Opera House for several blocks up and down Bowery Street. Additional accommodations for the audience were also introduced. The forward section of the parquette was equipped with cane chairs and labeled the "orchestra." Patrons could sit here for 50¢. Stage boxes were also made available at $3.00 and $5.00.

The fall season was not very old, however, before box office receipts began to show a noticeable decline. The east-siders were not turning out as they had in the past, and the two managers must have had some second thoughts about their new investment. The dip may have been caused by the start of the general fall and winter entertainment season in New York and in particular perhaps by the appeal of the Old Bowery and the Varieties. The east-siders loved the turgid melodramas served up with all the trimmings at the Old Bowery, and they had long claimed the Varieties as their favorite neighborhood concert saloon.

But competition can be a two-way street, and it is just possible that the Varieties was hurting in turn from the Pastor-Sharpley enterprise. In January, 1866, when Opera House receipts had fallen to $5,097, the Varieties suddenly turned off its sign and closed down for good.[25] This, plus the fact that "444" burned down on February 12, may account for the immediate improvement in

Opera House figures. February receipts rose to $5,800, and by the end of July the total receipts for the previous twelve-month period amounted to $70,211.50, or an average of around $5,850 a month.[26]

Sometime in the early summer of 1866 Sharpley withdrew from the Bowery operation. His name was missing in the ads beginning on August 4, and two weeks later the *Clipper* made it known publicly that "Mr. Sam Sharpley is no longer interested in the management of this establishment, he having sold out to Tony Pastor, who is now the sole manager."[27] There are no clues that might help to explain Sharpley's departure. The ads and printed programs had listed him as "Business Manager." This office was taken over sometime during the 1866-67 season by John F. Poole, former co-manager of the Varieties. Poole held this position off and on until the fall of 1874, when he took permanent leave to open the Olympic Theatre on Broadway as a variety house. Pastor replaced him with N. D. Roberts.

Although Pastor and Sharpley dissolved their partnership in the Opera House, they retained a joint interest in the touring company they had sent out in September, 1865, and kept on the road through the following fall. An ad for the "Tony Pastor Combination" in November, 1866, still listed both men as "proprietors."[28]

Pastor continued to send variety companies on the road under his name throughout most of his long career, even heading up his own traveling troupe for several weeks each spring and summer until the late 1890's. For the first few years he restricted his itinerary to the east coast. In 1871, however, he began pushing westward into the Mississippi Valley, and in 1876 he led his troupers on the first of many successful cross-country tours to California. His good fortune on the road was infectious, and as railroads began to expand during the 1870's dozens of variety managers followed his example and started hawking their amusement wares across the nation. William Pastor, who had returned from abroad in 1864 to ply the trade of a comic singer, generally looked after the Opera House while brother Tony was away, and later Frank Pastor and Harry S. Sanderson assumed this responsibility at the showman's successive houses on Broadway and 14th Street.

The Opera House remained dark for three weeks in July, 1866, so that the auditorium could be "fitted up in good style for the coming fall season."[29] Pastor returned to the city in early August after a brief swing through New England and officially opened the new season on August 8. Patrons found the auditorium sporting a new coat of paint and the domed ceiling and stage boxes touched up cheerfully with gold leaf. All the benches in the parquette had now been replaced by cane seats, and four large gas lamps had been installed in front of the house to light up the lobby entrance as well as the billboards announcing each week's attractions. "Everything looks as neat and clean as a new pin," said the *Clipper*.[30] Pastor called his showplace an "Opera House," said another paper of the day, "not because he had any idea of giving opera to his patrons, but because the name sounded well."[31] It seems that he was determined that the house should live up to its name. He gave it a face-lifting every summer and later continued the same care and grooming policy at his other houses.

If the fledgling manager had harbored doubts about being able to carry on successfully without Sharpley, they soon must have been dispelled. Business boomed, and the "No More Seats" sign became a common sight at the box office throughout the new season. Even nasty weather could not keep the crowds away. A *Clipper* reporter, for example, told his readers that when he attended the place early in February, 1867, "the night was a very disagreeable one, the rain coming down in torrents, and the walking in some places being ankle deep with water and slush. Notwithstanding these outside drawbacks, it did not prevent the Opera House from being crowded, for the house was literally jammed from gallery to parquette, and when the performance began there was not standing room in any part of the auditorium."[32] On Saturday night, March 16, 1867, the air was nippy and filled witth heavy snow, yet Pastor's was said to have drawn over a thousand patrons, "more than the Winter Garden, Kelly and Leon's, Circus, Barnum's, and Wood's combined."[33]

When Pastor took to the road again on June 29, he should have been happy. His maiden voyage as an independent manager had been successful, and he had every reason to expect that the upcoming tour, which was composed primarily of repeat bookings, would be profitable as well. But there was a matter of personal concern that must have dampened his spirits — his wife, Anna, had been ailing from her consumptive condition for several weeks. Her health deteriorated after Pastor's departure, and early in July she sought relief at the mineral springs in Saratoga. Her condition worsened, however, and Pastor left his company at the Morris Brothers Opera House in Boston to be at her side. She died on July 18.[34] The manager canceled the rest of his tour and returned to New York to arrange for the funeral. Anna Pastor was buried on July 22 in the Pastor family lot on "The Shadowy Way" in the Evergreens Cemetery in Brooklyn.

When the summer season began on July 29, Pastor did not appear on the bill for several weeks out of respect to his wife's memory. He remained a widower for four years, then married Josephine Foley of Hartford in 1871. "They met at the home of her relatives," said the *Hartfort Courant*, "and it was only a short time after that they were married."[35] Josephine Pastor outlived her husband by fifteen years.

Business continued to hold up well at the Opera House for the rest of the decade. The *Clipper* reported in November, 1867, that "Tony Pastor's Opera House has become a great institution on the Bowery side," and a year later, that "business continues first rate at this house, so much so that when nearly every other place in town has a poor house Tony has a good attendance."[36] From January through December, 1867, box office receipts amounted to $84,516, and for the same period in 1868 they climbed to $88,331.[37] Pastor invested much of his profit in a continual effort to improve the appearance and comfort of the house — fresh paint on the walls, new carpets on the floors, new gas fixtures in

30

the auditorium, fancy lace curtains on the windows, etc. The Opera House was closed down for extensive repairs during the entire month of July, 1869, yet receipts for the year totaled $85,911.[38]

Tony Pastor's Opera House was clearly a going concern. By 1870 it was the most popular showcase for variety in the city and a landmark on New York's east side. The manager's jumbo-size shows were attracting people from all over the city, and his annual tours were eagerly anticipated by countless thousands along the eastern seaboard. In the spring of 1870 he confidently arranged a five-year extension on his Opera House lease and threw a big party for his company to celebrate the occasion. Those managerial boots were now well broken in and fitting fine.

CHAPTER FOUR

Plenty of Beef and Mustard

Keeping a theatre attractive and comfortable is all well and good, but in the final analysis it is the show itself that must win and hold the public. Pastor knew this, and no variety manager ever worked harder to make his entertainment the best in town. To this end he became a severe taskmaster. The *Spirit of the Times* labeled him "The Bowery Autocrat,"[1] and so he was. No detail was too small to receive his personal attention and no one dared take for granted his approval on anything. He personally supervised the planning and construction of all new scenery, costumes and props, and when a new afterpiece was on the drawing board he hovered over the writer like a mother hen. He spent hours in his office selecting and negotiating for acts, and he put together the running order of each bill with studious care. More often than not, he was backstage at performance time to see that everything ran smoothly and according to instruction. "Show business and successful presentations were in the very marrow of his bones," said Morell in his biography of Lillian Russell, "and no trouble was too great for him to take to imbue his disciples with this same spirit."[2]

For all his severity as a manager, however, Pastor enjoyed a warm rapport with his workers. He ran a tight ship, but it was a happy ship and his crew was probably as devoted a group as could be found in early variety. He was a demanding boss, and for this they respected him; but he also was a warm-hearted and generous friend to all of them, and for this they revered him. "He was a little general," said Lillian Russell. "When he spoke his performers listened."[3] They listened and they responded because "they knew that whatever he said or whatever he did was the honest judgment of his heart."[4] And the public responded too because they had come to know that the Opera House show was indeed the best in town.

The bills were hearty, robust affairs seasoned well to the particular tastes of the east side. They followed the traditional variety format — a medley of songs, dances, comedy, circus acts and drama — but their geniality and overall high quality week in and week out seem to have been truly exceptional in variety circles. The Opera House opened with the promise that the management would employ "the services of some of the Most Talented Artistes in the Country."[5] And this was no empty promise! Many a run-of-the-mill act played the Opera House, but so did many a top-rung act, and the weekly bills regularly featured at least two or three top favorites.

Audiences saw such noted circus acts as the Coutillier Brothers, who performed derring-do on the flying trapeze, and Conchita Ronsati, who walked up a wire from the stage to the ceiling of the auditorium; such favorite songstresses as Viola Clifton, Jennie Engel, and the Weston Sisters; and such popular minstrels as Eph Horn, a real old-timer, Delehanty and Hengler, William Hoey, Hughey Dougherty, the stump orator, Billy Sheppard, noted for playing the "Anvil Chorus" on the banjo, and the inimitable Billy Emerson. Emerson was one of minstrelsy's finest balladists. His rich tenor voice made hits out of such songs as "The Yaller Gal That Looked at Me," "Nicodemus Johnson," and "The Big Sunflower."

Many a new act was broken in at the Opera House. Pastor had sincere sympathy for beginners, and besides, beginners were always willing to work cheaper than established acts. A good many of these newcomers went on to become popular variety stars. There was Ella Wesner, for example, one of variety's first male impersonators. She specialized in English music hall songs, monologs and characterizations, and one of her most popular take-offs concerned an inebriated Dapper Dan who kept dozing off in a barber's chair. Gus Williams, a German-dialect comic, was another who got his start with Pastor. He became a celebrated performer in the 1880's and 1890's. Then, too, Ed Harrigan and Tony Hart, on the threshold of their colorful career as a team, toured with Pastor's forces in the summer of 1872, then played for six weeks at his Opera House in the fall. They were a blackface act at this time and appeared in such sketches as *The Little Fraud, After the War,* and *The Colored Gentlemen.* The team went on to achieve extraordinary success in the second half of the decade.

By the late 1860's the rapid growth of variety entertainment was attracting performers with unique abilities. Pastor, always on the lookout for something new and bizarre, was among the first to recognize the value of these acts and to utilize them to any great degree. There was Johnny Forbes, for example, the champ drummer who demonstrated his rhythmic skills while performing military maneuvers around the stage; Harry Gurr, who sang, ate bananas, and played musical instruments while submerged in a tank of water; Mlle. de Granville, billed as a female Sampson, who lifted heavy weights with her teeth; and Professor O'Reardon, who created music of sorts by variously striking a number of partially-filled water glasses with two small mallets. He called the glassware collection a Tumbleronicon. Pastor even stepped into Barnum's world of freaks in March, 1871, to offer Colonel Routh Goshen, "the largest man living," and General Grant, Jr., "the smallest man living," in songs, burlesques, and comedy.[6]

34

One area that he seems to have tapped more often for novelty items than any of his colleagues was athletics. The east-siders took great delight in demonstrations of physical prowess. Pastor himself is said to have been particularly fond of prize fighting and "would travel all night in a buggy to get to the scene of an illegal finish fight."[7] He made sure that his customers saw frequent exhibitions of fisticuffs by contemporary fighters like Sam Collyer, Dick Hollywood and Barney Aaron. Sometimes these athletes even appeared in afterpieces especially tailored to their pugilistic talents. During the week beginning on May 21, 1870, for example, Collyer and Aaron appeared in *Dan Donnelly, Champion of Ireland*, and an ad promised that the drama would feature "a correct representation of the famous Donnelly and Cooper battle" with Aaron appearing as Donnelly and Collyer as Cooper.[8] Collyer also did a turn in the olio, playing the banjo and performing a triple clog dance with his two sons.

One of the first athletes to appear at Pastor's was Walter Browne, champion oarsman of the United States, who performed Indian club exercises in early June, 1867. He returned in February, 1870, but this time he left the clubs at home and entertained the audience by flexing his muscles in a series of "living statuary" poses. The Opera House was the scene of a truly bizarre variety attraction in March, 1868, when "the Champion Pedestrian of the World, Young Mills . . . [performed] his extraordinary feat of walking a mile inside of eight minutes, one hundred and twenty-six times around a circle of forty-two feet."[9] Something similar was demonstrated in early November, 1874, by two other "footmen," Ed Mullen and W. E. Harding. Very pedestrian entertainment, to be sure! But the east-siders loved it, and Pastor's early example helped to establish a practice that lasted well into the twentieth century. The later vaudeville stage was visited regularly by boxers, baseball players, wrestlers, marathon walkers, and even by six-day bicycle riders racing on a treadmill. The practice can still be seen today on certain television variety shows.

Most of the specialty performers at the Opera House were hired by the week. Some acts were engaged for two if they were particularly good and had new material to offer, while crowd-pleasers, of course, might be kept on for weeks at a time. In an effort to woo a steady clientele, Pastor tried to put on a basically new show each week, but this did not necessarily mean a change in performers, simply a change to some degree in the entertainment offered.

The Opera House maintained its own stock company and *corps de ballet*. The first consisted of a more-or-less permanent band of favorites engaged for upward of a year at a time. They carried the main roles in the afterpieces, helped out in the visiting sketches, and did an olio turn every now and then. Among the more enduring members of this group were Addie Le Brun, D. L. Morris, G. W. Thompson, Frank Kerns, Thomas A. Riggs, Helene Smith, Frank Girard, who was also Pastor's stage manager, and James Collier, who designed much of the Opera House scenery. Most of the larger resorts had such companies, and Pastor most likely had been a stock member at "444." The *corps de ballet* was directed by a

Monsieur Szollosy and consisted of ten "young" ladies. The dancers offered a weekly terpsichorean specialty and were usually on hand to decorate the afterpiece.

"The ballet is a great feature of Tony Pastor's Opera House," said the *Clipper* in April, 1867. "It is decidedly one of the best that we have had in the music hall business in this city."[10] An ad in the same issue of the paper indicated some of the conditions of employment: "Ballet Girls Wanted for Tony Pastor's Opera House, 201 Bowery. None but first class needed. Those who perform Solo Dances preferred; must have a good wardrobe. Engagements steady for one year."[11]

Few variety managers gave as much care and attention to mounting the afterpieces as the Bowery Autocrat. He dressed them up with fresh costumes and scenery and always insisted on ample rehearsals — ample, that is, for variety. The stock performers simply went over their parts several times the preceding week; then, on Monday, when the new specialty acts had arrived, the little playlet was whipped into final shape. If the piece was a particularly ambitious effort, however, the incoming acts were often required to show up for a rehearsal on Sunday, a day when the house was closed. It was standard procedure for specialty performers to participate in as many different parts of the program as the management desired. In Pastor's bill for the week of October 14, 1877, for example, Harrigan and Hart not only appeared in their own sketch, *After the War*, but they helped out in another, *High Jack, the Heeler*, and Harrigan took part in still another, *The Christmas Pudding*, as well as in the afterpiece, *The Irish Diamond.* Performers had to work hard in variety. There were no unions in those days.

During the Christmas season each year, Pastor topped off his show with an elaborate holiday pantomime. These annual spectacles were a big hit on the east side. Most of them were based on popular nursery rhymes — *There Was an Old Woman who Lived in a Shoe* (1867), *Hickety Pickety, My Black Hen* (1868), *Ba Ba Black Sheep* (1870), *Goosey, Goosey Gander* (1873). Familiar *commedia* characters moved in and out of these pieces, and Pastor appeared regularly as either Harlequin or Clown. They were far from being mute affairs. There was plenty of comic dialog and singing. The pieces were decked out in storybook costumes and scenery, and the 1867 holiday treat featured what the manager called "a gorgeous transformation scene costing over three thousand dollars, eclipsing everything ever before presented in pantomime."[12]

Most of Pastor's afterpieces were burlesques and sensational dramas, and most of them were written for him by John F. Poole. Current theatrical hits were always ripe material for travesty. One of Poole's first spoofs at the Opera House was *The White Crook* in early June, 1867. It was a take-off in the main on *The Black Crook*, the musical extravaganza currently breaking attendance records at Niblo's Garden and causing something of a sensation with its daring displays of the feminine leg. Pastor's burlesque featured "a female jockey dance, as well as a march and drill of all the male members of the company dressed as female policemen."[13]

Lydia Thompson and her British Blondes appeared in *Ixion; or, the Man at the Wheel* at Wood's Museum in the fall of 1868 to further dazzle and shock New Yorkers with sizzling exhibitions of feminine pulchritude. Poole quickly prepared a travesty on the show for Pastor. Here was a burlesque of a burlesque! The Opera House version was called *Ixion in the Bowery* with Addie Le Brun as Venus and Pastor himself as the fleet-footed Mercury. "Most of the choisest airs in the burlesque, as produced at Wood's Museum, are retained," observed the *Clipper*, "while several new ones have been introduced, all of which are given with considerable applause, particularly 'Beautiful Dreamer,' 'Taffy was a Welshman,' and 'Ring the Bells for Sarah.' "[14]

Travesties on Shakespeare had long been popular in the minstrel halls, and variety was quick to pick up the idea. The east-siders hooted and howled through numerous of these burlesques at the Opera House — *Richard III, the Crookedest Man in New York* (October, 1868), for example, and *Romeo and Juliet; or, the Beautiful Blonde who dyed for Love* (March, 1869), and *Othello and his Man Friday* (May, 1869). This last one probably took its cue from the spectacular production of *Robinson Crusoe* currently at Wood's Museum. The *Clipper* announced that "on Monday, Tuesday, and Wednesday, Tony will appear as Othello and on Thursday, Friday, and Saturday, Othello will be played by Tony."[15] Poole was responsible for writing what turned out to be one of Pastor's most talked-about afterpieces — his burlesque of *Hamlet* in February, 1870.

At that time Edwin Booth was in the middle of a revival of *Hamlet* at his own theatre, and George L. Fox, then at the height of his clowning career, had a burlesque of the play in production at the Olympic Theatre on Broadway. "Tony is determined," said the *Clipper*, "that the east siders shall have a 'Hamlet' as well as Broadway."[16] Pastor called his burlesque *Hamlet the Second*, and the *Clipper* observed that Poole "has taken in nearly all the principal events of the tragedy, and from beginning to the close has burlesqued every scene and situation in a most laughable manner."[17] Pastor played the title role dressed in black velvet with a martial cloak and a cap with a long plume. A large and grotesque pumpkin served as Yorick's skull. Addie Le Brun and Helene Smith sported breeches for the parts of Laertes and Horatio; Nelse Seymour, a tall and lanky fellow, wore armour and a silk stovepipe hat as the ghost; and Thomas A. Riggs falsettoed his way through the part of Ophelia in knee-length yellow locks. Comic and sentimental songs and topical allusions were sprinkled liberally through the piece. Ophelia, for instance, always entered to the popular air of "Walking Down Broadway," and the First Gravedigger, played by Frank Kerns, sang "Any Ornaments for Your Mantelpiece" as his spade littered the stage with tin cans, hoop skirts, and other bric-a-brac. The finale was a jaunty rendition by the entire cast — including the corpses — of the popular minstrel number, "Shoo Fly."[18]

37

The sensational dramas at the Opera House covered a wide range of subjects. *Wide Awake; or, a New York Boy in China* (September, 1868) was a fanciful extravaganza in which a Bowery Boy, played by Pastor, made a balloon ascension, landed in China and, after much ado with the local citizenry, succeeded in winning the hand of the Emperor's lovely daughter. *The New York Volunteers; or, the last of Libby Prison* (February, 1867) was an excursion into American history. The *Clipper* supplied an unusually detailed report on the production:

> *The first scene is taken from the London Comedy, 'Ours,' the situation being the same . . . . To aid and heighten the effect of this scene, as the volunteers are about leaving their homes for the battle field, a full military brass band is introduced on the stage, and this is so effectively done that it brings down the house. The rest of the piece shows us the life of the volunteer soldiers, the fatigue of a long march, their fare and pastimes. The last scene represents the interior of 'Libby Prison,' that has been made infamous during the late rebellion, with all its horrors as related by many an escaped man who has cause to recollect the place as long as he lives. The attack on the prison by the Union volunteers is very cleverly done, and the tableau is a very imposing one. No pains have been spared by the management in placing this piece upon the* stage. . . . *The piece itself is very cleverly written, and is well adapted for a music hall afterpiece. Tony Pastor's Ephraim Shapp was a good performance . . . . Taken altogether, it was one of the best dramatic performances we have seen in a variety place of amusement, and we seldom see so much pains exhibited in placing a piece on the stage for a variety company.*[19]

Topicality was the warp and woof of variety, and a good many of Pastor's little dramas dealt with current events on the local scene — *The Rich and Poor of New York* (July, 1867), *The Mechanics Strike; or, the Eight Hour System* (August, 1868), *The Orphan Girl; or, New York in the Streets* (November, 1870). If such "local dramas" did not contain enough excitement for his Bowery fans, Pastor offered other pieces which, judging by their titles at least, must have been well endowed with the lures of melodrama — *The Forest Fiend* (November, 1866), *Gamblers of the Mississippi* (September, 1867), *The French Spy* (December, 1872), and *Daredevil Pat; or, the Dashing Rider of the Plains* (February, 1873), to name only a few. This last little drama was based on a "dime novel" written by the manager himself.

For his Irish patrons, Pastor produced dozens of pieces dealing with current conditions in Ireland or with Irish history and lore, pieces like *The Fenian Dream; or, Ireland Free at Last* (December, 1865), *The Fairy Shamrock; or, the Lakes of Killarney* (September, 1868), and *Life in Ireland* (March, 1874). He also saluted the German element in the neighborhood with numerous pieces in which a "Dutchman" was a central figure. Most of these were farces like *A Dutchman in a Double-Bedded Room* (May, 1869) and *The Dutchman in Strange Lodgings* (April, 1870).

We would like to know more about these burlesques, pantomimes, sensational dramas, and farces but the scripts have vanished with the passing years. Pastor later registered a number of his afterpieces with the Copyright Office of the Library of Congress but a search of the files revealed only the registrations, no copies of the works themselves. Except for occasional and brief journalistic comments, the hundreds of afterpieces presented at the Opera House — and elsewhere, for that matter — seem to exist today only as so many titles.

Pastor certainly set a bountiful table for his east side guests! In the eyes of his loyal fans, however, the most attractive dish on that table was Pastor himself. Toward the end of his first year in the Opera House, the *Clipper* came out with a short poetic tribute to his success:

> *In his snug chapel, where holds Tony forth,*
>   *He is not on'y Pastor, but the deacon,*
> *And if, when you see him, you wish to see*
>   *New pastures, your taste is not correct, I reckon.*
> *New songs, fresh farces, and good witticisms*
>   *To charm the public all unite,*
> *While Tony, ever indefatigable,*
>   *To each night's sport contributes his mite.*[20]

It was always magic time when Pastor's name card was displayed and he sauntered onto the stage to "contribute his mite" to the fun. "Well, here I am again," he would say with a devilish grin, and the roar from the audience was always deafening and conspicuously affectionate. He was the darling of the east side. His voice had not improved with the years, and his dancing was awkward at best — "sometimes pathetic" was the way Gilbert described it.[21] But these deficiencies did not matter to those fans who were hopelessly charmed by that "witchery of personality." Take, for example, those two Boweryites who visited the Italian Opera one evening: "Coming away, one gentleman was overheard to ask the other what he thought of the 'oppra.' To which quoth his companion: 'Talk about yer Susseeneys and yer Brigneoleys, and all yer other d---d furriners, why Tony Pastor'd lick the skin o' the teeth off hafe dozen of 'em.' "[22] It was this kind of spirit that filled up Pastor's auditorium. Of course, there were dissenters here and there. Charles Cochran, for instance, an English music hall artist and manager, wrote that Pastor "was a poor artist, and they used to tell the story of a man who came to the box office and asked: 'Has Mr. Pastor been on yet?'--'Yes!'--'Then I'll go in.' "[23] The majority of Opera House patrons, however, certainly would have agreed whole-heartedly with the *Clipper's* observation that "a 'Tony Pastor' performance without the presence of the popular host himself seems very much like 'beef without mustard.' "[24]

In his early years in the Bowery Pastor appeared on stage in the garb of a circus clown, in the sloppy outfit of a rube, or in some special attire appropriate

39

to the spirit of the particular selection he was singing. When he sang patriotic songs, he often appeared as a Union soldier or as Uncle Sam. But he gradually moved away from strictly comic or individualized attire and, by 1873, was appearing regularly in a "coat of light-blue silk velvet, white vest, pantaloons and hat."[25] Soon after he moved his operation to Broadway in 1875, he appropriated white tie and tails as his standard stage wardrobe. It mattered little what he wore as long as the Pastor charm came through, and it always did — the warm, friendly, down-to-earth disposition, the bubbling energy, the impish gleam in the eye, and the almost child-like joy and enthusiasm that pervaded everything he did.

Pastor was well aware of the importance of matching style of delivery with the peculiar bent or attitude of a number. Indeed, one of his own songs voiced this very awareness: "It may be full of sentiment, wit, interest, and fun. But so much depends upon the style in which it's done."[26] When he sang a sentimental song he stood poised and swayed rhythmically to the music, but for a light-hearted number he bounced around the stage with roguish delight, twisting the grand mustache and kicking up his heels. "Tony is as lively as a flea in his budget of songs," exclaimed the *Clipper* in April, 1867, "particularly the one entitled 'The Ballet-Girl,' with terpsichorean movements by Tony, which are very laughable."[27] He usually sang alone, but every so often he warbled a duet with Addie Le Brun, Jennie Engel, or some other songstress. His turn was never complete, however, until he asked the audience to join in on the refrain of a number. "Okay, everybody help me out now," he would say, and the response was usually loud and hearty.

Pastor was his own best star, and he knew it. The Opera House ads and postbills promised the public week after week that "Tony Pastor will Appear at Every Performance." Although he curtailed his "dramatic" efforts toward the end of his stay in the Bowery, rare was the Opera House bill that did not feature his personal turn of comic and sentimental songs. There was always plenty of "beef" in the Opera House shows, and more often than not the genial manager was on hand himself to furnish that extra dab of "mustard" that his fans so richly enjoyed and demanded.

CHAPTER FIVE

Reformer in the Wings

Practically every modern account of Pastor's managerial career has something to say about his so-called pioneer crusade to wipe variety's runny nose and tame its coarse manners so it might have a fighting chance to attract notice from respectable circles. Most of these accounts emphasize his accomplishments on 14th Street, where there is little doubt that he succeeded in establishing a showcase for family-style variety freed from drink and smoke and "clean as a newly barked willow whistle."[1] Some accounts even go so far as to suggest that his crusade did not get under way until he moved to this location in the fall of 1881. The idea of refining variety was supposedly a sudden inspiration on his part, an innovation, "a daring venture"[2] that hit him in transit from Broadway to 14th Street.

The truth of the matter is that family-style variety on 14th Street was not an innovation with Pastor at all, but rather the culmination of a policy he had been pursuing in one way or another and with varying degrees of success ever since he first took to management back in 1865. He insisted, moreover, that it was the very idea of taking a broom to variety's stable that led him into management in the first place.

"I had long believed," he said of his "444" days, "that the variety show should attract the patronage of women and families and determined to make an effort to demonstrate my theory."[3]

His theory was not exactly a new one. As we have already noted, several of the larger concert saloons in New York and elsewhere had been trying to woo the ladies to special smoke- and liquor-free matinees since the beginning of the decade. Pastor did not admit any indebtedness to these affairs, but their introduction at Rivers' Melodeon, at the Broadway Music Hall, and at "444" during the time he was appearing there could hardly have escaped his notice. Nor is it likely that he was unaware of the disinfected variety shows presented along with moral dramas and curiosities at Barnum's prim-and-proper Museum on Broadway.

Moreover, Odell uncovered information leading him to believe that "444" had discarded some of its concert saloon trappings by 1864. "The '444' had developed into a real variety hall," he writes, "the first known to the city. No waitresses advertized here!"[4] If he is correct and Butler's establishment had indeed gone respectable to some degree by 1864, then this could very well have been the catalyst for Pastor's entire scheme of reform.

There are some observers, like Montrose Moses, who have suggested that there was puritan zeal behind the scheme. Moses surmised that Pastor's earlier singing at temperance meetings "may have been the beginning of his determination to clear the vaudeville stage of its traditional association with liquor."[5] Others have proposed that the showman's reform efforts could have been dictated simply by his unabashed fondness for the fairer sex. Pastor admitted that "I wanted the ladies, for I have always liked them."[6] He was known to be sympathetic toward the movement for women's rights, which was in full swing during the 1860's. Sophie Tucker, who appeared at Pastor's 14th Street house in 1908 as Sophie Taylor, conjectured that "maybe Tony foresaw that the country was going feminist."[7] But she quickly added what was undoubtedly the main reason behind his move, namely that "maybe he just figured that if you could sell five tickets to a family you made more money than by selling just one."[8]

Pastor may indeed have borne the markings of the puritan, but he was also an opportunist, and he apparently saw the refinement of variety as a potentially sound economic maneuver. As a matter of fact, his own words support this view. During the early 1860's, he wrote, "the vaudeville houses were patronized almost exclusively by men. During my stay at 444 I studied the situation closely, and determined that if women could also be induced to attend, the patronage could be materially extended."[9] It seems clear that the "opportunity" he had seen "waiting for the man ... who could disentangle it [variety] from cigar-smoking and beer-drinking accompaniment"[10] was not so much the opportunity of enjoying a moral victory or a greater popularity with the ladies as the opportunity to realize a handsome dollar-and-cents profit.

He claimed that he wasted no time in trying out his scheme, that he made his initial bid for family support on his first tour in the spring and summer of 1865, "advertising freely and pledging our reputation that the show should in no way offend." The papers of the day made no comment on this aspect of the tour, but we have the manager's own admission that the effort met with only "moderate success."[11] Pastor could not have been too greatly discouraged, however, because he opened the Opera House in late July with the confident boast that the management intended to make the place into "the Great Family Resort of the City—where heads of families can bring their Ladies and Children, and witness an exceptional entertainment—one that will please the most fastidious."[12] The Varieties concert saloon down the street had offered special matinees for ladies and children in the previous year but Pastor hoped to go one big step further. He wanted to attract mixed audiences to the evening shows as well. He conceded that realization of this "was a long time developing ...

because one had to temper the professional wind, as it were, to the limbs."[13] The evidence is slight and often sketchy, but there is enough to suggest that he worked at this task all through his ten years in the Bowery.

The Opera House offered a Saturday matinee from the outset, but the ads of early August did not stress that this performance was aimed primarily at the ladies. Pastor was doubtless hoping that they would turn out for the regular evening shows. And perhaps they did. On August 6, for example, he advertised that "the gentlemen [are] delighted and the Ladies in Exstacies" and that there are "front seats for ladies."[14] Opera House ads making similar claims appeared regularly over the years. Perhaps, however, it was his disappointment over the ladies' response in the evening that soon prompted him to emphasize the Saturday matinee as the most appropriate time for them to visit the house.

An ad in the *New York Herald* on August 25 announced a "Grand Matinee Every Saturday at 2½ O'Clock, when ladies and children can safely attend without escort. The attention of guardians, school teachers, and directors is called to this announcement."[15] A few weeks later a Wednesday matinee for the ladies and children was added, and an ad on October 23 proclaimed: "Children admitted half price at the matinees."[16] Pastor continued these semi-weekly matinees during his Bowery management, even supplementing them from time to time with extra afternoon shows for the family on special occasions: Washington's Birthday, Christmas, and New Year's Day. Records indicate that the attendance was good at these functions and that women and children were on hand.

Meanwhile, judging at least from accounts in the *Herald*, Pastor was taking steps to bring some degree of decorum and propriety to his auditorium in the evening. The *Herald* said on September 26, 1865: "We are glad to see that the management is bestowing as much attention upon the audience part of the house as upon the stage arrangements. The strict [watchfullness?] exercised over it has resulted in excluding rowdyish and troublesome elements." A few days later it reported that "the good order observed and the absence of peanut feasts and boisterous applause, which have become traditional [sic] with Bowery establishments, can, no doubt, in a great degree account for the respectable character of the audience which attend there." And on November 8 of the same year the paper announced that "the judgment with which this establishment is managed is procuring for it a large amount of family support. We observe that ladies and children now form a large proportion of its audiences."[17]

We should note, however, that the *Herald* may have had an ulterior motive for its favorable remarks about the Opera House. Trouble had arisen between the paper and the theatrical managers of the city in the latter part of September, 1865, when James Gordon Bennett, editor of the paper, had a personal disagreement with Barnum and had refused to print any of the showman's ads for his new museum on Broadway. Barnum had taken his case before a coalition of city managers representing the Academy of Music, Wallack's, Niblo's Garden, the Old Bowery, the New Bowery, and the Olympic Theatre. This group agreed to stand behind him in the dispute. When the managers received no satisfactory explanation from the newspaper for its treatment of Barnum, "it was unanimously agreed that they should withdraw after Saturday [October 1] all their advertisements from the *Herald*."[18] In writing of the events that followed this decision, Barnum said: "The *Herald* then began to abuse and vilify the theatrical and opera managers, their artists and their performances, and by way of contrast profusely praised Tony Pastor's Bowery show, and sundry entertainments of a similar character."[19] Toward the end of September, 1865, then, when trouble with the managers was anticipated, and after October 1, when trouble had arrived, the *Herald* may have been deliberately "puffing" the situation at the Opera House. The managerial embargo on the paper dragged on until September, 1868.

Two factors that certainly had a strong bearing on the character and behavior of the Opera House customers were the house rules on drinking and smoking and the general complexion of the show itself. Alvin Harlow claims in *Old Bowery Days* that at the Opera House Pastor "abolished the bar which had ever and always been an adjunct of the theater, and did not permit either drinking or smoking within its precincts."[20] The available evidence, meager though it is, argues against Harlow. We find in the *Clipper* for June 22, 1867, the notation that the Opera House was currently furnishing its evening patrons with ice water free of charge. The paper went on to say that "it is much pleasanter — to the ladies at least — to have their gentlemanly attendants sit by their sides and tell their tales of love sipping a glass of ice water than it is for them to jump up at the close of every act, rush out, and shortly after return with the smell of ein glass of lager or a Bourbon sour following them."[21]

The paper's remarks, to be sure, strongly suggest that no strong spirits were to be had in the auditorium itself but that they were close at hand. How close at hand? Probably as close as Tracy's Billiard and Refreshment Saloon, which the Opera House program for December 2, 1865, referred to as "adjoining the Hall."[22] Photographs and drawings of the Opera House exterior reveal that there were two front entrances to the building itself, one at 201 Bowery, which obviously led into the Opera House lobby, and another just south of this at 199 Bowery. None of the pictures show any identifying signs at the 199 Bowery entrance, but this could very well have led into Tracy's "adjoining" establishment. It may have been these quarters, moreover, that were renovated early in 1871 into what the *Clipper* described as "a large and commodious refreshment saloon, elegantly fitted up and supplied with chairs, tables, etc., adjoining the main entrance to the auditorium."[23]

And lest we think that temperance drinks were the main attraction here, a Pastor playbill for the week of October 14, 1872, sets us straight in no uncertain terms: "Best Quality of Ales, Wines, Liquors, and Cigars, to be had at the Saloon inside the Theatre." This little oasis was clearly a Pastor enterprise, for the same playbill bore the notation that Dody Pastor was the "proprietor."[24]

This evidence seems to indicate that Pastor indeed did not banish all drinking and smoking from the "precincts" of the Opera House, and, furthermore, that he even encouraged these activities by setting up a saloon "inside the

Theatre." But it does appear that the auditorium itself was placed off-limits to drinking (and most likely to smoking as well), which doubtless would have been a step in the right direction for any place trying to attract family support. Pastor probably realized that, while trying to build a new audience with one hand, he would have to cater to the old with the other. So, no doubt, he freed variety from its saloon trappings to attract those who preferred their entertainment straight but kept the saloon itself at close quarters to service those others who might want to catch a smoke between acts or who felt compelled to wash down all that Pastor beef with something stronger than ice water.

What about the complexion of the shows? If Pastor separated them from the saloon features of drink and smoke, did he also separate them from the coarseness and blue humor that long had been part and parcel of that class of entertainment? He once said that in trying to develop the idea that families could attend variety "one had to tone down a show that pleased the men to one that pleased the women."[25] Just what he might have been doing in this regard at the Opera House is conjectural. Opinions differ, and the scraps of contemporary data are hazy and inconclusive.

He had predicted in the *Clipper* on July 22, 1865, that ladies and gentlemen alike would be delighted with the "versatility of the performance and the high moral excellence of the programme,"[26] and he had opened the Opera House, as we have already noted, with the avowed intention of offering shows that would "please the most fastidious."[27] A later article in *Variety* recalled that the Opera House "shows were kept free of any offensive line or bit of business and before long the stag audience had become a thing of the past."[28] But the *Herald* in October, 1865, considered that at least one reason east-siders were flocking to the place was because the shows were "racy."[29] Gilbert states flatly that the acts Pastor booked at the Opera House and even later at his Broadway house were "coarse, vulgar, often obscene."[30] He holds that the manager did not present a "clean" show until he opened his 14th Street house in October, 1881.[31] Lloyd Morris, furthermore, has told us that "to the Sanctimonious, Pastor's was a sinful resort. Authors of books about New York City warned strangers to the city against its [Pastor's] 'dreary gaieties' and asserted that it was a place 'where the mob is tickled and good taste disgusted.' "[32]

Three contemporary books attacking the evils of New York concert saloons in general have been found, and none of them makes any comment one way or the other about the Opera House.[33] We get little help from the journals of the day; they seldom made any commitment about the "tone" of Pastor's entertainment, but merely stated that he offered a "good show" and that "women were frequently in attendance." It is quite possible that he offered one show in the evening and another at his ladies' matinee and that he leavened the afternoon fare in some way or other. The *Clipper* in June, 1870, for example, said that Pastor was offering "a good show every night, and something of the same order at the matinees."[34] But we can not tell whether this statement referred to the content or to the quality of the performances. Whatever stage reforms Pastor was trying to implement in the ladies' behalf, however, it is unlikely that his efforts would have been restricted for very long, if at all, to the matinees. He clearly wanted the ladies to feel free to attend regular evening performances, and to do so with open consciences.

The complexion of Pastor's Opera House entertainment is indeed thickly veiled and indistinct. It seems only reasonable to assume that any manager desiring to build his place into a "Great Family Resort" would try to gear his shows to family tastes. In all likelihood, then, Pastor was taking steps of one kind or another to sand-down variety's rough edges and sweeten its disposition, although once again, as in the matter of drinking and smoking, he probably moved cautiously so as not to lose altogether the support of variety's old guard who liked a little spice. How he might have managed such a compromise is a moot question. In any event, it appears that the Opera House was far from being a concert saloon and that Pastor was trying hard to make it into a more or less regular theatre.

During his last three years in the Bowery he introduced several promotional features. Ostensibly, these were aimed at further recruiting the ladies. In reality, the "Ladies Invitation Nights" and the distribution and raffling off of merchandise were maneuvers to bolster a slumping overall attendance. This slump was brought on by increasing competition and especially by the general depression that followed the financial panic of October, 1873.

After the Varieties and old "444" left the scene in 1866, the Opera House had virtually no serious competition in the field of variety. Business prospered. Early in the new decade, however, conditions were changing and Pastor may have had good reason to regret having signed that new five-year lease on the Opera House in 1870. "I was not long permitted to enjoy the prosperity I had won," he recalled. "Competition sprang up immediately and rapidly."[35] The only house that he mentioned specifically was the Olympic, Laura Keene's old theatre on Broadway, which converted to variety in January, 1874, and enjoyed good support for several seasons.

But a number of other new variety establishments had appeared earlier. In January, 1869, for example, the main hall of the Tammany building on 14th Street was made into a variety resort. The following September Robert Butler introduced variety to the Theatre Comique on Broadway. The Tammany venture collapsed, however, after only a few months. In early October, 1870, the Globe on Broadway, formerly the New York Theatre, opened as a variety house and, in mid-September, 1871, the newly-erected Union Square Theatre on 14th Street was presenting variety bills. Both houses were making a bid for family support. The Globe advertised a clean show where audiences could enjoy "fun, wit, and humor without vulgarity," and the *Spirit of the Times* noted that the Union Square was offering a show of "comedy and burlesque, music and dancing, good-natured satire and exhuberant fun unmixed with coarseness or vulgarity."[36]

These places may have been taking their cue from Pastor but there is no evidence to show any direct line of influence. Neither did very well and soon

46

switched to legitimate fare — the Globe in April, 1872, and the Union Square the following September. The Globe eventually returned to variety for a few seasons beginning in October, 1875. The Metropolitan Theatre on Broadway, recent home of the San Francisco Minstrels, converted to variety in August, 1872, and retained this format for a couple of seasons. Also, a number of smaller variety enterprises sprang up during these years on and around Broadway and in the upper reaches of the city.

The most popular and successful of all these new places was the Theatre Comique, especially after Josh Hart assumed management in the early fall of 1872. Hart had worked in variety's vineyards as a comic singer since the early 1860's and later had taken to managing a traveling variety troupe. Like Pastor in the Bowery, Hart announced first-rate and moral performances. The *Clipper* reported in December, 1872, that "Josh Hart, the manager, has by untiring energy, made the theatre one of the most successful in its class in this city, if not in the entire country . . . Obscenity, vulgarity and profanity are carefully expurgated from the performances which insures the continued attendance of the fair sex, who already represent a large portion of the audience."[37] Hart put on star-studded shows and shook the kaleidoscope as often and as vigorously as his Bowery colleague. By the end of 1872 the place had become a top-drawer variety resort, and business was excellent.

One of Hart's most valuable attractions was the team of Harrigan and Hart (no relation) who became regular headliners at the Theatre Comique in the fall of 1873. The manager wooed top artists with higher salaries than ever before had been paid in variety. Other houses were forced to match and even better Hart's figures and, as Odell says, "cut-throat rivalry set salaries booming and gave New York more 'variety' than the spice of life demanded."[38] During the season of 1874-75 Hart was regularly paying a top single act as much as $125 a week and a double as much as $300.[39]

These new houses, especially the Theatre Comique, soon began to siphon off Pastor's customers. Those who had been traveling over to the Opera House from Broadway soon found variety diversion closer at hand, while many curious Boweryites began to travel the other way to investigate the new places. Pastor's first obvious maneuver to stimulate business occurred in January, 1872, disguised as a chivalrous gesture in behalf of the ladies. He introduced a "Ladies Invitation Night." The *Clipper* noted on January 13 that "on Friday evenings of each week every gentleman purchasing a ticket has the privilege of taking in with him a lady free of charge."[40] Pastor recalled that the ladies were attracted by the lure and "commenced of course to tease their husbands, fathers, brothers, and sweethearts to bring 'em. That was the beginning of the women coming to the shows."[41] Elsewhere, however, he claimed that the women did not take to the idea, that "the charm did not allure."[42]

But the Ladies Invitation Night idea must have been successful to some degree, for it became a permanent feature at the Opera House. A *Clipper* reporter attended one of these functions in October, 1873, and "found the auditorium

47

crowded in every part, many ladies occupying the front seats in the gallery, which have been specially fitted up for their convenience ... The auditorium was about equally composed of ladies and gentlemen."[43] Pastor tried to further bolster business in December, 1872, by raffling off "several splendid sewing machines" at a Saturday matinee.[44] During the spring of 1873 he distributed candy and flowers to his female patrons, and in the fall he began letting those with escorts attend free at the matinees as well as on Friday evenings. Business was not up to expectations, and it soon got worse.

During the week of October 20, 1873, Billy Barry, the popular blackface comic, appeared at the Opera House in a sketch entitled *Wall Street*. The light-hearted piece was built around a janitor's woeful response to the financial crisis that had just struck the nation, the result in great measure of the too rapid construction of railways throughout the country. Barry's sketch made light of the initial situation, but the depression that followed hit particularly hard at the low income families in the Bowery and the shock waves were felt sharply at Pastor's. Stores closed throughout the neighborhood, unemployment was rampant, and money became tight, very tight. Pastor continued to serve up generous portions of beef with plenty of mustard, but his table was not always well attended. The depression and the competition from new houses was proving a double-barreled threat to Opera House receipts.

As attendance limped along through the remainder of the season, Pastor began thinking about moving his operation to Broadway. The entertainment business was holding up much better there. One of his closest friends at this time was Michael Leavitt, owner and manager of Mme. Rentz's Female Minstrels and soon to become one of the pioneers in the blossoming independent field of burlesque. Leavitt remembered that Pastor "became convinced that the location [the Bowery] had reached the end of its value as an amusement field. He frequently expressed the belief that his interests would be much improved by moving to Broadway."[45] The *Clipper* in March, 1874, contained the announcement that "Tony Pastor is to manage the Olympic Theatre during the season of 1874-75."[46] Something went wrong, however, and he could not secure the Olympic's lease. Ironically, the lease was picked up by John F. Poole, his former business manager, who tried to fashion the Olympic into a family variety house. As the new season opened with Pastor still at the Opera House and still plagued by disappointing receipts, his inducements to the public increased. The season was only a few weeks old when he announced that escorted ladies would be admitted free on Tuesday as well as Friday evenings and that "boys are admitted to the gallery at all times for 15 cents each."[47] In November, he was toying with the idea of sponsoring an "amateur night," permitting "amateurs and novices (who think they have talent for some specialty performances, and are anxious to go on the variety stage) to perform in public."[48] There is no evidence that he ever followed through on the idea.

Although amateur "hams" may never have taken to Pastor's stage, there was plenty of the real thing there on Monday evening, November 23. The show was stopped at ten o'clock and sixty hams were brought onto the stage. Brothers Tony and Fernando then appeared with a large box containing numbers corresponding to those printed on the evening's programs. Tony picked out sixty numbers, called each aloud, and the lucky program-holders filed up to the stage to receive their prizes.[49] Pastor made the ham raffle a regular Monday night feature and soon carried the "bank night" device to other performances as well.

On Wednesday evening, December 21, sixty turkeys were raffled off, and at a special matinee for kids on New Year's Day "a handsome toy" was presented to every child entering the auditorium.[50] Early in the new year he began giving away ten barrels of flour and ten tons of coal on Wednesday and Saturday nights respectively.[51] The lucky winners had these items delivered directly to their homes! Every lady entering the Opera House on Friday evening, February 10, received "a handsome valentine," and at the Friday evening show on March 5 "ten Dress Patterns were distributed among the ladies in the audience." [52] Pastor claimed that he also gave away "packages of coffee ... but with small success; but when I announced that on a certain date I would give away twenty-five silk dresses I caught them. Phew! Talk about Macy's on bargain day .... Next I tried bonnets, and so with the aid of milliners twenty-five hats of the latest fashion were displayed. It required twenty-five policemen to keep them in line."[53]

We find no mention of these items, however, in the ads and journalistic commentary of the day, nor of the "clocks" that Annie Yeamans, a songstress and comedienne of the period, said were also raffled off at the Opera House.[54]

The giveaway inducement was not original with Pastor. It has been used as a promotional gimmick by traveling minstrel troupes since the early 1850's, but Pastor seems to have been the first variety manager to employ the stratagem. We must not overlook the possibility, however, that his distribution of such provisions as coal, ham and flour may have been seen as an effort to aid the poor of the area as well as a spur to Opera House business. He had a big heart and the list of his charities over the years is a long one.

Although business apparently picked up somewhat on these special occasions, the overall picture remained gloomy. As Leavitt explained, Pastor still "found it impossible to secure the financial support he reasonably expected."[55] Around the first of March he was forced to lower his prices: admission to the parquette fell from 35¢ to 25¢, to the family circle from 25¢ to 15¢, and boys under twelve could now enter the gallery for 10¢ instead of 15¢. In Odell's words, "coal, flour and ham given away, and reduced prices showed the trail of the terrible panic of 1873."[56]

A special announcement appeared in the *Clipper* on March 27, 1875: "Tony Pastor will retire from the management of his Opera House, 201 Bowery, after the performance of Saturday evening, March 27, and it will be thereafter known as the Bowery Opera House .... He will continue to hold the lease of this property, but will sub-let it."[57] Pastor had been searching desperately for a Broadway location through the season and for a while in the fall had even thought of building his own quarters somewhere "between Sixteenth and

Thirtieth Streets."[58] This new house was never built and Pastor closed his last season in the Bowery without announcing any future plans. He took to the road with his company on March 29, leaving William Pastor to manage the now Bowery Opera House for a spring and summer season of traveling variety combinations.

It was not until the end of July that New Yorkers learned that the manager would return to their midst in the fall. "Tony Pastor is to assume the management of the Metropolitan Theatre, No. 585 Broadway, on Oct. 4," said the *Clipper*. "A preliminary season, beginning Aug. 2, will be managed by William Pastor and M. B. Leavitt."[59] Exactly when Pastor secured the Metropolitan is vague. Leavitt had obtained a lease on the house at $12,500 a year some time that spring or early summer. Somehow Pastor had managed to buy the lease from him.

"I had no desire to sell," said Leavitt, "but my friend's earnestness was such that I ultimately yielded, and accepted his proffered bonus of $8,000 for my lease."[60]

In any event, Pastor had found a new "Family Resort" for his variety enterprise and was destined to remain there for six years. It has been said that sometime in 1877 or 1878 he took over Pendy's Gaiety Theatre on Third Avenue between 125th and 126th Streets[61] but there is no indication in the records that he ever made such a move. Broadway was to be his home base until the fall of 1881.

It is uncertain how long he retained an interest in the Bowery Opera House. In August, 1875, it became known as Paul Falk's Volk Garden, and it continued under this name until the end of April, 1883, when Harry Miner obtained control of the premises, demolished the building, and erected the People's Theatre. Standing on the site today is a service station and parking lot.

CHAPTER SIX

Into the Lion's Den

It was on October 4, 1875, that Pastor officially threw open the doors of his new home at 585-587 Broadway. He announced the event with an ad in the *Clipper*, promising "all laughter-loving and time-killing amusement seekers" that "the location of his Opera-house on Broadway, the facilities of access, and Fashionable Surroundings, is not surpassed by any theatrical establishment in the city."[1] While the immediate neighborhood was not exactly what one could call "fashionable," it was certainly more respectable than the old Bowery location.

In the early 1860's it had been the city's Rialto, its theatrical center, but it had lost this distinction to Union Square during the city's postwar advance to the north. By the time Pastor arrived, the area was essentially a commercial neighborhood that had seen better days, a neighborhood that had already lost much of its first-class status to newer and more "fashionable" uptown areas and concerns. But it was still a wide-awake place of noise and bustle, its sidewalks crowded with shoppers, business men and sightseers, its streets alive with vehicles of all descriptions. Pastor's house was in the middle of it all. Directly across the street was the Metropolitan Hotel and Niblo's Garden, a block south the elaborate white-marbled and once-modish St. Nicholas Hotel, and a block north the Grand Central Hotel.

As far as variety competition was concerned, Pastor indeed had leaped into the lion's den. The Theatre Comique was south of him in the same block and the Olympic and the Globe one and two blocks to the north respectively. The "facilities of access" to the house seem to have been more than adequate. "All Stage Lines pass the door," said a postbill, "[and] the Bleecker, Houston and Prince Street Cars land passengers within one block of the Theatre."[2] With several large hotels in the area to draw from and with good means of transportation to bring in people from afar, the manager's new location was, all in all, a good one. The reputation of the house itself, however, was quite another matter.

The Metropolitan had a pockmarked history of ill luck and notoriety. It

51

had been opened originally by the Buckley Minstrels on August 25, 1856, and called Buckley's Minstrel Hall. The Minstrels held forth with only mild success until the following June. For a few years thereafter the house went through several changes in name, management, and format with good fortune always just a little bit beyond the managerial fingertips. It probably enjoyed its greatest popularity during the San Francisco Minstrels' five-year occupancy from May, 1865, to April, 1870. Upon the departure of this group, however, the place fell into decline and was frequently unoccupied for two years. Beginning in August, 1872, several different managers tried to introduce variety, but few were able to make a go of it. When the "naughty" Parisian Can Can was turned loose there in the fall of 1874, the respectability of the house fell rapidly. The *New York Times* called the performances in December, 1874, "a disgrace to the City" and "a disgusting exhibition."[3] The police made several raids on the premises, but to no avail — the high-kicking-skirt-ruffling dancers managed by one means or another to hold the stage until the end of May, 1875.

The house then remained idle until William Pastor and Michael Leavit opened their brief season on August 2. The *Spirit of the Times* noted the battle-scarred history of the place and was confident that Pastor was the one manager who indeed could restore its good reputation and bring it back into public favor.

"There is no man," said the paper, "who can be more safely counted on as capable of working this change than Tony Pastor. No one is a greater favorite with the masses."[4]

The Metropolitan had been renovated and refitted several times during its spotty career, and William Pastor and Leavitt made further alterations during the summer of 1875. When Tony opened his fall season the house contained a parquette, a family circle and several stage boxes. It had a capacity of around 1,800. Several rows of seats in the front of the parquette were now designated as the "orchestra." A new spacious entranceway had been added at 587 Broadway. The former entrance at 585 was used henceforth as an exit.

The fall admission prices were the same as at the Opera House in the Bowery before it fell upon hard times: 35¢ to the parquette, 50¢ to the orchestra, 25¢ to the family circle (or gallery), and $5.00 for a private box. Initially the house was called "Tony Pastor's Metropolitan Theatre." Two weeks after opening, it became "Tony Pastor's New Theatre," and by 1879 it was simply "Tony Pastor's Theatre."

The opening bill on October 4 was received by what the *Clipper* called "a very large and enthusiastic audience, many persons unable to obtain admission to the auditorium."[5] Assisting Pastor on the program were most of the performers from his touring company that previous summer. There was Gus Williams, for example, the Dutch dialect comic and Pastor's big star during the final years on the east side; Sanford and Wilson, comic musicians on a variety of instruments; McKee and Rogers, grotesque song and dance performers; Jennie Morgan, vocalist; William Carlton, Irish vocalist and comic; the Lenton Brothers, acrobats; Venus and Adonis, young velocipede riders; and a number of others.

Pastor's own turn that evening, prefaced by a short speech of welcome, was a howling success. He was called back for three encores and presented with several bouquets, one from a delegation of Elks. He had joined the Elks in 1869, and it is interesting to note that at that time the order was strictly a New York fellowship, the outgrowth of a minstrel-variety fraternity called "The Jolly Corks." It was on Pastor's motion in December, 1870, that the machinery was set in gear to make the Elks a national organization.[6]

According to contemporary accounts, Pastor's business held up well over the following weeks and months. The *Spirit of the Times* commented on October 16 that " the second week of the management of Tony at this house has been fully as prosperous as the one preceding it ... The success attending his change of base to Broadway from the east side we are heartily glad to chronicle, for the reason that he deservingly merits it."[7] The *Dramatic News*, brand new on the scene, noted a week later that "Tony Pastor has succeeded in making of one of the most run-down houses in the City, a financial success, and at each performance the houses are very large."[8] The same paper said in late November that Pastor "may claim the credit of being the first to make the theatre pay since the desertion of the minstrels, years ago."[9] The *Clipper* reported the following March that things were still going well: "Tony Pastor is doing a splendid business at his new theatre on Broadway, the result of good management, a constant succession of fresh attractions, and liberality in the presentation of the varied acts which make up the programme."[10]

There is not even a hint that Pastor had anything but good fortune during his first year on Broadway. There was no dip in his admission prices and no return to the vigorous give-away policy that had marked his final days on the east side. Although surrounded by competition, he apparently managed to draw his fair share of the business and perhaps a little more as well. One factor that certainly aided his success was the Theatre Comique's rapid decline during the year.

Josh Hart, for some undisclosed reason, relinquished the management to Matt Morgan at the beginning of the 1875-76 season. Morgan did not have Hart's magic touch and the Theatre Comique closed in late February, 1876, "after a season which was anything but successful."[11] Hart, meanwhile, had gone uptown to Broadway and 33rd Street to open the Eagle as a family variety house in October, 1875. He took along his policy of offering first-class bills and of paying inflated salaries to obtain them. But his magic touch failed him here and business was poor through most of the year. He abandoned his high salary policy early in 1876. Almost immediately, variety wages throughout the city began falling back to normal. The situation was stable again by spring. Hart struggled on at the Eagle well into the new season but conditions did not improve. The venture was finally dumped in February, 1878.

The pickings had been good for Pastor during his maiden voyage on Broadway, but the season ended on a personal note of sadness. Fernando Pastor had been too ill with consumption to perform his duties as treasurer during the season and the post had been filled from the outset by E. G. Browne. The end came on Sunday, April 16, the news reaching Tony in Washington where his company was just starting a week's engagement. He returned to New York to join the family on April 18 for "Dody's" funeral and burial in the family lot.

Death was to strike the Pastor clan again a year and a half later. William underwent an operation in the fall of 1877 for a tumor in the chest, and "after the surgeon had commenced his work he discovered that Mr. Pastor was also suffering from cancer, and the operation had to be abandoned. The Patient died from the shock given to his system by the knowledge that the operation had not been successful."[12] William died on October 23 and was buried beside Fernando.

The Globe and the Olympic proved to be no real competition for Pastor after the 1875-76 season. Both followed a rather erratic and stumbling course during the next few years under various managers, names, and formats. The Olympic was finally demolished in the latter part of April, 1880.

The Theatre Comique was another story. Harrigan and Hart took over its management in the fall of 1876 and made it into a formidable rival. "The Best Variety Show in the City," said an ad in the *Clipper*.[13] For two years Pastor had to share variety honors and receipts with his former proteges a few doors down the street. In the fall of 1878, however, the Theatre Comique broke away from the straight variety format, and the competition lessened. From the beginning of their management, Harrigan and Hart had thought about eventually replacing the standard variety show with a long play that took its material from city life among the Irish and Germans and that contained "variety" aspects within its make-up — sort of a glorified afterpiece. They experimented in this direction for two years and finally hit upon their highly successful "Mulligan Guard" series in the fall of 1878. *The Mulligan Guard Picnic* ran from September 23 to October 26, then *The Mulligan Guard Ball* held the boards from January 13, 1879, through the week of May 19 to close the season. In the years to follow, the two partners devoted themselves almost exclusively to staging plays of this type and business at their theatre was excellent.

But for those who wanted straight variety that was tops in quality and served up with all the trimmings, Pastor's became the place to go. As the newly-arrived *Mirror* reported in December, 1881, "when Harrigan and Hart began devoting their talents to the Mulligan series, Tony Pastor was left alone — king of the variety stage."[14]

Pastor carried to Broadway his desire to make variety into something suitable for the entire family. He dedicated his new house from the start to respectability and announced "that it will be his constant effort to cater only for Families, Strangers and others of the Best Class."[15] This notion was repeatedly put forward in his advertising, sometimes in simple declarations of intent, more often in bold claims of achievement. An ad in the *Clipper* in early November, 1876, for example, affirmed that the Broadway house is now "the acknowledged Vaudeville Theatre of the Metropolis. The resort most cherished by the Ladies, Children, and the Cultured Mass of amusement-seekers."[16]

54

This ad may well represent the first time that Pastor employed the French word "vaudeville," the term then applied to the "variety stage" in France and appropriated over here during the 1890's. It was just beginning to creep into use in this country. There were "Vaudeville Theatres," for instance, in San Antonio and Louisville in 1875 and another in St. Louis in 1876. It was Gilbert's opinion that Pastor "loathed 'vaudeville' as a sissy term for the correct 'variety.' "[17] But the manager actually employed the term quite frequently through the rest of his career, although more often in reference to his theatre than to the fare offered. The entertainment was usually referred to simply as a "variety show."

Gilbert may have been correct when he said that "the first in this country to use the word 'vaudeville' to describe a variety show was John W. Ransone, who assembled a specialty group in the eighties and toured the sticks."[18] Then we have Leavitt's statement: "I firmly believe that during the season of 1880 I used the term 'vaudeville' for the first time in connection with a variety entertainment in America."[19] Pastor probably thought the French term added a touch of dignity. We find him advertising his Broadway house under such fancy titles as "The Society Vaudeville Theatre of the Metropolis" and "Tony Pastor's Dramatic and Vaudeville Theatre — the recognized and legitimate family resort of New York."[20]

Whether smoking and drinking were allowed in any part of the manager's new "family resort" is uncertain. There was no statement one way or the other in any of the printed materials and contemporary accounts examined. An article in the *Dramatic News* in May, 1877, suggested that a goodly number of variety houses by that time had removed drinking and smoking altogether from their auditoriums. The paper noted what it considered to be a decline in variety's popularity and recommended that managers must find "something novel . . . in the business," but it was quick to warn that "the incentive of drinking and smoking, while witnessing a performance, is merely retrogression, and is a tacit confession that the performance will not draw of and by itself."[21]

It is clear, however, that in 1877 there were still plenty of variety establishments in the city offering patrons the accommodation of watching a show with a drink and cigar in hand. In fact, there were enough of these places in operation in October of that year to spur the New York police to resurrect and enforce the old 1862 law against drinking in the auditorium during a performance, a statute that had been generally ignored over the years but never had been repealed. The *Clipper* told of the action: "The sale of liquors, fermented or distilled, in the auditoriums of variety theatres while the performances are in progress, is to be stopped. On Thursday night [October 4] the police captains of the various precincts, in accordance with instructions issued by Superintendent Walling, detailed officers in civilian dress to stop the sale of beer or liquors in the Irving Music Hall, the London, Tivoli, Volk's Garden, the Olympic Theatre, and other places where similar performances are given . . . The bars in front of the theatres were not interfered with."[22]

It is quite possible that Pastor's theatre was open at the time of the raid.

While he and his traveling troupe did not return to inaugurate the winter season until October 4, William Pastor had begun a preliminary season at the house on September 10. No ads for the place between the week of September 17 and Tony's opening on October 4 have been found. Gilbert implies that there was "liquor" in the house, but does not say where it might have been available.[23] When we consider, however, that Pastor seems to have been successful in removing drink and smoke from his Opera House auditorium, it is highly unlikely that he would have "retrogressed" at his new Broadway house, the house he wanted known as the "Fashionable Family Theatre of the Metropolis."[24]

From the opening of the new theatre there were matinees each week for the ladies and children. "Ladies and Children's Grand Matinee Reception Every Tuesday and Friday" was the oft-repeated announcement printed in the *Clipper*.[25] These matinees were popular, too. The *Clipper* reported in October, 1876, that attendance at the afternoon functions the previous week was "so large that the auditorium could not accommodate all who applied for admission."[26] In February, 1877, the *Dramatic News* noted that "the Tuesday and Friday Matinees are very popular and are always crowded" and, a few weeks later, that "the matinees, indeed, are always crowded with out-of-town people."[27] Pastor apparently was drawing well from the neighborhood hotels.

Of course, he still wanted the ladies to attend with their families and friends during the regular evening hours. While he did not restore the "Ladies Invitation Night" feature, he did take pains to point out again and again that afternoon and evening performances would be identical and that both would be respectable and fit for the ladies to witness, even the children. In a postbill for October 16, 1876, for example, he assured the public that at the matinees "the same chaste programme will be rendered as at the evening representations," and in a *Clipper* ad in February, 1879, he boasted that "the programmes at this theatre are always arranged for the special enjoyment of ladies and children. The same entertainment, in its brilliant entirety, given at the matinees as at the evening representations."[28]

These claims for a "chaste" and respectable bill at all performances may have been more than a press agent's puff, for there are numerous contemporary and near-contemporary opinions attesting to the well-scrubbed complexion of Pastor's Broadway entertainment. The *Dramatic News*, for instance, reported in May, 1877, that "variety without vulgarity is the motto at Tony Pastor's Theatre," and the *Mirror* promised its readers in March, 1879, that Pastor's show "will always be found free from those objectionable parts so often heard on our variety stage, and it is clearly apparent he has determined to make his theatre a place of innocent amusement, where ladies and gentlemen, with their children, may go without hearing that vulgarity which is so odious to people of refined taste."[29] The *Mirror* evidently thought so highly of Pastor's programs by the end of 1879, that news of his activities was transferred from the "variety stage" column to the regular theatre section.

Pastor's was the first variety theatre to be so honored by this journal. The paper noted in December, 1879, that "Mr. Pastor never permits a word on his stage that can offend the ladies," and, a few weeks later, that "Mr. Pastor undoubtedly gives the best variety show in the city, and what is still better, the entertainment offered is always clean and wholesome."[30] Francis Wilson, who performed at the theatre as half of the team of Mackin and Wilson in April, 1878, wrote that "I can't say anything too good about Tony Pastor . . . Everything he did was clean and the best of its kind."[31] "One may laugh without blushing," said the *Mirror* in January, 1881. "This is the reason that ladies crowd the matinees and hold their own at the evening performances . . . Tony must be credited with doing more than any other manager to elevate the tone of this class of amusement."[32]

Pastor's touring company at this time was also drawing similar testimonials from papers around the country: "The fulfillment is always equal to the promise. There is nothing vulgar or offensive" (*Poughkeepsie News*); "Nothing of an objectionable nature, even to the most fastidious, is allowed upon the programme, and it is for this reason that Mr. Pastor's audiences are made up of the better class of our people" (*Philadelphia Evening Post*); "Baltimore has rarely had the opportunity of witnessing so high an order of variety entertainment, nor one in which so much of pure fun and innocent amusement are blended" (*Baltimore Herald*).[33]

In the face of the many claims for mixed audiences and clean fare on Broadway, it is difficult indeed to understand Gilbert's bold assertion that Pastor "first played to a 'double audience' (men and women) when he opened his Fourteenth Street Theatre in Tammany Hall, New York, October 24, 1881. It was the first 'clean' vaudeville show in America."[34] Gilbert must be wrong. Pastor the Reformer was certainly on the job at his Broadway theatre and in a much more open and vigorous way than at the old Opera House, and perhaps in a much more successful way as well.

CHAPTER SEVEN

The Pastor's Broadway Flock

Pastor's Broadway theatre was a virtual bargain basement for any variety buff with at least twenty-five cents in his pocket. The shows were whopping affairs lasting nearly three hours and stuffed full of the best specialty and comedy acts the field had to offer. The old *corps de ballet* was gone but the bills seldom wanted for pretty faces and well-turned ankles. Prominent were the Worrell Sisters, Jennie Morgan and Clara Moore, all songstresses, and the Four St. Felix Sisters, who sang and did a Dutch clog dance. Special mention must be made of the petite and trim Kitty O'Neil, one of the best jig and Irish clog dancers of the day. She was a dependable crowd-pleaser at Pastor's and the idol of the newsboys in the gallery. One of her big features was to spread sand on the stage and perform what came to be called a "sand jig." She was one of the first women to do this specialty.

Then too there were a number of young ladies who specialized in what was termed a "protean act." This was a song and dance turn built around a succession of quick costume changes. Protean acts were fast becoming the variety rage in the late 1870's, and Pastor's audiences were treated to the changeable moods and vestments of such "daughters of Proteus" as the French Twin Sisters, Lizzie Sims, the Richmond Sisters, Jennie Ward and Georgina Smithson. Miss Smithson was an English lass known far and wide in variety land as "The Gainsborough Girl." The *Clipper* carried an interesting description of her performance at Pastor's in April, 1878: "Miss Smithson, attired like the Duchess of Gainsborough, sang a song extolling the virtues of that lady; quickly changing her attire, she reappeared as an English servant girl and gave a flirtatious song, localized to the Central Park; after another rapid change, she was seen clad in a complete suit of armor, as worn by males, in which she gave an effective rendering of the flag song, and wound up by reappearing in the garb of a male dancer, and displaying choreographic skill of no mean order."[1]

There was a large fraternity of blackface, Irish, and Dutch (German) dialect

59

comics on the variety scene in the 1870's, and most of them appeared at Pastor's at one time or another, usually in a cluster. Notable among the burnt cork crew were Delehanty and Hengler, Fields and Hoy, Lester and Allen, the Dockstaders, and the incomparable McIntyre and Heath. This last team made their New York debut at Pastor's on March 22, 1880, then went on to earn riches and renown with a skit called *The Ham Tree* which they continued to perform in the leading vaudeville theatres of the country until the late 1930's.

Irish comics were rapidly coming abreast of those in blackface during the decade and by 1880 had just about taken over the lead. This came about not only because the Irish were everywhere in New York or because many of them took to the variety stage as a profession, but also because the general public was finding great delight in the high jinks of those funny fellows with the plug hats and side whiskers. Across Pastor's stage romped such sure-footed Irish jesters as Pat Rooney, Frank Mara, Sheehan and Jones, William Carlton, the Kernell Brothers, and Ferguson and Mack, one of the roughest knock-about teams in early variety. They started off their act calmly with a song and dance; but before long they were quarreling and tossing each other around the stage. The little Ferguson always got the worst of it, taking nasty spills all over the place. Their act ended with Mack imbedding a hatchet in his partner's trick wig, a bit of horseplay that may have contributed to Ferguson's total loss of hearing later in life. Topping the list of Pastor's Dutch comics were Bonnie Runnells, Morris and Fields, Charles E. Ellis, Harry Watson, and, of course, perhaps the greatest and most popular of them all, Gus Williams.

As at the Opera House, it was comedy that formed the backbone of the show. The weekly bills were always crowded with comic sketches and most of the afterpieces were designed strictly for laughs. The spectacular pantomimes were gone. We find only occasional titles suggesting an afterpiece of the "sensational drama" type — *The Working Girls of New York* (February, 1877), for instance, and *The Eighth Ward By Day and Night* (February, 1878). Many of the little playlets were farces, like *Dinkelspiel's Blunders* (March, 1880) and *Pastor's Evening Party; or, Fun Among the Actors* (December, 1880). The latter was sort of a backstage exposé of petty feuds, rehearsal woes, and general behind-the-scene shenanigans. The rest of the pieces were burlesques. One of the manager's biggest hits at his Broadway house was *The Emigrant Train; or, Go West*, a spoof on *The Tourists in a Pullman Car*, currently a big attraction at Haverly's Theatre. The travesty was written by William Carlton, the Irish comedian, and first presented on January 19, 1880. Like others of its species, it had a very simple dramatic framework on which variety acts were hung with gay abandon.

"In one emigrant train," says Odell, "were herded all sorts of dialect comedians that might be expected to appear in any 'variety' bill; and here they were gathered in a kind of dramatic thing suggestive, perhaps, of Harrigan and Hart . . . [or] Tourists."[2]

Sheehan and Jones appeared as Irish immigrants, Lina Tettenborn as a German immigrant and Bonnie Runnells as a German train conductor. The Four

Eccentrics were Negroes, the Sparks Brothers played Italians, and many other variety personalities moved in and through the piece. Despite all the evident "variety" within the work itself, *The Emigrant Train* was accompanied by the usual generous olio.

Pastor prepared his bills with a lavish hand and few customers, if any, could honestly complain of not getting their money's worth. "The Olio at Tony's," said the *Spirit of the Times* in January, 1881, "is never cut down on account of the success of the piece of the evening."[3] The *Emigrant Train* was clearly a success! Pastor played it for seven weeks, then took it along with his touring company the following spring and later revised it several times under various titles.

He continued to maintain a stock company to take part in the weekly afterpiece, offer a turn now and then, and assist visiting performers with their sketches, but he seems to have kept the company small. The *Clipper* made this observation in 1879 and suggested that such a policy enabled him "to present his patrons with a large list of fresh performers each week."[4] Pastor was still trying to win a steady clientele by offering a new show each week. Acts that stayed over offered new material, and each Monday saw a crowd of new performers. The number of artists on hand at any one time averaged about 35, and anywhere from 12 to 20 of these were new arrivals.

Pastor's Broadway theatre has often been referred to as "A House of Stars" because of the many performers who allegedly got their break there and went on to stardom on the variety and legitimate stage. "No man of the present generation developed so many great actors and actresses as Tony Pastor," said the *New York Herald* in 1908. "In his several theatres ... Tony was godfather to a host of performers who afterward became noted. Of these houses, it is probable that 585 Broadway produced the most remarkable talent."[5] Conspicuous among the many "godchildren" credited to the showman during these Broadway years were the Kernell Brothers, Nat Goodwin, Weber and Fields, May Irwin, and Lillian Russell.

Harry and John Kernell became a first-rate comedy team in variety during the 1880's and 1890's with what they called a "sidewalk conversation" act. This consisted of cross-fire dialog and explosive arguments between two Irishmen. The Kernells were a blackface team when they first appeared at Pastor's on October 16, 1876, and the manager took credit for having steered the two into the field of Irish comedy. "It was at my suggestion," he wrote, "after I had studied their work for a while, that they got up a little Irish sketch, playing the fathers of two boys who have a scrap. You must realize that the act was impromptu, the repartee absolutely spontaneous. They made such a hit that they immediately forsook their other roles and became Irish comedians."[6]

Nat Goodwin, later to become one of the most popular and most-often married light comedians on the legitimate stage, appeared initially at Pastor's on February 7, 1876, and "made a hit with his imitations."[7] Goodwin, then only 20, impersonated such well-known actors as Edwin Booth, Frank Mayo, Stuart

Robeson, Francis Chanfrau, and Richard Sothern. Pastor recalled that he had discovered the young mimic at an Elks' social: "I heard him sing and give imitations of actors at a social session of the Elks one Sunday night, and before he left the room I 'nailed' him. He, with Jennie Satterlee, I think it was, appeared in a sketch called 'Jerry Clip, the Stage Struck Barber,' and he was so good that before long he was coaxed away from me."[8] There was no mention of this particular sketch in the newspapers during Goodwin's engagement but Jennie Satterlee was in the stock company at the time.

Goodwin's booking at Pastor's, however, was not his first venture into the variety business. He had turned to variety in Boston the previous season when unable to find work on the legitimate stage. "I succeeded," he wrote, "in procuring an opening at the Howard Athenaeum under the management of John Stetson ... After my run at the Howard Athenaeum Tony Pastor offered me an engagement at $50 a week to appear at his variety theatre in New York. When I arrived I was terror-stricken at the way in which he had announced me. I was advertized as 'Actor, Author, and Mimic.' "[9] It was Pastor's recollection that on his opening night "Nat Goodwin ... was so frightened that I fairly had to push him out."[10] Goodwin claimed that "I remained with Tony several weeks [three to be exact!] and when I left Gotham my salary had grown to the sum of $500 a week, a tremendous salary in those days."[11] Tremendous indeed, and, according to Gilbert, unquestionably more than Pastor paid at that time and especially to an unknown performer. "Goodwin," says Gilbert, "could toss more money into a conversation than a mental-betting horse player."[12] The young entertainer never appeared again at Pastor's and shortly left variety altogether for the legitimate stage. If the manager gave Goodwin any particular help in developing his talent, no record of the fact has been uncovered. Perhaps the only real push he gave him was that push onto the stage on opening night.

Those who give Pastor credit for discovering Weber and Fields are in error. Gilbert even goes so far as to claim that the team had appeared for the manager at his old Opera House.[13] The truth is that these two entertainers first worked for Pastor at his 14th Street Theatre on June 15, 1891, when they had already developed their Dutch dialect comedy and were rising rapidly in popularity. That the team did not appear at the manager's Broadway house earlier, however, was not their fault. In 1876, at the age of 10, the two boys had assembled a blackface acrobatic song and dance act and were told as a joke, so the story goes, that they should take their act to Pastor and that the best time to find him in his office was at 7 o'clock in the morning.

Felix Isman, in his biography of the tandem comics, has reported what happened: "At seven the next morning the two boys posted themselves in front of the deserted theatre and asked every white male that passed if he was Mr. Tony Pastor. Four hours later the interrogation still was going on, unmindful of rebuff or insult. The question was put for the thousand and second time. 'Yes,' was the answer, and the answerer kept on into the lobby, where they overtook him. 'What can I do for you?' asked the great Tony. 'We're actors and we want to go to work,' they shouted in unison, and began forwith to turn flipflaps the length of the lobby. Antonio Pastor tossed them a chuckle. 'Come and see me again in four or five years,' he said as he turned away."[14] Pastor, who prided himself on his eye for talent and on his compassion for beginners, apparently had been unimpressed in his first encounter with a team that was to become almost legendary.

One of the leading comediennes of the legitimate stage in the latter part of the 19th century was the stout and jolly May Irwin. She and her sister, Flo, had entered variety in the mid-1870's as a song and dance team, and it often has been said that Pastor gave the girls their initial break on the stage. *Harper's Weekly* expressed this opinion in 1902: "It was toward the close of Mr. Pastor's occupancy of his house that a lady, who had just come to New York from Canada, called upon him and induced him to place her two young daughters on the stage. These young girls proved to be unusually bright and clever . . . One of the pair was slender and pretty, the other stout, jolly, and literally overflowing with wholesome, infectious fun."[15]

In 1908 the mother of Flo and May told what she insisted was the "truth" about her daughters' debut. "The papers," she said, "have never got it right about the start the girls got on the stage. They say that Tony Pastor put them on the stage. That isn't so."[16] She went on to relate that when the family was left almost penniless in Canada by the father's death, she had decided to place her talented daughters on the stage. She took them to Buffalo where a variety manager named Don Shelby gave the girls an opportunity to perform at his theatre in Rochester and later at his house in Buffalo. "Shelby never liked to read that Tony Pastor put them on the stage," she pointed out, "for he didn't. We went from Buffalo to the West, and it was in their second year on the stage, while they were playing in a Detroit house, that Mr. Pastor saw them. After a few months we went to New York, and they made their appearance at Pastor's."[17]

The girls did not, however, make their New York debut at Pastor's. Odell found them playing an engagement at Harry Miner's newly-opened Bowery variety house, the London, on January 22, 1877.[18] Their first booking at Pastor's was eight and a half months later, on October 8, 1877. In any event, the two became a celebrated team in variety and regular fixtures at Pastor's Broadway theatre. It was May, of course, who made the act. Her rise to popularity was due in no small measure to her appearances in the manager's succession of travesties on light opera. But her brilliance was somewhat dulled by another graduate of these burlesques, Nellie Leonard, better known perhaps under the name that Pastor is commonly thought to have coined for her — Lillian Russell.

Lillian Russell came to New York from Clinton, Iowa, in October, 1879, and got small parts first in a production of Edward E. Rice's *Evangeline*, then in the chorus of a *Pinafore* company. She came to Pastor's attention sometime in 1880 but the accounts of their meeting are at odds. Gilbert says the manager heard her sing while she was in *Evangeline*.[19] She, however, recalled that they met in her boarding house. "One afternoon," she wrote, "when mother was out, a friend named Mrs. Rose (who lived in the same house) said she had a caller for whom she would like me to sing. I consented. I never needed much coaxing to perform — whatever the time or place. So I went up to her suite and met a soldiery-looking little Italian who listened critically while I sang my little repertoire of concert songs. Then he suddenly turned to me and said: 'How would you like to sing those songs every night in my theatre for seventy-five dollars a week?' "[20] The "little Italian's" recollection of the meeting was simply that "a friend of hers brought her to see me. She was a girl at that time, singing in the rear row of a chorus." He recalled that her voice was "sweet, clear, and natural, and rang out like a bell . . . After I heard her sing, I didn't say a word, and she thought that I didn't like her voice. But I told her to come down to me right away and we'd see what we could do about it."[21] Miss Russell said that she hustled down to Pastor's for an audition the morning after their meeting: " 'Start next week,' said Pastor when his director pronounced my voice perfect. 'Oh!' I said miserably—'I can't. I haven't anything to wear on the stage.' Tony Pastor put a fifty dollar bill into my hand. 'Buy a dress with this,' he said. 'Pay me back at the rate of ten dollars a week out of your salary.' "[22]

Then there was the question of her name. "She was singing under her own name of Nellie Leonard then," said Pastor, "and I thought that wasn't good enough for her . . . We sat down together and each wrote on a sheet of paper names that we thought were good ones. I chose 'Lillian' and then put it with 'Russell,' and I still think the name suits her."[23] Miss Russell, however, told a different story. She claimed she needed an assumed name to hide her stage activities from her bluenosed mother and that she picked it out herself with the help of Harry S. Sanderson, Pastor's business manager: "When I went into his office the next day, I found Harry Sanderson, the house manager, awaiting me with a huge square of heavy cardboard on which were printed many names. Together we went over them — then suddenly, in opposite corners, I saw two that I liked. I fitted them together swiftly as I spoke them aloud. 'There,' I said, 'they stand out above all other names on that board. The L's in both of them make them musical. They're easy to say and to remember. LILLIAN RUSSELL — that's a lucky name. I'm going to choose it.' And thus I was rechristened as Lillian Russell."[24]

The young performer made her Pastor debut on November 22, 1880. The manager, evidently as wily as Barnum in his use of superlatives and window-dressing, billed her as an English ballad singer. His introduction of her to the audience that evening has been described by Morell in his biography of Miss Russell: " 'Ladies and gentlemen — friends and customers,' he said in his best ingratiating manner. 'Tonight I have a most unusual treat in store for you. At great personal trouble and expense I have brought here for your admiration and entertainment the beautiful English Ballad Singer. Ladies and Gentlemen, I give you a vision of loveliness and a voice of gold — Miss Lillian Russell.' "[25] The young songstress was an immediate hit with the "gallery gods." Pastor offered her a year's contract and she became a regular at the theatre over the weeks and months that followed. The newspapers, however, were little more than perfunctory in their praise. The *Mirror*, for example, noted simply that "Lillian Russell . . . is a pleasing balladist. Her songs are sweetly rendered."[26] But Pastor was convinced that his lovely discovery had big star potential, and he may very well have planned a burlesque of Gilbert and Sullivan's *Pirates of Penzance* in February, 1881, as a special vehicle for her talents and charms.

The manager's first burlesque of light opera and, as far as can be determined, the first presented at any variety house had been his spoof of Gilbert and Sullivan's *H.M.S. Pinafore* in February, 1879. The work had been first performed in this country at the Boston Museum on November 25, 1878, and first seen in New York at the Standard Theatre on January 15, 1879, where it settled down for a run of several months. The immediate result of its New York triumph was a *Pinafore* craze. Several New York theatres ran the comic opera simultaneously, amateur productions were legion around the country, and dozens of companies toured it through the backwoods. Not until *The Mikado* appeared in 1886 was another Gilbert and Sullivan comic opera to create such a national stir. Pastor's condensed version of the work was called *T.P.S. Canal Boat Pinafore* and was written for him by John F. Poole.

This production and the other Pastor burlesques of light opera that followed were longer than the standard afterpiece, running close to an hour instead of the usual twenty minutes.

"Mr. Pastor," said the *Mirror*, "has shown a great enterprise in presenting to his patrons a burlesque of this popular opera; and it will, doubtless, meet with success. The scenery, characters and plot will be closely adhered to, the costumes correct and appropriate, and each character represented as in the original version . . . During the action of the boat, Her Majesty's crew will indulge in nautical recreations, in which twelve clog dancers and twelve song and dance men will appear."[27]

Gus Williams was the Rt. Hon. Sir Joseph Lager, ruler of the entire navy, Frank Girard was commander of the Canal Boat, Alice Seidler played Josephine, Fannie Delano was Buttercup, George Kaine appeared as Ralph. Among the cousins and aunts were May Vernon, the French Twin Sisters, Amy Carroll, and Jenny Satterlee. As was his habit since moving to Broadway, Pastor did not take part in the afterpiece but was on hand with his parcel of comic songs as usual in the accompanying olio. The public took to the burlesque, and it held the boards through the week of March 31. It might have gone on indefinitely if the manager had not been forced to leave on his annual tour in early April.

As successful as the travesty had been, however, Pastor did not fashion a new afterpiece along the same line until the *Pie-Rats of Penn-Yann* two years later.

Gilbert and Sullivan's *Pirates of Penzance* had its world premiere at the Fifth Avenue Theatre in New York on December 31, 1879. The new comic opera was well received and supported, but it did not match the success of

Pinafore and the run lasted only to March 6, 1880. Variety and minstrel performers kidded the piece in sketches. The San Francisco Minstrels, for instance,
offered *Blue Fishes; or, the Pirates of Sandy Hook* at their house in February;
the Rentz-Santley Troupe offered a sketch entitled *Penn's Aunts among the
Pirates* during a visit to Pastor's in April. Pastor was the first manager to attempt
a full-scale burlesque of the work.

The first mention of the new travesty appeared in January, 1881, in an
interview by a *Mirror* reporter with Harry S. Sanderson. Sanderson told of
Pastor's plans to produce "a number of burlesque operas" during the year. "Our
first production," he said "will be the *Pie-Rats of Penn-Yann*. We shall put these
burlesques on the stage, with fine scenery and appointments, and have them full
of sparkling melodies and catchy music."[28] The *Spirit of the Times* noted
Pastor's plans with approval: "This is an unworked vein which ought to pan out
richly."[29] According to Morell, however, not everyone shared that journal's opti-
mism. "New York chuckled and reserved its seats in advance," he writes. "The
idea of Tony's rushing in where every other manager had feared to tread was at
once ludicrous and audacious. But the diminutive impressario knew what he was
doing. Travesty was, after all, pretty much in his line."[30]

Pastor introduced his burlesque on February 7, 1881, with a cast headed
by May Irwin, Bonnie Runnells, Florence Mertin, John Morris, and his lovely
"English Ballad Singer," Lillian Russell. The *Mirror* was on hand for opening
night: "For a first performance on Monday evening it was remarkably free from
the usual blemishes, and went off quite smoothly ... Most of the music is the
same as sung in the Pirates, which Mr. Pastor secured through the courtesy of
Arthur Sullivan, and the dialogue was supplied by W. S. Gilbert, Mr. Pastor
himself interpolating most of the local hits. The burlesque was costumed appro-
priately, while the scenic effects — noticeably, 'a wood near Penn-Yann,' and 'the
ancestral hall of the old stock' — showed more delicate touches then is generally
observable in burlesque."

The paper then went on to appraise the performers: "The cast was composed principally of the members of the variety company, and though many of
them betrayed an unfamiliarity with the concert music, yet especial credit is due
them for the zeal they displayed in their efforts to conquer its in-
tricacies ... Lillian Russell as Maria appeared to advantage, though her diffidence
militated somewhat against a positiveness that seems necessary in the character.
The lady possesses a sweet, flexible voice, which, with cultivation, will gradually
develop to her advantage."[31] Gilbert claims that "the play was an acute pain, a
record for lily painting ... The public remained apathetic."[32] On the contrary,
it was a hit, SRO signs were displayed throughout its four-week run.

Evidently pleased by his success and by Miss Russell's showing, Pastor
hurried another light opera spoof onto the drawing board while the *Pie-Rats* was
still playing to capacity crowds. The new piece was a tabloid version of Audran's
Olivette, currently a popular attraction at the Fifth Avenue Theatre. Pastor introduced his new travesty on March 7, 1881, with his young discovery in the title

role, supported by the Irwin Sisters, Frank Girard, John Morris, Dan Collyer, and others. The *Mirror* was taken with the production and especially with the performance of Miss Russell.

"Succeeding a highly-spiced and decidedly entertaining olio," the paper reported, "came the new travestie of Olivette at Tony Pastor's on Monday evening to a house crowded in every part . . . The choruses, though few, were well rendered, and showed evidence of careful training by some proficient baton. The costumes were new, rich and pleasing, and shone resplendently beneath the extra gas jets which were employed. Miss Lillian Russell as Olivette gave additional proof of her adaptation to the requirements of opera bouffe. She acted and sang most charmingly, and was faultlessly costumed. If the young lady does not allow adulation to conquer her ambition and elevate her too high in her own esteem, she will become a bright and shining light on the lyric stage."[33]

The *Olivette* burlesque was a success and, like its predecessor, held the boards for four weeks. Pastor signed Lillian Russell to another year's contract, then left on April 11 for his regular spring tour. His promising young songstress did not accompany him. Instead, as Morell writes, "she was farmed out to Frank Sanger and Willie Edouin who were then assembling a [variety] company for a tour to California."[34] She returned to Pastor's for more light opera burlesques in January, 1882. By then, however, the manager was operating in new quarters up on 14th Street.

By 1881 Pastor had become unquestionably the leading variety manager in the city. His likeness had appeared on the front page of the *Clipper* on March 11, 1876, and of the first issue of the *Mirror* on January 4, 1879. His immediate competition had folded — the Olympic had been torn down, the Globe abandoned, the Eagle, farther up Broadway, converted into a legitimate house, and Harrigan and Hart at the Theatre Comique were now concentrating on musical plays rather than straight variety. There were still many cheap variety houses of the concert saloon class around the city and several first-class family establishments as well, but most of the latter — places like Harry Miner's Theatre, the London and the American — were located south of 14th Street. Speaking of variety conditions in February, 1881, Odell notes that "since Harrigan and Hart had branched out into lengthy plays, Pastor's was about the only 'legitimate' theatre of 'Variety' in the city — uptown that is."[35]

By spring of 1881, Pastor had decided to move farther uptown. He looked to Union Square, the city's new Rialto and, sometime in late May or early June, leased the Germania Theatre on East 14th Street. The *Mirror* noted the move: "The theatre formerly known as the Germania . . . will hereafter be known as Tony Pastor's New Fourteenth Street Theatre. Mr. Pastor will be connected in no way with the old place on Broadway, but will transfer his company and name to his new establishment, and will conduct it as a first-class variety and vaudeville theatre, devoting his undivided attention to it."[36] Frank Pastor, who had taken over the summer supervision of the Broadway house in 1878 after William's death, continued to book variety combinations into the theatre while Tony was away on tour. The Broadway house was closed in the fall and, according to Thomas A. Brown, the theatre historian, was finally altered into stores on June 20, 1883.[37] The structure was torn down sometime in 1897, and today the location is the site of a twelve-story office building.

CHAPTER EIGHT

Greener Pastures Uptown

Union Square extends from 14th Street to 17th Street. In the 1850's it was a fashionable residential area; elegant mansions skirted a central green where an equestrian statue of George Washington surveyed a scene of quiet and leisure. The statue was still there in 1881, but the scene had changed. The green had shrunk, and the area itself was now a busy and bustling mercantile center. The fashionable homes had given way over the years to a complex of commercial firms — the Union Square Hotel, the Morton House, the German Savings Bank, Brentano's, the "literary headquarters" of the city, and Tiffany's, the great jewelry house, to name only the more prominent.

The Square was also the city's theatrical center. The *Mirror* had its offices here as did the costume house of Roemer and Koehler. The Union Square Theatre fronted the Square on 14th Street, and a block to the west was the Academy of Music and the Germania Theatre. Wallack's place was located on the corner of 13th Street and Broadway, and not far away was Pike's Opera House. The area in front of the Morton House and the Union Square Theatre was popularly referred to as the "Slave Market" because of the throng of "at liberty" performers who idled around there hunting for jobs during the summer. The theatrical identification of the Square was well suggested by the lithograph of "Union Square in Midsummer" printed in the *Mirror* on August 12, 1882. The print is framed by the likenesses of contemporary show personalities, and in the lower left-hand corner we find the mustached countenance of a relative new-comer to the Square — the king of variety himself, Tony Pastor.

"Tony Pastor's New Fourteenth Street Theatre" was actually a part of the Tammany Building on the north side of East 14th Street between Third Avenue and Irving Place. Early in 1867 the Tammany Society had decided that its headquarters on Park Row was too far downtown for the Society's political and social purposes and had initiated plans for a new house in the area of Union Square. Work on the new quarters was started in July of that year and completed the following spring. The building was constructed of red brick with white marble trimmings and contained a number of committee rooms and halls. The main hall on the second floor and a smaller one beneath it were fitted out as theatres. It was the smaller theatre that Pastor took over in 1881.

Its first occupant had been Dan Bryant, the minstrel manager. Bryant moved in with his blackface troupe in May, 1868, naming the place Bryant's Minstrel Hall. Business was only fair, however, and Bryant gave up his tenancy in June, 1870. The house was occupied off and on by various groups over the next few years, but stood empty and silent for long periods at a time. In September, 1874, Adolf Neuendorff leased the little theatre, christened it the Germania, and presented German dramatic programs there until early May, 1881. It was shortly afterward that Pastor appeared on the scene.

The auditorium of the theatre was about 52 feet square with a family circle, a parquette, several rows of orchestra seats, two private boxes on each side of the stage, and a total seating capacity of a little over 1,000. It was a cozy little place and lent itself well to the intimate performer-spectator relationship so native to variety and so often missing in the new vaudeville palaces built after the turn of the century. Although Pastor made no attempt to enlarge the auditorium during his twenty-seven years there, he did give the entire place a thorough face-lifting every summer. The *Mirror's* comment in October, 1885, was a common one: "The auditorium has been freshened up, the proscenium newly painted, and neat velvet and lace decorations placed in the front of the boxes."[1]

(More than paint, velvet and lace was called for in 1888 when a fire in the Tammany Building on June 6 nearly gutted the little theatre.[2] When the house was finally reopened on October 22, its former capacity and general layout remained unchanged but several new features were in evidence. Iron, brick and plaster had replaced wood throughout the house, and a new exit from the gallery had been provided. A new proscenium arch spanned the stage, supported on each end by two large columns and decorated in bas-relief with a center panel of Terpsichore flanked by medallions of Satire and Comedy. Patrons entered the lobby through a new portico with Corinthian columns, bevel-plate glass doors, and a colored glass transom. The walls of the lobby itself were now freshly plastered and floor tiled with white marble. "Everything shows elegance and good taste," said the *Mirror*. "The decorations are bright and charmingly contrasted; the proscenium arch and boxes are rich and artistic; the seats are sufficiently roomy and the floors are richly carpeted."[3])

As soon as Neuendorff and his troupe pulled out of the theatre in May, 1881, the auditorium had been "thoroughly redecorated and refitted"[4] under the supervision of Frank Pastor, who was also minding the Broadway store while brother Tony was away on tour. When the work was finished in late July, Frank announced that "Tony Pastor's New Fourteenth Street Theatre" was now available for "first class Legitimate Entertainments only." He boasted that the house was "thoroughly Equipped and Appointed" and "unsurpassed in location, being of convenient access by three lines of elevated railway, two lines of crosstown cars, one block from Second, Third and Fourth Avenue cars, and all Broadway stage lines."[5] There were no takers, however, until October 10 when N. D. Roberts brought his *Humpty Dumpty* and Specialty Minstrel Troupe into the house for two weeks. The troupe closed on Saturday evening, October 22, and two days later Pastor and his traveling company arrived home to open the fall season officially.

Admission was the same as at the Broadway house: 35¢ to the parquette, 50¢ to the orchestra, 25¢ to the family circle, 15¢ for children, and $5.00 for a private box. Customers could also obtain a reserved seat in advance for $1.00, but just where these seats were located and how many were available is not known.

All sections of the little house were jammed on opening night despite the fact that a steady downpour all day had turned the city streets into mud ponds. "Only here and there was there a vacant seat visible downstairs," said the *Clipper*, "but these vacancies by no means represented seats unsold, unless possibly by the speculators. There were a hundred or more persons who, unable to obtain seats, patiently stood up the whole night."[6] Many of those present were dyed-in-the-wool Pastor fans. Some managers, like Dan Bryant, had followed the city's move northward only to discover that they had lost much of their loyal following. This was not the case with Pastor. His Broadway fans trailed after him in droves. The *Mirror* later noted this loyalty and remarked that Pastor's uptown move was "a foregone success" because " it is the man, and not the location, which is the trade mark of a lucky manager."[7]

The opening night show was loaded with variety favorites. Frank E. McNish performed his comic acrobatic act called "Silence and Fun." He featured handstands and the like on top of a pyramid of chairs and barrels. Lillian Western presented her well-known musical act in which she dressed in male attire and played an assortment of instruments. Lizzie Simms was on hand with a protean dance; the French Twin Sisters, one an alto and the other a soprano, provided some sweet harmony and cut a few capers; Ella Wesner offered some of her famous male impersonations. Lester and Allen performed blackface shenanigans while Ferguson and Mack fractured the audience and probably themselves as well with more of their roughhouse Irish comedy. Rounding out the roster were Lester and Williams, Dan Collyer, Frank Girard, and Pastor himself with a fresh packet of songs. Several floral horseshoes were passed over the footlights to the showman at the end of his turn and a large number of friends and well-wishers stayed around long after the show to add personal notes of congratulations.

This was the bill that Gilbert singles out as constituting not only Pastor's first "clean variety show" but, indeed, "the first — as such — given in this country."[8] He discusses some of the performers on the bill, all of whom appeared for Pastor before, but he does not suggest how their acts might have differed from the usual on that particular night.

We have already noted the many claims for clean fare and mixed audiences at Pastor's Broadway theatre as well as at other "family variety houses." Did

Gilbert overlook these claims or ignore them or dismiss them as mere puffs? If Pastor did scrub his opening bill on 14th Street with unusual vigor, such is not announced by him nor noticed by the papers of the day. There is no disputing the fact that the 14th Street house became noted far and wide as the "model home" for family-style variety "to which," as Fred Stone, the actor, said, "a child could take his parents."[9] But, as pointed out earlier, Pastor clearly built this model home on a foundation he had been laying for years past.

It is the concensus among modern writers that by the time he had settled down on 14th Street, if not before, he had gone out of the liquor business altogether and had confined smoking to a special retiring room. Indeed, there is no mention of a bar or saloon in any of the contemporary accounts of either the old or restored house. It was in 1895 that the showman remarked: "I have labored industriously to make the variety-show business a successful one by disassociating it from the cigar-smoking and beer-drinking accompaniment."[10] It is unlikely that he would have recalled such a goal and in such terms if it had not been already achieved.

Pastor opened his new house with the promise that here, as at his Broadway establishment, he would be "catering to the ladies, and presenting for the amusement of the cultivated and aesthetic Pure Music and Comedy, Burlesque, and Farce."[11] He continued to offer "Ladies and Children's" matinees on Tuesdays and Fridays and announced at the outset that these would be "made especially attractive."[12] While we do not know all that he did to dress up these afternoon sessions, the occasional distribution of bouquets was one of his features. The *Mirror* noted in January, 1882, that "Tony's Bouquet Matinees are so successful that they will be repeated. How he does it is a mystery; but the bouquets given to the ladies are worth more than the price of admission at any florist."[13] During the Christmas season of 1882, moreover, he gave a wax doll to each woman at the Tuesday matinee, and by Christmas, 1883, he was also giving these dolls to children at both matinees. These so-called "Doll Matinees" became a regular and popular holiday feature. But bouquets and dolls, along with linen souvenir programs and autographed photos on special occasions, seem to have been the extent of his gifts; there is no indication that he returned at any time to the desperate "bank night" tactics of his final days in the Bowery.

The ladies regularly packed the auditorium for the matinees, but what must have been particularly pleasing to Pastor was the fact that they were turning out also in ever increasing numbers for the evening shows as well. The *Mirror* remarked in November, 1882, that "the entertainments are not vulgar or coarse in any respect and ladies may, and do, enjoy them as well as their husbands, fathers, and lovers."[14] A little over a year later the *Clipper* was high in its praise of the manager's family policy:

"A crowded and enthusiastic house evening of February 18 showed that Tony Pastor's efforts to procure the 'best in the market' are thoroughly and deservedly appreciated. It was decidedly a 'family' audience, a large number of ladies, many of them coming in twos and threes, without escort, showing that it is politic to manage an establishment of this description in such a manner that no gentleman need fear to bring his wife, sister, or mother to 'see the show,' or even allow them to go by themselves. This state of affairs reflects great credit upon the management."[15]

This state of affairs continued through the decade as more and more families came to realize that "a visit to Pastor's is certain to ensure a delightful evening, for the performance is always novel, amusing and clean."[16]

Pastor's 14th Street entertainment policy remained essentially the same as on Broadway. His customers were treated to a big show replete with songs, dances, acrobatics, plenty of comedy, and a "constant accession of Novelties, with complete and thorough change of programme each and every week of the season."[17] The farcical or burlesque afterpiece still topped off the weekly bill, and a small but versatile stock company was still maintained to assist in its production.

It must have been a happy day for Pastor when Jacques Kruger, a highly gifted comedian, joined the stock group in late October, 1881. Kruger became a dependable crowd-pleaser and a prolific writer of afterpieces for the management. He was responsible for such pieces as *The Professor* (October, 1881), a spoof on William Gillette's play of the same name at the Madison Square Theatre; *Charles Duno; or, the love of a Dry Goods Clerk* (December, 1881); and *Wanted 1,000 Milliners* (October, 1882). He was at least partially involved in assembling the manager's new crop of burlesque light operas. Gilbert is wrong when he says that Pastor had "junked his musicals" by the fall of 1881.[18] Pastor actually produced several more light opera travesties and indeed achieved one of the biggest successes of his career with a burlesque of *Patience* in January, 1882.

Gilbert and Sullivan's *Patience* had had its American premiere at the Standard Theatre in New York on September 22, 1881. It settled down there for a long run, and Pastor started preparing a burlesque on the piece during the final weeks of the year. He delayed production, however, until Lillian Russell returned to play the title role. "Miss Russell," he recalled, "was my ideal of that role."[19] Pastor, we remember, had farmed out his pretty young songstress in the spring of 1881. After a summer of touring, followed by an eight-week season at the Bijou Opera House in the title role of Audran's *The Snake Charmer*, the young performer returned to the fold to begin rehearsals on the new burlesque. The spoof, entitled *Patience; or, the Stage Struck Maidens*, was offered as the feature of the evening on January 23, 1882, with Miss Russell supported by such Pastor favorites as May and Flo Irwin, Jacques Kruger, Dan Collyer, and Frank Girard.

"We trace the nimble fingers of Mr. Kruger in the burlesque," said the *Mirror*, "which is not a mere rehash of the original, but a genuine travestie. The twenty love-sick maidens have become twenty stage struck girls; the bold dragoons are members of the Coney Island militia, and Bunthorne has changed from an esthetic poet to a crushed manager." The paper found "the scenery and costumes new and elegant," the chorus "not only large but thoroughly drilled," and it pronounced Miss Russell as "the best representative of Patience on the

American Stage" and the production itself "as the crowning achievement of Tony Pastor's management."[20]

Sullivan's original music was retained, but Gilbert's lyrics were rehashed and all the English allusions localized. The production was a decided hit and ran for two months. During this time, Lillian Russell became a most talked-about young lady. She received several handsome offers to play elsewhere but she turned them down, remaining loyal to the contract with Pastor for the rest of the season.

Pastor closed *Patience* on Saturday evening, March 18, only to open with a new light opera burlesque the following Monday. This time it was a travesty by Kruger on Edward Solomon's *Billee Taylor*. Solomon, an English composer, had had his work premiered in this country by D'Oyly Carte at the Standard Theatre on February 19, 1881. The show enjoyed a run of over 100 performances. Pastor called his burlesque *Bilee Taylor; or, the Lass who Loved the Sailor*, and once again the *Mirror* was highly impressed:

"Tony Pastor has made another hit with the burlesque of Billee Taylor, to our thinking very much better than the original opera. Lillian Russell as Phoebe is charming; she sings the music like a transmigrated nightingale, acts like a materialized Grace, and looks like Venus after her bath. Flora Irwin is a rollicking lad as William the Tailor, and looks as handsome as a dream. Kruger is more awfully funny than ever he is wont to be; his make-up as Ben Barnacle is killing, and his singing 'All on Account of Eliza' was encored to suffocation . . . The Charity Girls looked very neat and pretty, and sang well. The burlesque will, we think, beat even that of Patience in popularity."[21]

Although the *Billee Taylor* burlesque seems to have been well received, it ran for only two weeks. Morell claims that Pastor would have run the production longer if his star had not decided to become temperamental. "Unfortunately for Tony," he says, "Lillian suddenly became a problem child at this time. She had ceased to live with her husband, Harry Braham, and the friends she subsequently made dinned into her pretty ear the suggestion that she was not appreciated, that she was wasting her gifts and that she had only to assert herself to bring Tony Pastor to his knees . . . The consequences were disastrous for everyone. After playing *Billee Taylor* for three weeks [only two weeks] she quit the cast in a huff."[22]

Miss Russell did leave Pastor in early April but the circumstances surrounding her departure are vague. The *Clipper* claimed she left because of illness,[23] and indeed she was announced as ill and unable to appear on two nights during the first week of the *Billee Taylor* run. Moreover, there were ads in the *Clipper* for several weeks beginning in February, 1882, proclaiming that "The Lillian Russell Comic Opera Company will commence its season at Tony Pastor's 14th St. Theatre [on] Monday, April 10, 1882, in a New Comic Opera."[24] The company never appeared at Pastor's and perhaps was never formed at all. What ever the truth of the matter, Lillian Russell — the transmigrated nightingale — left Pastor's employ and never again appeared at his theatre or under his banner.

Pastor did not let his young star's departure dampen his interest in producing further burlesques of light opera. On February 26, 1883, he came out with a Kruger travesty on Varney's *The Musketeers*. He called his version *The Riflemen of Vassar*. It ran for two weeks but, despite the comic talents of Kruger and May Irwin and the singing of Flo Irwin, the piece was only moderately successful. The *Mirror*, however, liked the production and expressed the hope that "Mr. Pastor will do more of these burlesques, as they are novel and his company can do them attractively."[25]

The manager obliged on March 12 with a Kruger burlesque of Audran's *The Mascot*. He called his spoof simply *The Mascot*, and once again Kruger and the Irwin Sisters were featured and drew high praise. Yet, the production was replaced after only one week with a revival of *Billee Taylor* on March 19. Rose Temple appeared in Lillian Russell's former part of Phoebe. Kruger and Flo Irwin repeated their original roles. The *Mirror* called the production a "capital burlesque" and noted that "the music is admirably sung and the piece well mounted."[26] But the revival was not the hit that Pastor had hoped for and played for only one week. Although he had a good company in general and certainly two fantastically funny and popular comics in Kruger and May Irwin, he did not have another Lillian Russell in either Flo Irwin or Rose Temple.

Pastor lost both of his prized comics during the next season of 1883-84. The *Mirror* had earlier praised May Irwin's talents as being "proportionate to the size of her figure" and had predicted that "like a dough that is mixed with good yeast, May is bound to rise."[27] Rise she did! She became such a big attraction at Pastor's that she caught the eye of Augustin Daly who managed to entice her away in the fall of 1883. May then moved on under the coaching of Daly and others to become one of the most famous and beloved comediennes on the legitimate stage. She gained a special kind of fame in 1896 when she and John C. Rice, the actor, broke attendance records at nickelodeon resorts with what has since become a classic film episode, *The Kiss*. The episode was taken from the climax of their current Broadway success, *The Widow Jones*.

Kruger had the urge to move into the legitimate field at least as early as July, 1883. "Jacques Kruger is trying to get a release from Tony Pastor," the *Mirror* noted. "He yearns to star."[28] The comedian stayed on with Pastor, however, writing and appearing in such afterpieces as *The Dudes at Long Branch* (November, 1883) and *Duno the Dude* (December, 1883), until sometime in February, 1884, when he was loaned to Nat Goodwin for four weeks. "After his engagement with Goodwin," said the *Mirror*, "he will return to Tony Pastor's Theatre."[29] Kruger did not return. The same journal revealed in March that "Tony Pastor has given Jacques Kruger an absolute release."[30] Kruger went on to enjoy a popular career for a number of years as a character comedian on the legitimate stage. The defection of Lillian Russell, May Irwin, and Jacques Kruger was repeated often during Pastor's long career. He gave an opportunity for training and exposure to many who, after their popularity had been achieved, left him for bigger and better things.

Pastor made no effort to produce another light opera burlesque for nearly three years. He was holding off until he could find a personality with some of that Lillian Russell magnetism. He came across a likely candidate in Chicago while on tour in the early fall of 1884. Her name was Hilda Thomas, a pretty and petite young balladist, who joined the 14th Street regulars in October of that same year. Pastor worked steadily with her and early in 1885 the word went out that "Tony Pastor thinks of again producing burlesque opera, this time with Hilda Thomas in the principal parts."[31] Nothing more was heard of the matter for over a year. Then the rumor mill had it that the manager was contemplating a take-off on Gilbert and Sullivan's latest red-hot success, *The Mikado*. But something went wrong and the *Mirror* announced in March, 1886, that "Tony Pastor has abandoned the production."[32] What happened is not recorded. Pastor never again tried to produce a light opera burlesque. The issue was dead. A colorful chapter of his career was closed.

But the energetic manager closed one chapter only to open another. "After several years of success with comic operas," he wrote, "I decided to see what London and Paris might teach me."[33] So began in the summer of 1887 the first of his annual prospecting trips into the treasure troves of England and the Continent in search of new ideas and fresh attractions. He had been thinking about making such a trip for several years and even had divided his yearly tour into a spring and fall season in 1883 so he would have a few weeks off in between for this very purpose. The fear of deep water still haunted him, though, and he had never been able to get himself up the gangplank. Michael Leavitt, who made the trip almost annually, tried again and again to persuade his friend to accompany him, but to no avail.

Finally, on June 18, 1887, Pastor actually took to the high seas, convoyed by his wife and Leavitt. Leavitt took credit for the victory: "It was not until I went so far as to engage a cabin for him on the 'Umbria' of the Cunard line in 1887 that he consented reluctantly to face the terrors of the deep. Even after he was safely ensconced in his stateroom he was so very much perturbed that he clung to his bed until a few hours before reaching Queenstown. Once ashore, Tony was like a baby with a new toy."[34]

Pastor's guide around the London show spots and the city itself was George W. (Pony) Moore, the former American minstrel and now manager of St. James Music Hall. The two had maintained a friendship since the early 1840's when, as a young volunteer at New York's Croton Hall, Pastor had toted water for Moore. The minstrel entertainer made England his home in the 1850's and is frequently credited with having introduced the English to blackface minstrelsy. He began serving as Pastor's "London agent" in the late 1870's and supplied the manager with a shower of English music hall stars, including the Wilkinson Brothers, St. George Hussey, Maud Beverly, Marie Loftus, Georgina Smithson and Queen Vassar, a handsome and dashing songstress who made a big hit with New York audiences and later married Harry Kernell.

Pastor and his wife were in Paris seeing shows and doing the sights when a

76

TONY PASTOR'S
COMBINATION!

⁕

PROGRAMME This Evening.

Grand Overture........Full Orchestra

SERIO-COMIC SONG......Miss B. STANLEY

FANCY DANCE......M'lle MARIE BERTHA

FAVORITE BALLAD -Selected..........Miss IDA DUVAL

The Great Sensation--The Nerves!
JOHNNY WILD and MISS STANLEY.

DOUBLE CLOG DANCE.....Mast's SHERIDAN & MACK

COMIC VOCALISMS!
Introducing his Latest and Best Compositions, by TONY PASTOR

Comic Ethiopian Sketch, entitled
CAN'T SHAKE HIM OFF!
JAMES GAYNOR AND JOHNNY WILD.

TERPSICHOREAN EVOLUTIONS........M'lle BERTHA

COMIC BANJO SOLO- Original........ **JAMES GAYNOR**

FAVORITE SONG..........Miss IDA DUVAL

Burlesque Tragedy, entitled
OTHELLO!
WILD and GAYNOR.

BUDGET OF COMICALITIES!
Original, and performed only by TONY PASTOR.

New Double Song and Dance......Mast'rs Sheridan & Mack

To conclude with TONY PASTOR'S Pantomime, entitled
THE HAUNTED BARBER SHOP!
BARBER ... Jas. Gaynor | PIERROT A Clown Tony Pastor
COLIN .... Johnny Wild | GERTRUDE ..M'lle Marie Bertha
Other Characters by the Company.

ADMISSION ....35 CENTS

☞ No Reserved Seats. No Extra Charges. Front Seats
Reserved for the Ladies. Last appearance of the Troupe in
this city.

NEWARK DAILY ADVERTISER STEAM PRINT.

Postbill for Pastor's first traveling
company in Newark, New Jersey, on
March 25, 1865.

Cover of *Tony Pastor's Union
Songster, circa. 1862.* (Cour-
tesy of The University of
Iowa)

Cover of *Tony Pastor's 444
Combination, circa. 1864.*
(Courtesy of the Harvard The-
atre Collection)

PASTOR'S CHARACTERIZATIONS as . . .

a soldier,

a sailor,

a rural character

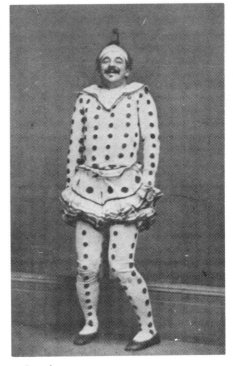

and a clown

as he appeared singing such songs as "When the Cruel War Is Over," "Monitor and Merrimac," "Lucy Long" and "I'm a Young Man From the Country." Photographs: 1864. (Courtesy of the Harvard Theatre Collection)

Program for the first week at Tony Pastor's Opera House, July 31 - August 5, 1865. (Courtesy of the Hoblitzelle Theatre Arts Library, The University of Texas at Austin)

Program for the week beginning October 14, 1872, at Tony Pastor's Opera House.

TONY PASTOR'S OPERA HOUSE
201 BOWERY, OPPOSITE SPRING STREET.

TONY PASTOR .... PROPRIETOR
Robert Butler .... Stage Manager
Professor Braham .... Leader of Orchestra
Samuel Sharpley .... Business Manager

TRIUMPHANT SUCCESS
OF THIS
GREAT FAMILY RESORT
Universal Acclamations of Delight
From a Crowded and Fashionable Audience.

The Inauguration of this Beautiful Temple of Amusement a Brilliant Success!

THE ADVENT OF TONY PASTOR'S GREAT TROUPE
Greeted with an Overwhelming Reception.

AN OVATION TO GENIUS!

CARD TO THE PUBLIC.—The Manager wishes to return his thanks for many favors previously bestowed upon him in this city, and takes pleasure in announcing the opening of his beautiful Female of Amusement, which he designs making the Great Family Resort of the City,—where heads of families can bring their Ladies and Children and witness an unexceptionable entertainment,—one that will please the most fastidious. He has procured the services of some of the Most Talented Artistes in the country, and has no hesitation in assuring that to entertainment of a similar character, depending entirely upon its own merits, has ever rendered the same degree of universal satisfaction as the performances of this company; their popular concerts meeting with unqualified success upon each occasion, and unexceptionably admitted by the Press and Public to be the most superior, popular and pleasing organization in the world.

The People's Universal Favorite

TONY PASTOR

In New Comic Songs, Humorous Ballads and Admirable Adaptations.

MISS ERNESTINE DeFAIBER,	MR. JAMES GAYNOR,
In Beautiful Dances and Beautiful Ballets.	In Unrivalled Banjo Solos and Utopian Utterings.
M'LLE MARIE BERTHA,	JOHNNY WILD,
In Comic Songs and Comic Dances.	In Consecutive Comicalities and Correct Karacteristics.
MISS AMELIA WELLS,	MR. ROBERT BUTLER,
In Pleasing Farces and Piquant Peculiarities.	In Laughable Pantomimes and Laughable Lectures.
MISS ELLEN COLLENE,	SHERIDAN and MACK,
In her Pleasing Dances.	In Double Clog Acts and Double Songs and Dances.
MISS CARRIE AUSTIN,	MR. WILLIS ARMSTRONG,
In her Wonderful Zouave Drill.	In New Negro Narratives and Neat Negro Acts.
MR. WALTER CALDWELL,	MR. DOTY LULY,
In Xtravagant Xcentricities and Racy Recollections.	In Hibernian Humors and Herculanean Feats.

Select, Popular and Multifarious MUSIC by
THE GRAND ORCHESTRA AND MILITARY BAND
Under the direction of the Distinguished Musician, Mr. J. Braham.

Friday Evening, August 4, 1865.
PROGRAMME.

Grand Overture .... Orchestra
A GOOD NIGHT'S REST,
Butler, Armstrong and Miss Amelia Wells.
Dashing White Sergeant .... Miss Ernestine De Faiber
Favorite Dance .... Miss Ellen Colene
The Great Sensation.
THE NERVES!
Johnny Wild and Mlle. Bertha.
Double Clog Hornpipe .... Masters Sheridan and Mack
Tony Pastor's Olio of Fun!
Dance, Highland Fling .... Miss Ernestine De Faiber
INFLUENCE OF MUSIC,
Johnny Wild, Gaynor, Butler, Armstrong, Sheridan and Mack.
Young Gal from the Country .... Miss Amelia Wells
Dance .... Miss Ellen Colene
Comic Banjo Solo .... James Gaynor
Greek Hornpipe .... Mlle. Marie Bertha
Zouave Drill .... Miss Carrie Austin
The Intensely Funny Negro Burlesque,
TENPIN JOHNNY,
Johnny Wild and Gaynor.
Dance, Characteristic .... Miss Ernestine De Faiber
Comic Song Original, and sung only by Tony Pastor
THE HAPPIEST DARKIES OUT,
Masters Sheridan and Mack.
Selections .... Orchestra
The performance to conclude with the Laughable Farce, entitled
SMITH AND BROWN
Jonathan Smith .... Robert Butler | Mrs. Somerton .... Miss Amelia Wells
Timothy Brown .... Johnny Wild | Mrs. Brown .... M'lle De Faiber
Mr. Somerton .... Willis Armstrong | Mr. Smith .... Mlle. Bertha

Doors open at Seven o'Clock.   Performance to commence at Eight o'Clock.

Grand Matinee on Saturday,
At Half-past Two o'Clock.

ADMISSION:
Parquette .... 35 Cents
Family Circle .... 25 Cents

TonyPastor'sOperaHouse
PROGRAMME.
OVERTURE   ORCHESTRA
The Roaring travesty, called
HIGH JACK, THE HEELER
High Jack, the Heeler ... Ben Mason | Cully, the Cutter ...... Harry Kernel
Old Simmons the Slummer ... C.F Seabert | Mike the Killer .... Billy Carter
Pete, the Pincher ...... Ned Harrigan | Bill the Biter .... Johnny Manning

Miss Jenny Engel's . Portfolio of Songs

LA GIZELLA.   Marie Goreuflo & Malinda Nagle

BILLY CARTER'S BANJO SOLOS

AFTER THE WAR,
Original, HARRIGAN & HART.

COMIC SONGS TONY PASTOR

The Comic Sketch entitled
THE CHRISTMAS PUDDING
Frank Glover .... Ben Mason | Dr. Marrowbone .... C.F. Seabert
Mr. Pettibone .... Frank Girard | Clem Titus .... Billy Carter
Uncle Timothy .... Ned Harrigan | Deacon Johnson ...... Johnny Manning
Simon .... Harry Kernell | Mrs. Pettibone .... Tony Hart
Snkey .... | ...... Miss Amelia Goreflo

SERIO-COMIC SONGS - "NELLIE"

The Peculiar African Domestic Sketch called
THE YOUNG SCAMP
Old Eph Simpson ...... Ben Mason | Young Eph the Scamp ... Master Cawthorne
Mr. Hargraves .... | .... Frank Girard

the American Star Comique
GUS WILLIAMS
In his Original Dutch Character Songs and sayings

MADAM ZITTELLA & THE VARRELLA BROS.
In their wonderful Gymastic Feats and Fleights

OVERTURE .... J. BRAHAN'S ORCHESTRA
To conclude with the Laughable Comedy, entitled
THE IRISH DIAMOND
ANDY, THE IRISH DIAMOND .... "NELLIE"
G. Titus .... C.F Seabert | Mary .... Miss Amelia Goreflo
Deacon Brown .... Frank Goard | Mrs Blake ...... Miss Colen Herd
Mr. Mercurey .... Ned Harrigan | Lady Mountjoy ... Miss Amelia Goreflo

Matinees Tuesday and Saturday.
Friday, Ladies Invitation Night, a Lady admitted free with each gentleman.

Best Quality of Ales, Wines, Liquors and Cigars to be had at the Saloon inside the Theatre.
Tony Pastor, Proprietor

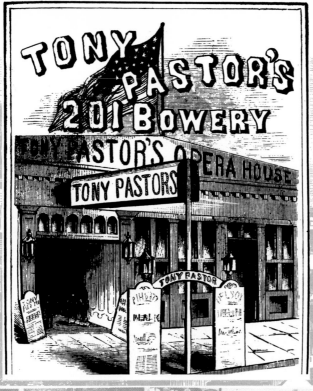

Pastor's Opera House and scenes of the neighborhood, *circa. 1867*. The center picture shows the Bowery as seen from Delancy Street.

Art: courtesy of the Harvard Theatre Collection; Photograph: courtesy of the Hammacher Schlemmer Company, New York.

THE DEAN OF THE VAUDEVILLE STAGE

TONY PASTOR

circa. 1900

May Irvin, early 1880's. (Courtesy of the Harvard Theatre Collection)

1878.

TONY PASTOR'S THEATRE

585 & 587 Broadway, Opp. Metropolitan Hotel.

TONY PASTOR........................SOLE PROPRIETOR

Monday, Dec'r 20, and during the Week

PROGRAMME

Overture.................... H. T. Dyring and Orchestra

The performance will commence with the funny sketch

STRATAGEM

Jerry, a Servant........ Dan Colyer | Old Cruncher............Frank Girard
Harry Jinkins.... ..... John Kernell | Jennie Oruncher....Miss Edith Orelius

Character Changes and Descriptive Ballads

Miss Joyce Martelle

BARNEY | REYNOLDS AND WALLING | DAVE

Will appear in new act arranged by Dave Walling, entitled

CONAMORE

Hector.... ....Barney Reynolds | Jessie................Dave Walling

MISS FLORENCE MERTON

In a choice Selection of Popular Ballads.

The Champion Lady Jig Dancer

Miss Kitty O'Neil

TONY PASTOR'S CHRISTMAS CAROLS

JOHN | The Kernells | HARRY

In a bit of Song and some Original Conversation, introducing Harry's great hit

The Dizzy Serio Comic

Miss Lillian Russell

Will Sing Alice by Archer, and the beautiful Ballad by C. C. Muller,
How to Catch a Beau

Dutch Deception

The Funniest Dutchman in the World

Harry Watson

In his Dutch Courtship Specialty, assisted by Miss

Alice Hutchings

The FRENCH TWIN SISTERS

In splendid execution Jig, Clog and Reel Dancing

Sheehan & Jones

In their Absurdity

An Every Day Occurrence

Jerry Driscoll ....{ John | Mrs. McManus, ...
Mrs. Jerry Driscoll.....{ Sheehan | ....Robert Jones
Policeman Murphy .... Frank Girard | Mary Ann McManus... Jennie Christie

Niles and Evans

The Famed Wits and Punsters, in their Comical and Amusing Specialty

Bric-a-Brac

Ferguson & Mack

Original and Eccentric Irish Comedians. Presenting a line of Character Creations that are distinct from all others of same order, and illustrated in Extemporaneous Dialogue and Repartee

The performance concluding with the screaming Farce

DUTCH AND IRISH RIVALS

Jacob Kransmeyer, a love sick Dutchman.... **HARRY WATSON**
Pat Maloney, an Irish Masher.............**HARRY KERNELL**
Mr. Pemberton, a husband who is not jealous ....Frank Girard
Mrs. Pemberton, a mischief-loving wife.... ....Miss Jennie Christie

3 MATINEES TUESDAY AND FRIDAY and Christmas Day

Program for week beginning December 20, 1880, at Tony Pastor's Theatre at 585-587 Broadway.

Pastor's 14th Street Theatre in the Tammany Building sometime after adoption of the "continuous" policy in 1896. (Courtesy of the Hoblitzelle Theatre Arts Library, The University of Texas at Austin)

Lillian Russell in the title role of Pastor's production of *Patience*, January-March, 1882. (Courtesy of the Harvard Theatre Collection)

An earlier picture of the entrance to the Theatre taken sometime between 1881 and the fire of 1888. (Courtesy of the Hoblitzelle Theatre Arts Library, The University of Texas at Austin)

Program for the week beginning January 15, 1883,
at Tony Pastor's New 14th Street Theatre.

Pastor in a characteristic stage pose, *circa. mid-1890's.*
(Courtesy of the Harvard Theatre Collection)

Drawing of Pastor in
The Morning Telegraph,
October 22, 1903.

Pastor with Tom Lewis (left) and Lew Dockstader (center) at New York's Polo Grounds, July, 1908.
One of Pastor's last public appearances. (Courtesy of the Hoblitzelle Theatre Arts Library, The University of Texas at Austin)

cablegram arrived telling him of his mother's death on July 10. According to the *New York Times*, "Mrs. Cornelia Pastor's remains were temporarily placed in a vault in the Cemetery of the Evergeens to await the return of her son, Tony." The paper went on to mention that "all her sons, with the exception of Tony, are dead."[35] (No record of Frank Pastor's passing has been uncovered, but his name no longer appeared in the papers after the summer of 1883.) Tony and his wife cut short their Paris visit and sailed for home. They arrived on July 31 and the funeral was held on August 3, followed by burial in the Pastor lot.

The manager's first transatlantic talent hunt had been productive. He had made numerous friends and had reviewed dozens of acts in London and Paris. He had returned with two popular European performers in hand — Albert Clive and his trained dog from the Circus D'Ete in Paris and Little Tich, a burlesque song and dance man from the London Pavilion. Both toured with him that fall, then appeared for several weeks at his 14th Street theatre. Little Tich, whose real name was Harry Ralph, had expected to encounter wild Indians on the tour and "it was only Mr. Pastor's assurances," he wrote, "that prevented me investing in a huge Colt's revolver."[36]

There were no Indians, but the little entertainer did have an anxious moment with a fan in Syracuse. A burly individual heartily complimented the Englishman on his performance, then accused him of not fully appreciating the praise. "You're an unnat'ral, ongrateful varmint," said the big bruiser, lifting the performer off the floor by his coat lapels. Pastor was sent for in a hurry. "Mr. Pastor walked up," Little Tich recalled, "and, laying his hand on the man's shoulder, requested him to vanish. Round spun the stranger. His eyes had come right out of their caves now, into the open. Out shot two number 19 grappling-irons. Up went Mr. Pastor; and *bang!* he was *bounced* into my empty chair. 'Sit down,' roared the other. 'Don't open your head at me! Sit down!' Before we had recovered from our surprise — or Mr. Pastor from his 'bouncing' — the wild man . . . was passing down the street."[37]

Little Tich and Albert Clive in 1887 were the first of a large contingent of foreign artists hand-picked by Pastor over the years. He now had his sea legs and an annual expedition abroad became a regular part of his professional calendar. This new enterprise added further lustre to his already enviable image as an astute and energetic showman and, by the end of the 1880's, had earned him a patrician title among his New York admirers — "The Impresario of 14th Street." He claimed indifference to the title, but in truth he wore it with pride and style.

CHAPTER NINE

The Impresario of 14th Street

The 1880's were Pastor's golden years. The decade found him at the peak of his powers and one of the most popular and respected men in the theatrical world of New York, perhaps of the country. The papers liked to write about him, and people were proud of his friendship, of being seen in his company, or of just receiving a salutatory smile and tip of the hat as he passed. The waiters at Baron Mulbach's on 14th Street treated him like a visiting potentate when he dropped in for a bowl of oyster stew or a glass of lager, and so did the clerks at the Morton House when he stopped by on Mondays to pick up his weekly supply of cigars. Invariably he had a funny story to pass along, and once he supposedly kept a crowd at the Baron's "laughing for an hour in discussing a bee in a molasses barrel."[1] To most people he was the same affable and good-natured person off the stage as he was on.

But he did have a dark side, and his close associates knew that it did not take much to raise his dander. He had become a staunch Democrat during the post-war years, and the subject of politics could send him into a table-pounding rage. So could pinochle! He was hopelessly addicted to the game and a notorious poor loser. According to Lew Fields, the comic, "any man who would play pinochle with him all the time, and let him win, could have an engagement for the rest of his natural life."[2] Then, too, he was easily ruffled by criticism of himself or his house. "He had no sympathy for those whose hands bore heavily on their pens," said Epes Sargent,[3] who wrote about vaudeville under the pseudonym "Chicot" for several New York papers in the 1890's. The *Dramatic News* once reported that Pastor had hissed at a performance of *La Tosca*. The manager wrote a curt note to the editor: "I desire to state most positively that this is not true, and that no action of mine warrants such statement. I never was guilty of such an ill-mannered act in my life."[4]

Pastor was not a particularly handsome man. He was short and now quite stout, a far cry from the "dapper little chap of about 110 pounds" whom Harry

S. Sanderson had seen at Rivers' Melodeon in 1861.[5] But the ladies found him cute, charming, and gallant, and they loved his grand mustache, waxed and rolled into straight, fierce points. "It was a beautiful mustache," said Lillian Russell, "and tinted with artistry."[6] For a heavy man he was surprisingly light on his feet, and his walk was a combination swagger and roll that oozed confidence and breeding. His wardrobe was extensive, and Miss Russell remembered that he was "always dressed with exquisite taste whatever time or place you found him."[7] He delighted in jewelry, changing fancy rings with the days of the week and invariably displaying a glittering diamond solitaire in the front of the dress shirt that he always wore.

Whether on the stage or off, his shiny opera hat was now as much a trademark as his rounded figure and bristly mustache. He was seldom seen or pictured without it. On the stage he used it as a prop, popping it open to emphasize a certain word and wearing it at various angles to capture the style of a particular song. For a romantic ballad the hat was traditionally held collapsed against the hip, for a comic song it was perched precariously on the back of the head or tilted rakishly over one eye. In his *Cosmopolitan* article on vaudeville, C. R. Sherlock recalled that one of Pastor's common attitudes for a jaunty number was "with his fists shoved deep into his trousers pockets and his bristling tile at a rakish angle over his shiny forehead."[8]

Referring to a cartoon of the manager on its front page, the *Mirror* asked in 1880: "Who's this? Tony Pastor? Yes, there can be no possible mistake as to whom those smiling features, that Napoleonic mustache, the expanse of shirt bosom, the diamond headlight and crush-hat belong. No picture of our genial friend Tony would be complete without the latter accompaniment."[9]

Perhaps those New York admirers who labeled him "The Impresario of 14th Street" were inspired as much by his princely appearance as by his managerial acumen. He just had that look about him of the successful and prosperous entrepreneur.

There were a number of peculiarities in Pastor's make-up that alternately amused and puzzled those around him. For one thing, he was fondly attached to a pair of old patent leather boots that laced to his knees. He wore them simply because they were comfortable and apparently was unconcerned that they were totally at odds with his otherwise fashion-plate elegance. Impeccable from head to knee, that was Tony Pastor! Then there was his quaint theory about the hair needing air. "Every half block," said Sargent, "he would lift his headgear and let the air escape and cool air flow in."[10]

He was also a dog fancier and owned several of various breeds. He frequently took one of the pets to the office and kept a small kennel in one corner for just such an occasion. A visitor often found himself interviewing the manager amidst yaps and growls from a poodle or a spaniel while Pastor punctuated the conversation by tossing scraps dutifully furnished by the cook at the Baron's.

One of his most curious habits, perhaps, is described by Gilbert: "Once a woman tripped on the steps of the Academy of Music, injuring herself fatally.

Thereafter when Pastor went by the Academy, as he had to daily to get to his theatre, he would pause, raise his hat, and bow, a curious genuflection he never explained."[11] This may have been nothing more than the act of an eccentric; then again, it may have been the honest action of a highly compassionate and religious man.

Pastor was known to be "a strict and devout Catholic,"[12] highly prone to charity and easily moved to sentiment. A crucifix hung on his office wall, and there was a shrine backstage "to which," as Gilbert says, "he would repair (after checking up on the box office)."[13] There was a poor box located in the lobby. "Just inside the door," Edwin Goewey wrote in his article on Pastor, "he would pause, cross himself, then drop a coin in the poor box, which remained in the same spot from the day he took over the house until he left it."[14] Edward Marks was a song plugger in the 1890's and later established the Edward Marks Music Publishers. He remembered that "backstage at Pastor's a placard prominently and permanently warned against taking the name of the Lord in vain . . . I hold it to his credit, because he was no tin saint. He wasn't indifferent to a pretty ankle."[15]

There are those who hold that Pastor strongly disliked any kind of profanity or lewdness and never resorted to abusive language himself, even on those occasions when anger got the better of him. "I never heard Pastor use a profane word that I can recall," said Francis Wilson. "Though he had been a circus clown, he had a certain dignity which always impressed me."[16] Gilbert has told us that "jiminetty" was one of the showman's "favorite expletives and the height of his profanity, which occasionally included 'so help me Bob!' "[17] Yet, Arthur Roberts, a London music hall comic of the period, had a different tale to tell. He recalled that on one of Pastor's visits to Paris he purchased a handbook on conversational French with the intention of trying to communicate with the natives in their own tongue.

"As we walked along the Paris streets," said Roberts, "Tony studied the volume with laborious care. He read extracts aloud to hotel managers, commissionaires, cabmen, waiters, and attractive young ladies behind the counters of the Parisian shops. Of course nobody understood a syllable he said. The men gesticulated wildly. The girls looked prettily and politely puzzled. Tony, who was taking everything with the utmost seriousness, got quite angry and indignant. He swore in the very worst American that he knew — and his vocabulary was marvelous."[18]

Something else about Pastor that was considered "marvelous," and rightly so, was his warm-hearted benevolence, his frank, unabashed, and sometimes foolhardy generosity. Behind the elegance and buoyancy there was a loving and charitable nature. "Brother Pastor," wrote Charles Edward Ellis in his history of the Elks, "in his life, in his many quiet deeds of charity, was a living exemplification of the principal motto of the Elks — Charity. It might be said truthfully that no man ever lived who gave more than he did of his money, of his time and sympathy to alleviate the distress and suffering of his fellow man."[19] It also might be said truthfully that no man ever lived who was such an easy touch! He was one of the incorporators in 1882 of the Actors' Fund, a charity organization devoted to the care of the aged, sick, and needy members of the theatrical profession. He was one of the Fund's strongest boosters and, at the same time, perhaps one of its biggest rivals. As the *Mirror* remarked in 1884, "he is a whole actors' fund by himself." [20]

It was comparatively easy to talk Pastor into donating his theatre and company for a benefit of one kind or another — a special matinee, for example, in behalf of the victims of the Brooklyn Theatre fire (December 17, 1876) or a performance to raise money for the George Washington Camp, Number One, of the U. S. War Veterans (February 22, 1886). It also was easy to get assistance from him of a much more personal kind, and most of his Good Samaritan gestures were, as Ellis said, "quiet deeds of charity." His office was a virtual welfare agency for the needy of the profession, and business was always brisk.

"He dispensed his gifts right and left," said Harry S. Sanderson, "and had a certain pocket in which he placed each night seven one-dollar bills and twelve quarter-dollars. This fund invariably reached the hands of the needy." [21] Sime Silverman, co-founder and editor of *Variety*, wrote: "Did someone die; someone taken ill or injured; in fact anything in connection with a real variety artist was first reported directly to Pastor's, generally to Mr. Sanderson. Both the venerable Dean and Mr. Sanderson were instrumental in relieving and assisting untold hundreds of cases of want." [22]

Such a report once came to Pastor's notice as he was reading a newspaper over lunch at the Baron's. He read that a theatrical company was stranded in Salt Lake City. An "old friend," who was lunching with the manager at the time, remembered what happened: "He went across to his theatre and had his manager get the details. When he learned that it was a bona-fide case of stranding, with a business manager who had skipped, Tony had his own bank wire to Salt Lake City enough money to get the company out of debt, pay their fares to New York, and feed them on the way. How many times he did that sort of thing nobody knows. His friends use to remonstrate with him about his generosity, but it did no good. He simply could not be kept from lending his money ... He never seemed to keep any account of the money he loaned, and I know he must have passed out a good many thousand dollars during his career, without a slip of paper to show for it." [23]

Apparently there were those in the profession who were quite ready and willing to take full advantage of Pastor's generosity. "Any one," said the same old friend, "actor, manager, agent, could 'touch' him successfully ... When he used to go on the road with his own company it was a shame to see the way stranded actors used to wait for his arrival. It was worst in Chicago. They would meet him at the train with hard luck stories, and Tony would always stand for them." [24] The manager's generous streak may have had some effect now and then upon the nature of his bills. "More than one actor," said Sargent, "deliberately borrowed money of Mr. Pastor that he might plead his inability to return the loan and offer to play for a week for a sum less the loan, and always Mr. Pastor accepted the offer."[25]

One did not have to be in the profession to receive a financial assist. Pastor helped the less fortunate wherever he found them. "If he refused to help a derelict," said Sanderson, "there must indeed have been more than ordinary cause."[26] Sanderson recalled a meeting with Pastor in the early 1870's: "I was making a call on a friend when Tony came in during the conversation. The ill-fortune of a worthy old lady was mentioned and, as it was Christmas Eve, comment was made on the change in her circumstances. Tony soon took leave, and after his departure my hostess exhibited a ten-dollar bill that Tony requested her to hand to the old lady. Billy Delehanty (of the well-known Delehanty and Hengler team) remarked: 'Oh, that's nothing for Tony; he's always doing that.'"[27] Indeed, he *was* always doing that. He seems to have been deaf to the advice of one of his own songs, "Up a Tree," whose sentiment was one of thrift: "So while you have it, keep it, or you'll soon be up a tree."[28] He had it, but kept giving it away, and he may indeed have spent his final years "up a tree."

His charity was by no means confined to almsgiving alone. He was equally generous with professional encouragement and advice and was admired as a sympathetic and kindly patron of the young beginner. "A word of encouragement," he insisted, "is a great thing. Just a pat on the back as a man leaves for the footlights and told that he has done well when he comes off, helps him a lot. Perhaps he has been a frost, but a bit of approval will help him to do better next time, and it's a pretty good thing to dispense. We don't any of us get too much of it."[29] He gave such encouragement in abundance and would sit for an hour or more, if need be, talking with an act and offering pointers for improvement. It was almost as if he considered the performers as children who needed fatherly supervision. Maggie Cline was a big attraction at the manager's theatre in the early 1890's, and Harvey Higgins reported in an article on the origin of vaudeville that "Maggie Cline told me it was the happiest day of her life when 'Tony' engaged her for his theatre . . . 'He was just like a father to a beginner. He thrilled at any extra applause given an artist, as much as if it were rendered for him.'"[30]

Pastor was noted for giving a newcomer a particularly generous and warm introduction to the audience. "The Pastor dignity and eclat on occasions like this," says Morell, "were something wonderful to behold. Gently leading the bewildered — and sometimes palsied — tyro out onto the stage by one shaking hand he would pause for a moment, smile benignly at the audience, say a few words of introduction and then, with an explosive pop of his opera hat and a nod in the direction of the orchestra leader, start the ball rolling."[31] Perhaps his almost paternal concern for his performers had something to do with the fact that he himself remained childless throughout his life. He loved children, and one of his greatest charities was certainly the annual Christmas Party for the Children of the Stage, a gesture he initiated in the early 1880's and continued until shortly before his death. The *Chicago Record* described the big affair of 1906:

83

"Good old Tony Pastor gave his annual party to the children of the stage in New York, Sunday, first providing an entertainment for them in his theatre and afterward taking them to supper and a Christmas tree in Tammany Hall ... Our dispatches give this account of the happy affair: 'First, the entertainment was given in the theatre. It consisted of fourteen numbers, all of the performers being little actors and actresses under 12 years old. At the conclusion of the concert the little ones marched to the basement of Tammany Hall, where luncheon was served, and after that they again formed in line and marched to the main hall in the Tammany Building, where three Christmas trees were laden with presents.' " 32

Charity, magnanimity, sympathy, and kindness — these were slogans that Pastor lived by. The Impresario of 14th Street had a heart as big as the shows he produced.

The great popularity and affection that he enjoyed both within and without the profession was ably demonstrated at his theatre on the afternoon and evening of March 21, 1890, upon the occasion of his twenty-fifth anniversary as a manager. One story has it that the idea of commemorating this milestone came to him quite accidentally while he and his wife were taking an evening stroll up Irving Place. A "ragged pensioner," who had repeatedly and successfully hit the manager for a handout in the past, approached for another try:

"Mr. Pastor's face took on a severe expression. 'Don't you know any better than to accost me when I'm with a lady? Not a cent tonight ... 'See here, Tony,' he said, rejoining the indignant and retreating manager. 'Yer ain't goin' ter give the go-by ter an ol' fren'? Why, I knowed yer years ago. Yer uster give me a nickel now and then, way back in '65 wen youse was down at de ol' stan, four-forty-four Broadway. Say, me an' you ain't goin' to part like dis. A cold night, too, an' me widout de price of a bed or a coffee an' sinker.' 'Oh, give him something, Tony,' said Mrs. Pastor, and her obedient husband went down in his trousers' pockets and Monsieur le Tramp went off happy ... The words of the beggar set Mr. Pastor a thinking. 'The fellow's right,' said he to Mrs. Pastor. 'It is just twenty-five years ago that I began as a manager in this city. What was the date? Let me see — why, it was in March — the 21st.' 'Then you must commemorate it with a special performance,' said she, and forthwith Mr. Pastor began making arrangements."33

At the matinee on March 21 the little house was "crowded to suffocation by friends anxious to do honor to the occasion." Included in the throng was a large delegation from the Actors' Amateur Athletic Association of America, " of which Mr. Pastor is a beloved member." DeWolf Hopper, the actor, and other officers of the Association occupied a stage box. The manager was greeted with a "ringing reception" and presented with "two immense azalias in full bloom (sent by Annie Pixley), an immense basket of flowers from Monroe and Rice, and another basket from Manager Edwin Knowles." After Pastor had finished his turn, "DeWolf Hopper stepped to the front of his box, and, in a few words, presented the veteran with a set of resolutions from the Five A's and a magnificent medallion badge from members of the club . . . It was a beautiful affair, and Mr. Pastor's voice choked several times as he replied to the highly appreciated compliment. As he ended his speech, the club arose, and, at the end of their cheers, took their boutonnieres from their coats and gave Mr. Pastor a bombardment of violets. The attaches of the theatre, the orchestra and stage hands presented their manager with a costly easy chair."[34]

That evening another capacity crowd was on hand, including hundreds of luminaries from both the variety and legitimate stages. "Rare and costly floral offerings came from the Nobles of the Mystic Shrine, Edward Harrigan, Add Ryman, the Julians, and others."[35] As Pastor was leaving the stage after singing his usual package of topical songs, Abe Hummel, legal mind for many of the big theatrical figures of the day, stepped out from the wings, "drew him back and presented him with a gold medal encrusted with diamonds. The medal was designed by Tiffany and is of old gold, encircled with ten blue-white stones."[36] The names inscribed on the back of the medal read like a Who's Who among performers and managers. Included on the list were Augustin Daly, Daniel Frohman, William Harris, Evans and Hoey, Harry Kernell, Harry Miner, Theodore Moss, Proctor and Turner, John Stetson, Denman Thompson, and Gus Williams.

"After giving the genial Tony a full minute to gaze at the elegant testimonial of his *confreres*, Mr. Hummel made a brief but eloquent speech. Mr. Pastor was completely surprised, but stammered out a few words of thanks. Then the two gentlemen linked arms and walked off the stage, while the audience shouted itself hoarse in enthusiastic recalls."[37]

As Pastor looked back over a quarter of a century of variety management, he had every reason to be proud of his accomplishments. He was still the "king of variety," and he had achieved and made successful the refined type of variety he had sought from the beginning. But he was somewhat alone in that.

Although there were some variety establishments around the country devoted to family-style entertainment, most were still stag resorts, mere saloons. A few houses in New York advertised a "family policy," places like the London, Harry Miner's 8th Avenue Theatre, the Olympic in Harlem and, in nearby territory, Hyde and Behman's Theatre in Brooklyn and Waldman's Newark Opera House. Pastor's, however, seems to have been the only house receiving regular endorsement from respectable circles. "The one vaudeville theatre in New York that is patronized by the ladies," said the *Mirror* in 1887, "is Tony Pastor's."[38] Much of the variety available in the city during the 1880's was supplied at regular theatres by visiting combinations; or in establishments of the concert saloon class, like the popular Koster and Bial Music Hall on 23rd Street; or at the countless dime-museums that had sprung up during the decade — Huber's Palace Museum, for example, and Doris' 8th Avenue Museum, Worth's Museum, the Star Museum, and the Harlem Museum.

The situation had not changed much by 1890. Pastor's was largely in a class by itself. The decade had been good to the old campaigner: his competition had been low, his popularity high and, despite the fact that Madison Square had superseded Union Square as the city's Rialto by 1885, his 14th Street business had remained impressive. Truly, Pastor must have looked back with general satisfaction. If he could have looked ahead, however, he might have been troubled. Conditions were to change rapidly in the next decade. A variety boom was to bring great changes to this form of entertainment and stiff competition to the genial and beloved "Impresario of 14th Street."

CHAPTER TEN

A Ride on the Ferris Wheel

The decade known as the "Gay 90's" had barely begun when New York began showing symptoms of variety fever. The old resorts were flourishing and new ones were appearing in rapid succession, several in the city's new theatrical stretch along Broadway between Madison Square and 42nd Street. Scores of New Yorkers were catching the bug. By the end of the decade an epidemic would be sweeping the entire country.

Some of the new variety houses took their cue from Koster and Bial's glorified concert saloon on 23rd Street. These places offered customers the pleasures of smoke and drink in an environment of tables and chairs. Others followed Pastor's example and put on variety bills alone in a regular theatre. The first were generally labeled "music halls," the second "variety" or "vaudeville theatres." These terms were used loosely and interchangeably and should not be accepted as distinct categories nor as indicating the particular character of a place. Most of the new houses, whatever their title, were striving for respectability, and the growing use of the term "vaudeville" in place of "variety" was clearly an attempt to stress such respectability.

Among the first of the new variety haunts was the New Park Theatre at Broadway and 35th Street. This former legitimate theatre was owned by Hyde and Behman, variety managers in Brooklyn, and donned the motley in late August, 1892, under the management of Archie Ellis.

"It shall be my aim," Ellis stated in a *Mirror* interview, "to present clean, attractive entertainment that women and children can enjoy ... I think that straight variety on Broadway can be made to pay. The prices are cheap, 25, 50, and 75 cents, and we shall never go above that figure. It will be a long entertainment, too, lasting until 1:15, so that people, even after having seen another performance, may drop in and enjoy themselves for a half hour or so at a small expense. I am confident that the plan will succeed."[1]

The plan succeeded until the spring of 1895 when mushrooming competition forced a return to legitimate fare. The house then became the Herald Square Theatre.

On October 24, 1892, George J. Kraus opened the Imperial Music Hall on West 29th Street between Broadway and Sixth Avenue. At least a portion of the house was equipped with tables and chairs. The place seated some "1,200 persons" and the variety bills ran "continuously from eight until twelve every evening."[2] The fact that some people were staying away because of the Hall's saloon features prompted a comment from J. M. McDonough, business manager for the house. "That smoking and drinking do prevail to some degree," he said, "has given rise to the impression in some quarters that it is not a proper place for a man to take his family. But a single visit will destroy that illusion."[3] While there is no indication that the Imperial ever became a favorite "family" resort, it did enjoy hearty support for several years before being converted into the famous Weber and Fields Music Hall in the fall of 1896.

Both the Imperial and the New Park were featuring a show that ran from eight in the evening to midnight and later. On January 9, 1893, F. F. Proctor, owner of Proctor's 23rd Street Theatre, went them both one better. He turned his house into a "vaudeville" theatre with a show that ran "continuously" from noon until 10:30 in the evening. "After Breakfast Go to Proctor's, After Proctor's Go to Bed" became a popular slogan. The idea, according to the *Mirror*, was to supply "an entertainment so arranged that patrons may understand and enjoy it whenever they drop in without reference to what follows or precedes the portion of the programme they witness ... It is for the benefit especially of women that may, for instance, be shopping, and want to drop in to be entertained for a long or a short time."[4]

Some women apparently considered the place a sort of boarding school for their offspring. In their 1943 biography of Proctor, William M. Marston and John H. Feller write: "Some mothers sent their children to Proctor's right after breakfast with their lunch in a bundle and told them to stay all day and come home in the evening."[5] With low prices of 50¢, 35¢, and 15¢ and with attractive accommodations and an immaculate show, Proctor's became a first-class family house. Respectable audiences attended freely, and it was here that many persons undoubtedly contracted the variety bug for the first time.

The continuous performance idea involved the presentation of three shows in succession, each running about three and a half to four hours. There was a "milkman's matinee" starting around noon, a "supper show," and an evening show. The top acts, however, appeared only in the matinee and evening shows, sometimes only in the latter. The house orchestra gave way to a piano player, and reserved seats became a thing of the past as customers shuttled in and out at their pleasure. To discourage patrons from remaining in their seats for more than one show, thus cutting down the turn-over in ticket sales, some managers employed what came to be called a "chaser." This was an act so bad that its repetition was certain to drive some customers to the street.

Proctor was the first to introduce the "continuous" idea to New York, but the idea itself seems to have been originated by Benjamin F. Keith in Boston during the mid-1880's. "Other managers have laid claim to the title," wrote Sargent, "but they could not prove their points. It would seem that to Mr. Keith belongs the credit."[6] We will have more to say about Keith a little later.

Roof gardens were becoming popular in New York during the 1890's and one of the first was opened in June, 1893, by Rudolph Aronson. Aronson was manager of the Casino on the east side of Broadway at the corner of 39th Street, the home of light opera in New York, and he established a lavish roof garden on top of the theatre. Here people could eat and drink under the stars while watching a bill of light opera, ballet, and variety.

Meanwhile, Koster and Bial were making headway in their efforts to upgrade the clientele at their 23rd Street Music Hall. Carmencita, a Spanish dancer immortalized on canvas by Sargent and Chase, had appeared there for a lengthy engagement beginning in February, 1890. She had aroused the curiosity of New York, especially of the city's more polite circles. Curtained boxes skirted the balcony of the Music Hall. "In these," writes Henry Brown in *In the Golden Nineties*, "ladies consumed with curiosity to see the latest craze of the hour would defy the proprieties, and it eventually became the smart thing in society to get up a party to see Carmencita from the half draped boxes."[7]

Impressed by this turnout of the carriage trade, Koster and Bial had begun a campaign to improve the tone and general character of their resort. The campaign was paying off so well by the spring of 1893 that the managers decided to transplant their operation farther uptown. The new site was to be Oscar Hammerstein's Manhattan Theatre on 34th Street midway between Broadway and Seventh Avenue. Koster and Bial were to manage the new hall, but Hammerstein was to be a partner in the venture. Theirs was a stormy association since, as Gilbert has told us, "Oscar would fight with a mirror."[8] The new Manhattan, equipped with a second-floor cafe where "people can eat and drink, and at the same time get a view of the stage,"[9] opened on August 28, 1893, and was called simply Koster and Bial's Music Hall.

While we can not say exactly what it was that prompted this boom in variety during the early 1890's, the rage created by Carmencita certainly contributed to it, and so did the great popularity enjoyed at Pastor's by two bouncy English entertainers, Bessie Bonehill and Jennie Hill.

Miss Bonehill was a male impersonator whose act was built around songs and character studies from London. She was already a noted London attraction when Pastor first saw her during the summer of 1889. He was taken by her at once and wasted little time getting her signature on a contract for four weeks at his theatre in the fall. "I saw Bessie Bonehill," he recalled, "and knew that she would be an American favorite."[10] He was right. She was an immediate hit when she opened in New York on October 28, 1889. Audiences loved "her pathetic Newsboy, her gallant Cavalier of gay Prince Charlie's time, and her natty midshipman."

"No variety performer that has come from England," said the *Mirror*, "has

89

either merited or received the degree of popular favor enjoyed by that extremely clever young woman with that extremely disagreeable name . . . Her line of business is not new by any means, but she infuses into it a freshness, an incisive intelligence and an accurate skill that are *sui generis*, and that even the gallery boy is quick to see and admire. She has a bright face and a flexible figure; she is a nimble and graceful dancer, and what is more conspicuous still, she has plenty of brains lodged in her shapely head . . . If Bessie Bonehill comes back she will have a warm welcome."[11]

She did come back a year later to open the manager's fall season in late October, 1890, and that "warm welcome" indeed was there. Pastor, astute and generous as always, backed her up with a topnotch array of variety specialists headed by the locally popular Russell Brothers and Maggie Cline. The Russells dressed as Irish servant girls and performed a roughneck song and dance act. Maggie Cline had been a big crowd-pleaser at Pastor's for several years, singing lusty songs with a vim and vigor that had earned her the nickname, "The Bowery Brunhilde."

The public descended on Pastor's house like locusts. "You will find the theatre packed to the doors," exclaimed the *Mirror* in early November, "(there hasn't been a vacant seat in it any night since the season opened) and you will hear more laughter and observe more genuine enjoyment than you are likely to hear and to observe in any other theatre in town."[12]

Bessie Bonehill ended her engagement on Saturday, December 6, and after the show that evening she entertained the Pastors and the company at her quarters in the Hungaria Hotel. Informal speeches were made and toasts were drunk all around, including one to another luminary of the London halls soon to make her American debut at Pastor's — Jennie Hill.

Jennie Hill had been billed in London as "The Vital Spark," and she specialized in rowdy songs of the street. Pastor had been the guest of honor at a dinner in her London home the previous summer and had signed her up at that time. He ballyhooed his star's reputation for weeks in the local press, and when she opened on 14th Street on February 23, 1891, the little shoebox-of-a-theatre was mobbed. The *Mirror* covered the event:

> The house was sold out before evening, and the count of the people turned away showed over fifteen hundred. Jennie Hill, the greatest of London music hall performers, was the magnet that drew the crowd . . .
>
> When she entered as a soap-boiler's daughter and proceeded with infinite zest and electrical vivacity, to describe her adventures 'On the Continong' the house gave her a thundering welcome and filled the intervals when the brilliant artiste paused for breath with such cheers, such hand-clapping, and such tattoos of enthusiastic feet and umbrellas as were never heard before under the dome of Mr. Pastor's theatre.

> *Her next character was a coffee-shop waitress, a type thoroughly*
> *cockaigne but so humorous and so artistically presented withal that*
> *the audience again went wild with delight.*
>
> *Then she sang a descriptive song 'Masks and Faces,' displaying*
> *remarkable versatility and considerable dramatic power. The fourth*
> *and last of her sketches was 'Arry,' a costermonger out for a Sunday*
> *stroll.*[13]

Pastor had been worried at the outset that his star's decidedly English patter might hamper her success and had "distributed in the audience a dictionary with definitions."[14] His concern was unnecessary, and so was the dictionary. Jennie Hill had a charm that went straight to the heart and audiences loved her, even if they could not always understand her specialized dress and mysterious lingo. New Yorkers flocked to Pastor's during her six-week engagement, and the line of stage-door-johnnies waiting to meet her after each show was always a long one. Even the *haut monde* was drawn to 14th Street to find out what the fuss was all about.

"Jennie Hill has become the rage," the *Mirror* stated in March. "There is as much curiosity to see her as to see Carmencita among the inhabitants of fashionable New York. Seats at Tony Pastor's are engaged far ahead, and latecomers are certain to find standing room only – and precious little of that. Miss Hill's popularity has eclipsed that achieved by her predecessor, Bessie Bonehill."[15]

The young English entertainer concluded her triumphant run on April 4. She was showered with flowers and gifts, among which was a medallion and a diamond-studded watch from Pastor himself. Two days later the manager left on his annual spring tour. Jennie Hill had provided a glorious wind-up for an overall glorious season.

Business continued brisk at Pastor's over the next two seasons as variety's popularity swung sharply upward. Since the new houses were locating to the north, they offered no immediate threat to the only first-class variety house in the area of 14th Street and Union Square. The veteran manager still had the territory to himself. Even after Proctor opened his elaborate and popular "continuous" house on 23rd Street, Pastor's prosperity held fast. There was no dip in his prices or in the quality of his bills. Twenty-five cents still bought a three-hour show packed full of some of the best local and foreign specialty and comic talent that could be found.

The old afterpiece, however, was gone from Pastor's bills by 1892 and had pretty much disappeared from variety in general by 1895. With it, of course, went the resident stock company as well. The primary reason for its passing was doubtless the refusal of more and more of the new headliners to participate. Also, the public's enthusiasm for the afterpiece had been gradually waning since the mid-eighties. Managers soon found that this expensive added feature simply was no longer necessary to draw in the business.

Among the local favorites appearing regularly on Pastor's stage during the

1891-92 and 1892-93 seasons were the following: Ward and Vokes, an extremely winning team of tramp comics; J. W. Kelly, "The Rolling Mill Man," who delivered a dry monolog in the character of a well-paid Irish mechanic out for his Sunday afternoon walk; and Frank Bush, one of the first Jew comics in variety, who specialized in dialect stories and songs and in triple-tongue concerts on a tin whistle. The Russell Brothers also were regularly on hand, as was the inimitable Maggie Cline who still sent audiences into near-hysterics whenever she gave full voice to "Throw Him Down McCloskey," a hearty ditty about a barroom brawl.

Lottie Gilson was another big favorite. She was an energetic soubrette who sang serio-comic songs and was popularly known in the variety haunts as "The Little Magnet." She was one of the first to use a singing "plant" in the audience. In the middle of one of her songs, an audience member would "unexpectedly" start singing along with her. She would feign surprise, stop singing, carry on a light-hearted conversation with the spectator, then ask him to stand up and do a solo.

Later on, Tin Pan Alley employed this device to plug new songs. Irving Berlin, the prolific tunesmith, introduced songs in this fashion as a boy. He has recalled that on at least one occasion, around 1905, he was a singing "plant" at Pastor's: "I was then plugging a song called 'In the Sweet By and By' written and published by Harry Von Tilzer. In those days, the music publishers used to plug their songs through singers who sat in the audience. I was one of those and was paid the handsome salary of five dollars a week. I sang with an act called The Three Keatons — father, mother and son, the famous Buster."[16] We will meet the Keatons a little later.

Pastor's leading importations during the 1891-92 and 1892-93 seasons included Lydia Yeamans, George Beauchamp, Lilly Burnand, Nellie Lingard, Katie Lawrence, Vesta Victoria, and Paquerette. The pretty and winsome Vesta, with her English comic songs and dances, and the angular Paquerette, with her comic impersonations of the French peasantry, seem to have been the most warmly received of these foreign artists. Neither, however, caught the public's fancy like Bessie Bonehill and Jennie Hill. Miss Bonehill paid a return visit to Pastor's in October, 1892, and once again was a big hit. Nellie L'Estrange, a serio-comic songstress from the London halls, created a mild stir there in late July, 1893, prompting the following comment from the *Mirror:* "Mr. Pastor may be assured that his enterprise in introducing foreign artists, and his care in the tone of his entertainment are fully appreciated by the public to which he has catered so long."[17] In the face of all the evidence, it is certainly difficult to understand Gilbert's claim that "Tony Pastor made no direct importations, just gathered them in after they clicked over here."[18]

Pastor's timeworn monopoly on 14th Street was finally broken in September, 1893, when Benjamin F. Keith and Edward Albee opened the Union Square Theatre a block to the west as a "continuous vaudeville" house.

Both Keith and Albee had backgrounds as circus grifters and sideshow spielers. Their paths had crossed in Boston early in 1883 when Albee was hired as general manager for Keith's Washington Street Museum. The Museum featured freaks and exhibits along with performances of light opera and variety. The latter proved to be the more appealing; the freaks and exhibits were soon discarded. In 1885 the two men formed a partnership to open Boston's Bijou Theatre as a "continuous" house, the first perhaps in the country. The Bijou opened on July 6 with a bill of specialty acts and a cut-down light opera. The show was called "vaudeville" to give it the stamp of respectability, and, according to Keith, the "acts were free from vulgarity and innuendo" and the house was "clean and respectable."[19]

Keith and Albee were to become noted later on for their almost fanatical insistence on clean houses and decorous vaudeville fare and, as Gilbert says, "years after, when the Keith-Albee-Orpheum chain linked every important vaudeville house in America, performers called it the 'Sunday-school circuit.' "[20] The Bijou Theatre was the first link in that chain.

During the next few years the partners began to expand their holdings. They opened the Gaiety Museum in Providence, the Bijou in Philadelphia, the Colonial in Boston, and in September, 1893, their first property in New York — the Union Square Theatre. They leased the New York house in April and it was handsomely remodelled under Albee's supervision during the summer. J. Austin Fynes, former editor of the *Clipper*, was appointed resident manager for the theatre. The initial bill on September 18 consisted of a series of specialty acts and a condensed light opera, *Ship Ahoy*. This was the Keith-Albee formula. Three shows a day beginning at noon were offered, and prices were 50¢, 25¢, and 15¢.

Robert Grau, brother of Maurice Grau, general manager of the Metropolitan Opera, was a booker during the 1890's. He recalled that "when the house was thrown open ... it was the prettiest, daintiest vaudeville theatre in New York ... Beyond a doubt, the house was a hit."[21]

The house was a hit, but not the show. It did not take with the public. Fynes blamed the light opera. "The opera is not right for New York," he said. "It gets by in Boston and Philadelphia. It's outclassed here where we have a Casino to show us the real thing. As soon as I am rid of it, there will be something doing."[22] Fynes dropped the light opera in March and established a straight vaudeville show. Business improved almost immediately. By the end of the year the *Mirror* was able to announce that "B. F. Keith's continuous performances at the Union Square Theatre have become one of the most popular forms of amusement among metropolitan theatre-goers."[23]

Fynes soon began to beef up his shows with stars from the legitimate stage. These celebrities gave readings and recitations and often appeared in one-act plays especially written for the occasion. Legitimate performers on the whole tended to look down on vaudeville but Fynes lured a good many of them into the fold with huge salaries. Among his recruits were Maurice Barrymore, Clara Morris, and David Warfield. The idea spread like wildfire. Such performers, according to

93

Sargent, were commonly referred to as "Gold Bricks," and their chief value was to "draw into the theatre people who did not know how good vaudeville could be, and so fix them in the habit."[24] Such stars also helped to add dignity to vaudeville and were greatly responsible for eventually bringing this dappled form of entertainment to the serious attention of the country's conservative press. It was not long before Keith and Albee followed Fynes' example at the Union Square and installed straight vaudeville and the guest-star policy at their other houses as well.

One might suspect that with its elaborate accouterments and low prices the Union Square Theatre would have presented an immediate challenge to Pastor's modest operation down the street where reserved seats were still $1.00. But Pastor held his own very well during those final months of 1893. Odell notes that "despite the strong opposition of Keith and Proctor, Pastor had come brilliantly to 1894."[25] After Fynes switched to straight vaudeville in March, however, Pastor's business took a nose dive.

Robert Grau visited the venerable manager in his "little bird-cage of a theatre" around this time and found that "the show 'hung fire'" and that "the house was not crowded, nor was it little more than apathetic. 'What's the matter with it all?' I asked of the Dean of the old-time variety show ... 'Bob, a chap up the street in the Union Square Theatre is putting us to sleep.'"[26]

The nap was brief. Pastor's awakened with a start on April 16 when Vesta Tilley arrived from England to begin a seven-week engagement. Miss Tilley, a male impersonator, was then one of the most esteemed artists in the London halls, even more popular there than Bessie Bonehill or Jennie Hill, and Odell has told us that "the great event for Vaudeville for that season, or perhaps for any season preceding, came on April 16 with the debut in America of Vesta Tilley."[27]

Getting Miss Tilley had been a windfall for Pastor. He had been trying to persuade her to come to New York ever since he first saw her perform in the summer of 1888. In later years the English star explained why she had been so slow in accepting the offer: "I felt from what I had heard of that city, that my particular line of work would not appeal to New Yorkers. It was not until after I had married that my husband persuaded me to take the plunge."[28]

The *Mirror* was on hand for her debut: "Vesta Tilley more than fulfilled the promises made for her. She is unquestionably the best product of the English variety stage that has yet come to us ... She is bound to be very popular, and she deserves it."[29] She *was* popular. Dressed in stylish male attire and sporting an air of aristocratic elegance, she sang songs like "Only a Chappie" and "Following in My Father's Footsteps." Pastor's little theatre did a wide-awake business during her run. The *Mirror* reported in late May that "Vesta Tilley is still the rage at Pastor's, where a large crowd applauded her clever songs and personations last week."[30] After the young artist closed her engagement on June 2, however, the house dozed off once again, and two weeks later it was closed down for a whole month, "owing," said the *Mirror*, "to Tony Pastor's desire to be free from business cares."[31] Certainly among those "cares" must have been the growing threat of the Union Square Theatre.

Conditions remained wobbly at Pastor's through most of the 1894-95 season. The manager tried to give business a shot in the arm in February by adding matinees on Mondays and Saturdays and by offering "Good Reserved Seats" for 50¢ and 25¢.[32] In early April he even began offering matinees six days a week.[33] How these particular maneuvers affected business is not evident, but things were clearly looking up during Vesta Tilley's reappearance for six weeks beginning on April 22. The manager surrounded her with such top favorites as the Russell Brothers, the St. Felix Sisters, Weber and Fields, and James F. Hoey, and the SRO signs went up.

The theatre was closed down after the London entertainer finished her engagement on June 2, and this time it stayed closed for the entire summer.

Pastor had been thinking about quitting 14th Street and opening a new theatre uptown since early fall and, in November, 1894, Sanderson had let it be known that his employer had "three sites for such a theatre under consideration, but I cannot give any particulars as yet."[34] No further word was heard on the matter during the season. Then, in August, 1895, Pastor announced that he had decided not to make a move after all. "I have renewed my lease of my Fourteenth Street Theatre," he told a *Mirror* reporter, " and will remain there for at least three more years."[35] What had prompted him to stay put? He said it was "the very favorable results of last season,"[36] but this has a false ring to it. He was no longer a young man, and perhaps his ambition and drive had begun to falter. Then again, perhaps he had backed off because of the swelling number of new vaudeville houses to the north, especially the two mammoth amusement palaces being erected by Hammerstein and Proctor.

Hammerstein's venture, the Olympia on Broadway at Long Acre Square, was to be a combination music hall, theatre, and concert hall. Proctor's resort, the Pleasure Palace on 58th Street, was to be an even more pretentious place, combining a music hall, concert hall, palm garden, roof garden, German cafe, and an oriental divan. Family-style vaudeville was to be the music hall feature at each resort. Both opened in the fall of 1895.

By 1895, Pastor's clean, family-style variety was no longer the exception in New York. Keith and Albee, Proctor, Hammerstein and most of the other new managers were now pushing the same policy. Furthermore, they were shooting high, seeking out only the best performers, bringing in big names from the legitimate stage, and demanding that all acts be polished to a high lustre and presented in snappy costumes and settings. Acts that smelled too strongly of corn or mildew were pushed aside. The old afterpiece was dropped altogether. Emphasis now was on freshness, finesse, and poise, on ruffles and lace and spit-and-polish. Competition for top attractions was becoming fierce and salaries were beginning to soar. Run-of-the-mill acts that had received $50 in the 1880's were now receiving twice that amount and more. The big artists were counting their earnings high in the hundreds. Hammerstein pointed the way to even larger salaries when he announced in March, 1895, that he had signed Yvette Guilbert, the popular French songstress, to open his Olympia in the fall at the sum of $3,000 a week.[37] Dame Variety was being decked out in an evening gown and high heels. This was variety with manners and class. This was vaudeville.

Competition from the Union Square Theatre became critical for Pastor in the season of 1895-96. Daily matinees at half price and reserved seats at reduced prices in the evening seem to have done precious little to help the situation. His bills were still as attractive as ever. Paquerette and Vesta Victoria paid return visits, and Bessie Bellwood, a cockney singer from London, appeared on November 25 to being a four-week engagement. All three drew well, but apparently not well enough. The Union Square continued to get the lion's share of the business.

Soon after the beginning of the new year, Pastor decided that nothing would help but adopting the "continuous" performance idea itself. "As long as he could," said Sargent, "Mr. Pastor held out against what he and Harry Sanderson, his right-hand man, termed the 'Ferris Wheel Shows.' At last the time came when something had to be done."[38] Pastor recalled his decision: "Always responsive to public demand, in 1896 I changed my house to continuous after Mr. Keith's example."[39] The *Mirror* commented on the change: "The new arrangement will go into effect next Monday, January 20. Mr. Pastor says that as he is paying his performers as much as other managers, he ought to get as much work out of them. Besides, he had made up his mind that the continuous is the only kind of show that will pay in that part of the city."[40]

Adoption of the "Ferris Wheel" policy brought several big changes to Pastor's theatre. The matinees gave way to three shows daily running without interruption from "12:30 p.m. to 11:00 p.m.," and the public was told to "Come any time [and] Stay as long as you Like."[41]

If Pastor's house orchestra was as bad as Edward Marks claimed, its passing may have been looked upon by some as a happy circumstance. "The second violinist," said Marks, "was deaf in one ear. And when the cornetist began to play, the whole orchestra was out of tune. They were strictly fromage de Brie, and Tony knew it. 'I know they're terrible,' he used to say, 'but they're my old boys and they can die here.' "[42] The orchestra was replaced by two piano players who alternated in some manner through the long and continuous program. Joe Laurie, Jr., the latter-day funnyman, writes: "Mike Bernard, Burt Green, Tom Kelly, Ben Harney, and William Brode; they all played there at one time or another. Tom Kelly and William Brode played the supper shows, while the others played the two-a-day acts."[43]

The change of policy also brought a change in the admission prices. Pastor advertised at the outset: "Best Seats 20 and 30 cents" with some still available at "75cts and $1.00."[44] The *Mirror* predicted that with the lower prices "the chances are that the genial Tony will reap the benefits in a succession of constantly crowded houses."[45]

Sanderson told a *Mirror* reporter in mid-January, 1896, that one aspect of Pastor's operation that would not change with the new policy was "the first-class shows with which the name of Tony Pastor has been identified."[46] The bill for the first week of "continuous" fare gave little argument to Sanderson's claim. The week was marked by "crowded houses," said the *Mirror*, and by a show that was "as good as ever."[47] Fourteen acts, headed by Pearl Andrews and Kitty Mitchell, were on hand to perform turns on Pastor's "ferris wheel." Miss Andrews was a dialect comedienne who gave impersonations of such Pastor favorites as Frank Bush, Vesta Tilley, and Maggie Cline. Miss Mitchell was a serio-comic songstress whom Pastor had discovered in Chicago while on tour the previous fall. She became a popular performer with his audiences. The old maestro himself was also on the bill and his "songs and parodies were as warmly received as usual."[48] How all the performers were distributed over the three daily shows is not recorded. We no longer encounter the promise of "Tony Pastor at Every Performance," and in November, 1897, the *Mirror* reported that "Tony Pastor continues to head the bill, but reserves to himself the privilege of singing only once a day,"[49] probably on the evening show.

He had indeed saved the day at his little theatre by adopting the "ferris wheel" policy at low prices. Attendance picked up almost immediately. From January 20, 1896, through the summer, his customers saw jugglers, whirlwind dancers, dialect and acrobatic comics, ventriloquists, tight-rope walkers, banjoists, hand balancers, musket drillers, trained animal acts, and the like. "They go on from 12:30 to 11 p.m.," said the *Spirit of the Times* in September, 1896, "without a stop or a dull moment, and only twenty or thirty cents for the best seats to see and hear the whole show or any part of it. There is nothing cheap about the Tony Pastor programme except the price of seats."[50]

CHAPTER ELEVEN

The Sunset Years

During the last twelve years of Pastor's life, those sunset years from 1896 to 1908, family-style vaudeville took hold throughout the country and became a huge and highly complex industry with a network of circuits and independent houses stretching from coast to coast. New vaudeville theatres sprang up everywhere. Many of them were built from the bottom up, while others were carved out of some of the finest old legitimate houses in the land. Elegance and wholesomeness was the rule and, as the twentieth century dawned, vaudeville found herself freed at last from the crippling stigma of earlier variety.

"Vaudeville manners," said an article in *Independent* in May, 1901, "are now on a par with those of the parlor . . . The vaudeville theatres of the Greater New York and of the leading cities of the land are more healthful places of amusement than those which produce problem plays, French comedies, and sex dramas."[1]

Vaudeville's growth during this period and after was stimulated and guided by a handful of managers, principally Keith and Albee, Proctor, Hammerstein, Percy Williams, Martin Beck, and John H. Murdock. Relations among them were constantly strained by the struggle for dominance in the new industry. Bernard Sobel called these managers and others like them "robber barons," whose history "may be described as a crazy-quilt, with patches of skulduggery, fraud, good faith, and betrayal."[2] Keith and Albee may well have been the most ambitious and scheming of the lot.

Sometime close to the turn of the century the two began to muse on the monopolistic advantages of consolidating the vaudeville houses of the country under one booking office. They seem to have taken their first step toward this goal in late May, 1900, when they persuaded a dozen or so managers, representing sixty prominent vaudeville theatres around the country, to unite in a Vaudeville Managers' Association (V.M.A.) "for mutual protection and to regulate the dates and salaries of performers."[3] The Association established central booking agencies in New York and Chicago to service the member theatres. In return for paying annual dues, the managers were guaranteed standardized bills of high quality and the artists, in return for paying a regular commission, were promised lengthy tours. There was much internal wrangling, numerous disputes with the performers themselves, and fierce opposition from independent managers, like Hammerstein, and from other agencies, like that of William Morris. A band of disgruntled artists organized into a "union" called The White Rats on June 18, 1900, to fight what they considered unfair salary cuts and booking abuses by the Association. The V.M.A., however, managed to stay intact and even to grow stronger over the years. New managers and theatres were rapidly brought into the fold, sometimes willingly and often through some type of "skulduggery."

On June 13, 1906, Keith and Albee took another giant step: they effected a merger of most of the principal vaudeville houses of the United States and Canada.[4] The V.M.A. spawned a new corporation called the United Booking Office (U.B.O.), which became practically a clearing house for vaudeville.

The U.B.O.'s course was a bumpy one, marked by revolts among its own and tigerish attacks from outside rivals. Klaw and Erlanger, for example, tried to infiltrate the field in April, 1907, with what they termed "Advanced Vaudeville;" they secured a number of theatres and arranged to have the William Morris agency book top talent for them. "Advanced Vaudeville" immediately locked horns with the U.B.O. So strong was the latter's position that Klaw and Erlanger found themselves hard-pressed to secure the top artists for their houses and quit the vaudeville arena after only a few months.

An agreement was signed between the two factions on November 9, 1907, and, according to Gilbert, Klaw and Erlanger were paid $250,000 by the U.B.O. to retire from the field.[5] New threats were forthcoming but the U.B.O. weathered them all and monopolized a major portion of the vaudeville industry for years to come. Keith and Albee dominated the new corporation at the outset in 1906 but Albee gradually pulled away from Keith to become, through "his goading ambition and ruthless methods," a virtual dictator of the industry.[6]

Tony Pastor was little involved in the managerial feuds and dogfights for power that formed the background of his last years. For one thing, he was getting old. Age sapped his energy and drive and tempered that once-restless ambition. More important, he was of the old school where the bonds between manager and performer were close and affectionate. His old-fashioned and sentimental nature rebelled against the cold, impersonal, and hard-and-fast tactics of big business that were taking over the vaudeville scene. Although he joined the V.M.A. at the outset in the spring of 1900, he soon became disheartened and withdrew to go it alone. "He was past the time of life," said the *New York World*, "where he could transform himself into one of the cogs of an amusement syndicate and he had no sympathy for that system of conducting theatricals."[7] He stepped to the sidelines with his ideals intact and tried to get along as best he could at his "little bird-cage of a theatre" just off Union Square. His "best," alas, was not always good enough.

100

It was in the summer of 1896 that a new-fangled novelty called "moving pictures" first appeared on the three-a-day bills at Pastor's. The machine itself was called a Kineopticon, one of several projectors on the market at the time. The novelty had stirred up quite a bit of excitement when introduced at Koster and Bial's the previous April. Fynes had made it an added attraction at the Union Square a month or so later and Pastor, not to be outdone, followed suit in August. The pictures lasted only a few minutes and were little more than simple demonstrations of movement—lapping waves, running horses, and the like. It was all quite crude, but fascinating, and Pastor beefed up his show with the Kineopticon and other similar machines on numerous occasions over the next few years. Most people thought the moving picture a fad that would soon wear out its welcome but it grew in popularity, and by the turn of the century had become a more or less permanent part of the show at many of the country's leading vaudeville houses. By July, 1899, Pastor had made the cinematic marvels of the American Vitagraph a feature on each of his daily bills. A new form of entertainment was in its infancy. When it grew up and learned to talk, it would destroy vaudeville.

The Vitagraph had its appeal but the big drawing attraction at Pastor's house continued to be the many talented performers, old and new, important and obscure, offered to the public week in and week out. Top artists of the day regularly shared the stage with Pastor veterans from the 1880's and even earlier, people like Lillian Western, Gus Williams, James F. Hoey, Ella Wesner, and old banjo comics like Billy Carter, Edwin Latell, and P. C. Shortis. Evil days had fallen on many of these old troupers, on some because their particular talents had grown rusty with age, on others because the new, civilized vaudeville of the day regarded their specialties as seedy and out of date. But hapless performers could always depend on Pastor for a handout or a spot on the bill, and he remained a steadfast friend to the old-timers until the end. "His sympathy . . ," says Gilbert, "got into the way of his business management, driving to madness his astute associate Bert [Harry] Sanderson . . . Cracked-voiced tenors and fumbling banjoists were continued on the bills, largely because Pastor knew them when."[8]

Others who likewise enjoyed the manager's generosity during his final years were the beginners who were looking for that first break and those established performers who were looking for a chance to try out a new act. Soon after going "continuous" in 1896 Pastor set aside the first hour of the Tuesday "milkman's matinee" for these artists to show their wares. "Almost every Tuesday afternoon," said the *Mirror* in December, 1897, "the 'Extra Turn' sign is displayed at Tony Pastor's and some team, trio or quartette . . . proceed to show what they can do in the way of entertaining an audience . . . Mr. Pastor is very kind to allow performers to give these trials, and he is occasionally rewarded by discovering an act which pleases the audience well enough to allow of its being presented in the regular bill."[9]

Pastor's fellow managers grew to respect his generosity and eye for talent.

101

They often sent representatives to his Tuesday afternoon bills with notebooks in hand. Later, some of them even adopted his "trial-run" idea itself. Many a top act owed its success to a "trial-run" at Pastor's. This was the case with The Four Cohans and The Three Keatons.

Managers had considered the Cohan family a good singing quartette but had been unwilling to hire the group as sketch artists. Pastor gave them a trial in a sketch called *Money to Burn* in September, 1897; then immediately booked them for a week on the regular bill. Their success was instantaneous. George M. Cohan recalled that "during the weeks at Pastor's we were offered fancy engagements right and left."[10] The team went on to become headliners in the main vaudeville theatres of the nation. The Three Keatons—father, mother, and little Buster—had been doing their knock-about acrobatic specialty in the hinterlands for a year or so when Pastor gave them a New York debut in December, 1899. They clicked, and the manager quickly signed them up for several return engagements. The Keatons, like the Cohans, went on to travel the circuits as a headline act.

Pastor's kindness to new acts was genuine but so were the pressures of current economics. New acts, willing as always to work cheaply for the opportunity to show their stuff, helped to balance the books. Vaudeville salaries, after all, were on the march. Being handicapped with a small house and forced to continue low prices to meet competition, he had to cut corners whenever and wherever he could. Another stratagem that worked well for him was to book performers while they were between engagements. "Finding out what dates an act had open," Gilbert writes, "he would wire it for this information, and, arranging his bill accordingly, would telegraph, 'Bring in your trunks,' and book them for the open time at a meager salary."[11]

Interestingly enough, Cohan recalled that after his family's initial success at Pastor's, the manager told them to "pull your trunks in this theatre any week you have open."[12] The Cohan family did just that on several occasions. So did the Keatons, and so did many other acts. The genial showman was so loved and respected by the profession at large that countless performers, even top-drawer artists, were usually willing to give him their open time for whatever figure he could offer. That anonymous fan who labeled himself simply "one who knew him" reported that "Pastor never had to pay as much for his top-liners as the other vaudeville managers, and if he ever got in a tight spot financially he could have them for nothing."[13] A glowing tribute to the manager's old-fashioned ideals and warmhearted rapport with his performers!

Many of Pastor's stars, like the Russell Brothers, Frank Bush, and Nat M. Wills, who did monologs and sketches in the character of a happy tramp, kept returning to his stage long after they had made the big time. There were others, like Maggie Cline, Vesta Victoria, and Vesta Tilley, who did not. Why, is uncertain. Some were obviously kept away by the lure of handsome money elsewhere. This seems to have been the case with Vesta Tilley. After her last appearance at the little theatre on 14th Street in the spring of 1895 she had returned

102

to England. But the growth of vaudeville competition in New York over the next few years brought her many flattering invitations to return.

"I received my share of offers," she recalled, "but I felt that as Tony Pastor had been the first to introduce me to a New York audience, it would be unkind of me to appear at any place opposed to him, and so turned them all down, until Mr. Warner came specially from New York to see me on behalf of Oscar Hammerstein."[14]

Hammerstein's offer was 1,000 pounds a week. Miss Tilley discussed the matter with Pastor during his summer visit to London in 1897. "I lunched with him and his wife at the Trocadero," she wrote. "He said I was worth all the money I had been offered as an attraction in New York, but that, of course, it would not be possible for him to pay any such terms as I had mentioned. He told me that the big competition was affecting his theatre . . . He advised me to accept Hammerstein's offer."[15] And she did.

Pastor was asked what he thought of such tall salaries. "Notorious!" he exclaimed. "Such indiscretion does more harm to vaudeville, I think, than anything else I know."[16]

Pastor continued to import English performers through his final years, but none struck sparks like his London music hall personalities of the past. Inflation at home was boosting prices on the foreign market as well. The top London entertainers, like Harry Lauder, were brought over by bigger managers with bigger pocketbooks. Two of his most successful visitors during this period were Marie LeBlanc, a character vocalist, in March, 1898, and Charles ("The Man Who Broke the Bank at Monte Carlo") Coburn, a comic and dialect singer, in October, 1900. Following Coburn's two-week engagement, the manager's importations fell off, and the few foreign artists he did bring over — with the exception of a marionette affair called Jewell's Automatic Electric Theatre in August, 1904 — passed relatively unnoticed. "Pastor used to import English performers with great frequency," said the *Mirror* in 1907, "but that was before the days of inflated salaries."[17]

In the closing years of the 19th century the newspapers were ever and always complimenting Pastor on his perpetual youth and vigor. "He is as young and energetic as ever," said the *Mirror* in January, 1897. Moreover, in June, 1898, the showman challenged all comers to a cakewalk contest to be held as part of a testimonial for Hammerstein. Although Walter Jones and Marie Dressler walked off with the prize cake, Pastor was said to have done some high stepping at the affair and to have "surprised even his warmest admirers by his agility."[18]

In truth, the old trouper was slowing down. That now-and-then agility was hard bought! Age was beginning to take its toll. Rheumatism and a failing memory were becoming irritable burdens; plus, he was just getting tired of the hectic pace he had set himself for over thirty years. Those managerial boots were wearing down at the heels. By the turn of the century he had discontinued both his summer trips abroad and his annual barnstorming tours and had stopped appearing regularly on his evening bill.

TONY PASTOR: DEAN OF THE VAUDEVILLE STAGE

The trip abroad in 1897 was Pastor's last. He and his wife spent the following summer visiting friends in Indiana and Michigan, and in succeeding years the warm summer months found them at their new country home in Elmhurst, Long Island.

Pastor had been thinking about moving from his West 94th Street residence to the leisurely little community near Flushing as early as the spring of 1898. Manhattan Island now had a teeming population of over one and a half million. The quiet and tranquillity of country living held strong appeal. By May, 1899, he had built or purchased a house in the Long Island community and by the end of June he and his wife had moved in. Fourteenth Street, however, was neither forgotten nor neglected. He commuted to the office each day and usually stayed around until the evening performance was well under way. Sometimes he took off on Saturday afternoons to catch a show at some other theatre. Sunday, when his house was closed, was just about the only time he had to play the role of country gentleman with any real gusto.

The move to Elmhurst signaled the end of Pastor's annual excursions outside of New York. The records indicate that the spring and fall tours of 1898 were his last. Indeed, his tours that year were not really tours at all, consisting merely of one week in April at Hyde and Behman's in Brooklyn and one week in late August at Waldman's New Theatre in Newark. Strangely enough, curtailment of this prominent feature of his long career seems to have passed unnoticed by the press. The traveling company was doubtless a victim of growing road competition, spiraling production costs, and the manager's own waning capacity. In September, 1908, the *Mirror* recalled the popularity of the manager's old traveling troupes and suggested that "he could have won great pecuniary success even in later years, no doubt, by sending out a company under his name in the old style."[19]

From the very beginning of his managerial career, as we have seen, Pastor had been a more or less permanent fixture in his own shows. Even after his 14th Street theatre went "continuous" in 1896 the notice "Tony Pastor Sings Every Evening as Usual" had been a common one. This time-honored tradition, however, like the tours and trips abroad, came to an end before the century turned. The strain was becoming too much for the old veteran, and, to make matters worse, he was having more and more trouble remembering the words to his songs. He took to the stage only four or five times during the 1899-1900 season, and only once — to celebrate his March anniversary — in the next. After a two-week stint in August, 1901, four years went by before he appeared again to add that little dab of mustard to the show. Each anniversary was acknowledged with linen souvenir programs for the audience and an open house in the front office for friends and well-wishers, but the old showman did not appear on the bill. One of the well-wishers on hand in March, 1904, was Charles Darnton, a writer for the *New York World*. He asked the manager when he was going to take to the stage again.

"If any one was to offer me this house loaded with $20 bills," Pastor answered, "I couldn't get up and sing a song — couldn't remember the words. Enough voice left? More than enough. One of these nights I'm going out on my stage and sing one of the old-timers."[20]

That night finally came in March, 1905, on the anniversary of his fortieth year as a manager. He sang "Sarah's Young Man" and "Down in a Coal Mine," and the packed house went wild. That old "witchery of personality" may have been a little frayed around the edges but it was still there. It continued to be there at each March anniversary for the next three years, the only occasions on which Pastor again stepped out of the wings to chase away those old "blue devils" with his repertoire of "glorious songs."

Up until shortly before the end, Pastor's little theatre gave all the outward signs of being a going concern. The week to week bills always boasted of two or more top performers. The reviews seldom failed to mention that attendance was good to excellent. One unidentified New York paper in 1900, for example, noted that "business is big" and speculated that "Tony must be worth upwards of $300,000 or over."[21] In August, 1901, the *Mirror* went on at some length about the old impresario's legion of devoted followers:

"The Pastorians, and there are hosts of them, think that Tony is the greatest man on earth. Nothing would shake their confidence in this belief, and no one is going to try to do so because Mr. Pastor invariably and completely makes good wherever occasion appears. It must be very comfortable to be. a manager and to know that every blessed regular patron is proud to be near to you, whether the nearness is the matter of an orchestra stall or just a gallery admission. But they're mightily and honestly and quite properly proud of Mr. Pastor down there in Fourteenth Street. And they ought to be."[22]

Good attendance, however, even excellent attendance, did not necessarily mean a respectable profit. Pastor's house, after all, was small, and his prices were low — 20¢, 30¢, 75¢ and $1.00. His customers over the years had come from all walks of life and economic classes. But as vaudeville started to expand, the more affluent patrons began drifting away to the bigger and grander houses uptown and their places were taken by persons of more modest means. He soon discovered that the 75¢ and $1.00 seats were not moving and that many customers who were unable to buy a cheaper seat were taking their money up the street to the Union Square Theatre. So, in the fall of 1903, he dropped the top price to 50¢. We can only guess what effect this change had on the profit margin. Some people might say that Pastor's donation of $300 to the Actors' Fund in March, 1905, was certainly not the typical act of a manager in distress.[23] But then, of course, when it came to giving away money, Pastor was anything but typical. He handed it out right and left until the very end.

The manager's final two or three years were dark ones, filled with frustration, pain and defeat. His rheumatism grew worse, palsy struck, and the bottom fell out of his business. "The last few years of his career," said Sanderson, "were a struggle against odds that would have swamped even a young man. Larger and modern theatres, the movement uptown, the great increase in salaries, rendered the struggle abortive."[24] There are two additional factors, important ones, that bore upon this struggle and should be added to the list: first, the appearance of dirt-cheap entertainment in the Union Square neighborhood, and second, the end of top acts filling in their open time on Pastor's bills.

Union Square had been declining steadily over the years. As first-class concerns left, they were replaced by cheap shops, plants, saloons and tenements. By 1905 the area had several penny arcades and 10¢ picture houses. A year later it broke out in a rash of vaudeville resorts peddling third-rate wares for a nickel and a dime. Ten-cent vaudeville houses had begun appearing in the western part of the country during the fall of 1904. One reason cited by the *Mirror* for Proctor's decision in April, 1905, to abandon the "continuous" plan at his 23rd Street house was the great scarcity of "chasers": "The performers who were formerly relied upon to drive the late stayers into the streets during the supper shows have all gone West and are now appearing as 'headliners' on the ten-cent circuits."[25] These cheap houses, some now charging only 5¢, moved eastward during the season and by the year's end had invaded Greater New York.

The persevering Pastor told a reporter for the *New York Sun* in late March, 1906, that "I owe my good health and my good spirits . . . to the fact that I am not worried by ambition."[26] Maybe not by "ambition," but we may suspect that he was plenty worried about the picture houses and the rock-bottom vaudeville haunts springing up around him, particularly the 5¢ house that only two weeks earlier had opened directly across the street.[27]

These new places were a boon to the growing number of low-income revelers in the area, and they soon were luring away scores of Pastor's customers. The Union Square Theatre also became a victim to these establishments. On February 24, 1908, after fighting it out for two years, the old house was converted into a 10¢ picture palace and rechristened The Bijou Dream.

"There have been many changes along the old Rialto during the past few years," the *Mirror* pointed out, "and people that knew the neighborhood in its prime would hardly recognize it now . . . Penny arcades and 5 and 10 cent theatres are the favorite resorts of those that now frequent Fourteenth Street, and the Keith and Proctor mng. [They merged their interests early in 1906], seeing the drift of things, will simply cater to the only kind of patronage that can be made profitable under existing conditions."[28]

We recall that in April, 1907, Klaw and Erlanger formed their "Advanced Vaudeville" organization and tried to challenge the supremacy of the U.B.O. The battle that erupted lasted well into the fall. A cartoon in the *Mirror* for July 20 showed Pastor standing safe and secure on a pile of rocks while waves labeled "Competition," "Syndicates," and "Agents" surged menacingly but harmlessly at his feet. The caption read: "Never Touched Father."[29] But the tide was low. It came in swiftly over the weeks to follow. The paper could have run the same cartoon a few months later with a new caption: "Pastor on the Rocks."

As the Klaw and Erlanger forces battled it out with the U.B.O. each side tried to outdo the other in corraling the headline acts, and the "blanket contract" became an effective weapon. This contract bound an act to a long and uninterrupted engagement. Acts that were wrapped up in this blanket no longer had the open time to bring their trunks to Pastor's and, as Silverman pointed out, "this stopped the big numbers from heading Mr. Pastor's shows."[30] This was a critical blow to the old manager.

By late summer his shows were filled out for the most part with second-string acts, old-timers, and raw recruits. A top performer on the bill was a rarity. Although they continued to be big shows, their quality fluctuated markedly from week to week. They were often listless and repetitious. Pastor apparently was no longer able to shake the old kaleidoscope with that vigor of yesterday. "It was not at all unusual," said Silverman, "for three or four singing and dancing acts to follow one after the other, while it occurred quite often that two or three full stage acts in the same parlor setting successively appeared."[31] The newspaper reviews were often severe. *Variety*, for example, said on October 12, 1907: "The show is so heavily overburdened, without variety, that it grows fearfully boresome." Again, on February 8, 1908: "The bill is far and away off quality this week, working into one of the most unprofitable entertainments the house has offered in a long time."[32]

With the headline acts gone and the general quality off much of the time, those uptown vaudeville buffs who had continued to support the veteran manager stopped making the trip down to 14th Street. Apparently the shows were no longer worth the effort. The end of vaudeville at the Union Square Theatre in late February left Pastor's the only regular vaudeville house in the area as well as the sole remaining "continuous" house in the city. But all this made little difference. Pastor's business was now too weak to rally. Hard times had fallen with a thud. Picture shows were now the big attraction in the neighborhood. A week after The Bijou Dream opened, he did away with his 50¢ seats in a desperate effort to stay in the race.[33]

The little theatre tucked away in Tammany Hall regained some of its old sparkle on the evening of March 23, 1908, when Pastor took to the stage to mark his forty-third, and what was to be his last, anniversary. The event had been publicized for weeks, and hundreds were on hand to salute that old impresario who now was being affectionately dubbed by his colleagues as "The Dean of the Vaudeville Stage." Josephine Pastor sat in a stage box with family friends, a delegation of the New York Lodge of the Elks occupied two others, "while all over the theatre were patrons who knew Mr. Pastor when he first entered the managerial arena."[34]

When the uniformed card boy placed Pastor's name on the easel, the auditorium erupted with cheers. The performer entered in his traditional formal attire complete with solitaire and shiny opera hat. He was thinner now, and his walk was stiff, but he radiated charm and confidence as he stood in the center of the stage smiling and bowing in response to the persisting ovation. *Variety* described what happened:

> *Nothing but a speech could reduce the house to silence, when Mr. Pastor said: 'Ladies and Gentlemen: I have been requested by several people I have known for the past two or three years to sing a song. It is an old song, and one I first sang as far back as forty-three years ago. I know some old songs (great laughter) and I know some new songs (laughter), but I will sing "Sarah's Young Man." It was a good song then; there's none better now.' (Great applause)*
>
> *Upon Mr. Pastor reaching the end, a spontaneous wave of cheers and applause spread over the auditorium. One of the Elks said: 'We are all getting old,' as several were seen to furtively apply their handkerchiefs. 'Who's getting old?' demanded Mr. Pastor with asperity, turning to the boxes, whereat the crowd laughed and cheered again like children.*

Pastor then began to sing another one of his old favorites, "Down In a Coal Mine."

> *He was interrupted by the ushers in a line and making two trips, completely filling the stage behind him with floral horseshoes, wreaths, bouquets and cut flowers. James J. Armstrong, on behalf of the Elks, mounted the stage, making a speech in which he dwelt upon the esteem Mr. Pastor was held in by the entire profession, proclaiming the Dean as the inaugurator of 'decent vaudeville.' The Elks in a body arose to sing 'Auld Lang Syne,' and it was an impressive moment.*
>
> *Mr. Armstrong remarked: 'Brother Pastor, I am not so very young, am I?' but Mr. Pastor bristled up, retorting, 'I don't know; you can't prove anything by me.'*
>
> *Looking at the flowers behind him, Mr. Pastor remarked: 'Aren't they beautiful?' and then created loud laughter by saying: 'I don't care what happens, you can't cut me out of my third verse of "Down in a Coal Mine." I'm here to stay.'*
>
> *After singing, Mr. Pastor replied to the applause with another speech, when he said: 'I trust you will kindly allow me to retire. There are a number of artists to follow, who wish to be heard, and I bid you one and all good-night, inviting you to see me on my next anniversary – the 44th.*[35]

But there would be no forty-fourth anniversary.

By the spring of 1908 there were three main picture houses on East 14th Street between Broadway and Third Avenue – the Bijou Dream, the Unique, and the Dewey. On June 6 a fourth picture palace appeared on the scene – Pastor's.

"A regulation picture show," said *Variety*, "with illustrated songs as a side divertisement, took the stage of the Tony Pastor Theatre this week. The 'picture show' runs one hour and fifteen minutes ... The Pastor picture regime is a joint venture of Mr. Pastor's and the American Vitagraph Co., the former supplying the house while the latter furnishes the reels. Admission to the orchestra is ten cents."[36]

It was said that the move was only temporary "to give the vaudeville 'regulars' a vacation from the amusement" and that "Pastor's is scheduled to resume with vaudeville on August 3." But a rumor was circulating that the manager had decided to quit 14th Street altogether and move "to a larger theatre in the uptown district."[37]

On June 23 the *New York Herald* announced that the old showman was definitely vacating his theatre in the fall and that "it will become a burlesque house under the management of Messrs. Murray and Samuel Kraus." The paper went on: "Mr. Pastor said that until he retired from the management of his present theatre he would not be able to make known his future plans. 'I am getting along in years and do not care to undertake a long lease of another theatre. I likely will have another playhouse, but cannot say at this time where it will be located, save it will be far north of here. I am sick and tired of Four-teenth Street.' "[38]

In truth, Pastor would have been willing to stay put in his little theatre if the Tammany Society had been willing to let him renew the lease on a year-to-year basis. The Society had insisted on a new long-term lease and, conditions on 14th Street being what they were, the aging manager had refused. "My lease expires on September 15," he stated in a *Mirror* interview on July 11, "and they wanted me to renew it for five years, but I decided after proper deliberation that I did not care to sign a lease for so long a period."

When asked about his plans he replied: "The moving pictures will be continued until August, when I will resume my regular vaudeville programmes, continuing until September 15. After that I have not decided definitely what I shall do, but you may depend upon it that I will remain in harness... I have not the slightest intention of retiring, as I love my work, and would be lost if I did not have my daily routine of duties to attend to." He went on to say that he had received several offers to return to the stage as a performer. He did not want to travel, however, "as I am fond of home... The chances are that you will find me in a new location further uptown."[39]

According to *Variety*, Pastor reintroduced vaudeville at his house on July 13 as an accompaniment to the pictures: "Four vaudeville acts are played weekly in Pastor's, and the Dean's representative, Harry Sanderson, is again signing vaudeville contracts."[40] There are no ads or reviews in the papers to guide us on this matter. Apparently, the venture was not successful for by the end of July Pastor had decided to "allow the new lessees to take immediate possession, so that necessary alterations could be made in time for the opening of the burlesque season on August 29."[41]

The alterations were begun at once, and workers were already replacing the old front stoop with a street-level entrance when Pastor came down to the office for the last time to collect his things. He had made the little room a virtual treasure house of pictures, mementoes and other memorabilia gathered over his long career, and we can only imagine what emotions were touched and memories awakened as he packed everything away — the gilded pictures of Gus Williams, May Irwin, Maggie Cline, Lillian Russell and others of his former stars; the handsome diamond-studded medal of the Order of Elks presented to him by his company on New Year's Day, 1877; the white vellum album given to him on his thirtieth anniversary in 1895 by his brother managers and containing photographs of Augustin Daly, A. M. Palmer, Daniel Frohman, Maurice Grau, Edward Harrigan and Oscar Hammerstein, to name only a few; and the framed telegram sent to him on his forty-second anniversary in 1907 and signed by Keith, Albee, Proctor, Hammerstein and practically every other major manager of the day. It read as follows: "Your career and examples have made it possible for many of us to follow in your footsteps. Loved by everyone in all branches of our profession, you have been a help and guide to many who have reached the highest pinnacle of success. We extend the hand of friendship and the sincere wish that you may be spared many years in the position which you occupy as 'The Dean of Vaudeville.' "[42]

Pastor's palsy had been growing worse during the summer, and he had been spending more and more of his time in the quiet of Elmhurst. Sometime in July, however, despite his failing health, he found time to attend a benefit baseball game at the Polo Grounds: "His growing paralysis had come down hard upon him that day and as he walked out on the field he tottered and fell. Lew Dockstader and Edward Rosenbaum ran toward him to help the old man to his feet again and they wanted to drive back to town with him at once. He smiled bravely though and went out on the field and shook hands with the men that crowded around him. And he was there that day because a baseball game was being played for the benefit of half a hundred little children — not children that could sing and dance around him as the stage children did every Christmas when he gathered them around him in Tammany Hall and stripped the Christmas tree for them — but half a hundred kiddies on crutches in a children's hospital."[43]

This may have been Pastor's last public appearance. Early in August he became ill and was confined to bed. *Variety* said on August 15: "On Wednesday [August 5] the condition of Tony Pastor was very serious ... By telephone from his house on Tuesday evening [August 11] Mr. Pastor was reported much improved ... His affection for 'Pastor's,' from which he parted last week, oppressed him greatly, which with the intense heat this summer caused the veteran's collapse."[44] A rumor spread that "Mr. Pastor was made ill through worry over business reverses," but the *Mirror* commented that aside from the loss of his theatre, "there is no truth in this report, as Mr. Pastor has always been thrifty."[45] On August 22 *Variety* noted that "the Vaudeville Dean was on the high road to complete recovery ... It is said he will be able to leave his room in about ten days."[46]

Pastor's recovery was brief. He was able to get out of bed and walk around for awhile, "but was shortly forced to take to his bed again. Since that time he had been sinking rapidly, and his weakness became every day more noticeable."

110

On August 26 he "sank into sleep ... and his friends were summoned to his bed side."[47] The Dean did not wake up again. The end came at ten o'clock that evening.

The news of Pastor's death traveled rapidly throughout the country and, in fact, to many parts of the world. Josephine Pastor received scores of letters and telegrams of condolence. "The family seemed pleased," *Billboard* said, "that the first telegram ... should come from Lillian Russell, who owed her start and her stage name to Tony Pastor."[48] The United Vaudeville Managers held a special meeting on August 27 to frame a letter of sympathy: "We hold in great and reverent respect the memory of the departed dean of American vaudeville, who leaves behind so brilliant a list of historical achievements in a profession which loved him dearly and will feel keenly his loss."[49] Another message was sent from the office managers and heads of departments of the U.B.O. and of the Orpheum circuit, and there were countless others from the big and small of the profession and from Pastorians all over the nation.

Pastor's funeral was held at 10:00 o'clock on Saturday morning, August 29, at Bartholomew's Roman Catholic Church in Elmhurst. A solemn requiem mass was celebrated. "The floral offerings were remarkably beautiful and were so numerous that they filled five carriages."[50] Dozens of theatrical personalities were present along with delegations from the Elks, the Actors' Society of America, the Lambs Club, the Comedy Club, the White Rats, and other organizations of which the showman had been a member. Interestingly enough, Pastor had been the only manager ever accepted into the ranks of the White Rats association.

Immediately following the church service, the remains were conveyed to the home of the Brooklyn Lodge of Elks, where they lay in state. Special services were held there on Sunday afternoon. "The spacious clubhouse of the Elks was crowded to suffocation and thousands of people stood in the street during the services." The remains were then borne to the Evergreens Cemetery. "Four hundred members of the New York Lodge walked several blocks as an escort, and when the funeral procession finally started there were over sixty carriages in line."[51] The interment was in the Pastor lot.

The amount of Pastor's estate was finally made public on October 7, 1910. He had left four pieces of real estate worth $65,000, jewelry valued at $1,532.00, and cash in the amount of $6,001.34.[52] Apparently there were some who were not startled at the low cash figure. *Billboard* reported that the news "caused little surprise among the theatrical manager's old friends. Some said that they had not expected there would be that much."[53] One of these old friends remarked that "when Keith took the Union Square and began to present modern vaudeville there, Tony's business began to fall off and his profits to shrink. This did not seem to affect his lending to any extent, however. It only curtailed his own spending money ... I am surprised that his estate amounted to as much as it does. He must have made a Million Dollars in his time, and I thought he had given away almost that much."[54]

TONY PASTOR: DEAN OF THE VAUDEVILLE STAGE

It seems´ that Josephine Pastor was able to realize a comfortable income from her husband's real estate, either by sale or through rental, for on December 5, 1910, she donated $2,400 to the Children's Festival Fund. This Fund had been newly-organized to carry on Pastor's traditional Christmas parties for the Children of the Stage. "It is because of his wide charities while living," said Mrs. Pastor, "that Mr. Pastor died a poor man, and I want his little friends of the stage to feel that his thought for them lives after him."[55]

Tony Pastor's long and eventful career had come to an end, but his idea of clean and refined variety had now taken hold throughout the land and was to remain a highly popular form of family entertainment for nearly three decades. It is unlikely that the generous Pastor would have been overly disturbed to learn that most of his latter-day competitors — men like Keith, Proctor, Williams and Albee — left huge fortunes at the time of their deaths.[56] He might have been sorrowed to learn that his own early reformative efforts in variety were too often forgotten by later writers. Marian Spitzer, for example, wrote in the *American Mercury* in 1924 that Albee was the savior of vaudeville and that "it is to him that all the credit must go for cleaning up an institution that was looked upon by our grandparents as a sewer of iniquity."[57] Joe Laurie, Jr., however, would certainly have pleased Pastor with his observation in 1953 that it was "Tony Pastor who made it possible for all of them to cash in with his idea of clean vaudeville ... He left more than money; he left a good feeling in the hearts of all the people who knew him. There never lived, then or now, in or out of vaude, any better liked theatrical manager than Antonio (Tony) Pastor!"[58]

Notes

INTRODUCTION

[1]The material herein appeared originally under the title "The Cradle of Variety: The Concert Saloon" in the *Educational Theatre Journal*, December, 1968.

[2]Quoted in Alvin Harlow, *Old Bowery Days* (N.Y.: D. Appleton and Co., 1931), p. 374.

[3]For information on the evolution of the English music hall see Maurice Willson Disher, "Music-Hall," *Oxford Companion to the Theatre*, ed. Phyllis Hartnoll (Oxford: Oxford University Press, 1951), pp. 551-57.

[4]Quoted in "The Variety Stage," *Harper's Weekly*, XLVI (March 22, 1902), 380.

[5]George C. D. Odell, *Annals of the New York Stage* (15 vols.; N. Y.: Columbia University Press, 1927-1931), VII, 288.

[6]*Ibid.*, VI, 589.

[7]*Ibid.*, VII, 289.

[8]Ad for "Mechanic's Hall," Petersburg, Va., *Clipper*, XII (May 13, 1865), 24.

[9]"The New York Concert Saloons," *N.Y. Evening Post*, Jan. 2, 1862. V. V. file, Harv.

[10]"Changes in Vaudeville," *Chicago Chronicle*, sometime in 1899. V. V. file, Harv.

[11]Matthew Hale Smith, *Sunshine and Shadows in New York* (Hartford: J. B. Burr and Co., 1869), p. 440.

[12]Lloyd Morris, *Incredible New York* (N. Y.: Random House, 1951), p. 51.

[13]*Ibid.*

[14]Douglas Gilbert, *American Vaudeville* (New ed. of 1940 work; N.Y.: Dover Publications, 1963), pp. 10-11.

[15]Ad for Rivers' "Melodeon," *Clipper*, VIII (May 5, 1860), 23.

[16]Ad for "Broadway Music Hall," *Spirit of the Times*, IV (June 8, 1861), 224. This weekly journal was first published on September 10, 1859, by George Wilkes, a former co-editor with William T. Porter of *Porter's Spirit of the Times*. It was essentially a political and sporting paper. Its coverage of the theatrical scene was brief in the 1860's but increased over the years.

[17]Undated program for the "Canterbury." V. V. file, Harv.

[18]"Music and the Drama," *Spirit of the Times*, IV (July 20, 1861), 320.

[19]James Dabney McCabe, Jr., *Lights and Shadows of New York Life* (Philadelphia: National Publishing Co., 1872), p. 596.

[20]"Theatrical Record: City Summary," *Clipper*, VIII (Sept. 15, 1860), 174.

[21]Ad for "Gaieties Concert Room," *N. Y. Herald*, LXXXIV (Jan. 17, 1860), 7.

[22]Odell, VII, 187.

[23]Quoted in "The Concert Saloon," *N. Y. Times*, XI (Jan. 5, 1862), 5.

[24]*Statutes at Large of the State of New York*, ed. John W. Edmonds (5 vols.; Albany, N. Y.: Weed, Parsons and Co., 1869), III, 323-24.

[25]"The Concert Saloon Reform," *N. Y. Times*, XI (April 25, 1862), 5. For further information on how the different resorts reacted to the Legislative action see *ibid.*, April 26, 1862, p. 8; also "Enforcing the Concert Saloon Law," *N. Y. Herald*, LXXXVI (April 25, 1862), 5.

[26]Ad for "American Concert Hall," *N. Y. Herald*, LXXXVI (Aug. 28, 1862), 7.

[27]Ad for "Canterbury Music Hall," *N. Y. Herald*, LXXXVI (Aug. 28, 1862), 7.

[28]"Concert Saloons," *Spirit of the Times*, X (May 2, 1864), 181.

CHAPTER ONE

[1]Quoted in "Pastor the Last of a Famous Group," *N. Y. World*, Aug. 28, 1908. T. P. file, Harv.

[2]The year 1837 was cited by Edith J. R. Isaacs, "Antonio Pastor," *Dictionary of American Biography* (21 vols.; N. Y.: Charles Scribner's Sons, 1934), XIV, 290. The year 1832 was proposed in Charles Edward Ellis, *An Authentic History of the Benevolent and Protective Order of Elks* (Chicago: Published by the author, 1910), p. 325. The year 1835 was mentioned in "Our Dramatic Portrait Gallery: Tony Pastor," *Clipper*, XII (Sept. 17, 1864), 181. The year 1840 was cited in "Antonio Pastor," *National Cyclopedia of American Biography* (45 vols.; N. Y.: James T. White and Co., 1918), XVI, 30.

[3]Inscription on tombstone of Antonio Pastor in the Pastor lot on "The Shadowy Way" in the Evergreens Cemetery, Brooklyn, N. Y.

[4]Tony Pastor, " Life of Tony Pastor," *Tony Pastor's Songs* (N. Y.: Frank Harding, 1891), p. 2.

[5]*Ibid.*

[6]"Our Dramatic Portrait Gallery: Tony Pastor," *Clipper.*

[7]Pastor, "Life of Tony Pastor."

[8]Richard Moody, *America Takes the Stage* (Bloomington, Ind.: Indiana University Press, 1955), p. 39.

[9]Pastor, "Life of Tony Pastor."

[10]*Ibid.*

[11]*Ibid.*

[12]*Ibid.*

[13]"Pastor the Last of a Famous Group," *N. Y. World.*

[14]Pastor, "Life of Tony Pastor."

[15]Quoted by Charles Darnton, "Tony Pastor, 39 Years a Manager," *N. Y. World*, March 26, 1904. T. P. file, NYPubl.

[16]George L. Chindahl, *A History of the Circus in America* (Caldwell, Idaho: Caxton Printers, 1959), p. 40.

[17]Pastor, "Life of Tony Pastor."

[18]According to the *Clipper* for Oct. 27, 1866, Frank was born on November 13, 1837. (See "Our Dramatic Portrait Gallery: Frank Pastor," XIV, 226). The same paper for Oct. 24, 1868, stated that William was born on Sept. 6, 1840. (See "Our Dramatic Portrait Gallery: Billy Pastor," XVI, 229).

[19]The only information we have on this is Pastor's statement that his father "died when I was a very small boy, and I was obliged to start out very promptly to carve out my own fortune." (Quoted in "Mirror Interviews: Tony Pastor," *Mirror*, XXXIV [July 27, 1895], 2).

[20]Quoted in J. Milton Traber, "Pen Sketch of 'Tony Pastor,' the Father of Modern Vaudeville," *Billboard*, XXIII (Feb. 18, 1911), 5.

[21]Ellis, p. 299.

[22]"Dean of Vaudeville Celebrities," *Variety*, II (March 24, 1906), 5.

[23]Quoted in Traber.

[24] Pastor, "Life of Tony Pastor."

[25]*Ibid.*

[26]Quoted in Traber.

[27]*Ibid.*

[28]Quoted in "Tony Pastor Looks Far Back," sometime soon after March 22, 1906. Amer. Vaud. file, NYPubl.

[29]Quoted in Traber.

[30]George C. D. Odell, *Annals of the New York Stage* (15 vols.; N.Y.: Columbia University Press, 1927-1931), VI, 176.

[31]Quoted in Traber.

[32]"Tony Pastor," *Clipper*, XXXVIII (March 29, 1890), 1.

[33]Quoted in Traber.

[34]"Our Dramatic Portrait Gallery: Tony Pastor," *Clipper*. The *New York Clipper* was founded as a weekly sporting journal by Frank Queen in 1856. It also gave some attention to the theatrical scene, and this attention increased markedly after the Civil War. Frank Luther Mott wrote that the paper "may be said to be the only theatrical paper of the decade from 1865 to 1875." (Frank

Luther Mott, *A History of American Magazines* [3 vols.; Cambridge: Harvard University Press, 1938], III, 198).

[35]"They Talked of Tony Pastor," an unidentified N.Y.C. paper sometime soon after the death of Pastor on August 26, 1908. T. P. file, Harv.

[36]"The Passing of Tony Pastor," *Green Book Album*, I (Jan., 1909), 192.

[37]Quoted in Traber.

[38]Pastor, "Life of Tony Pastor."

[39]"Tony Pastor at the Washington," unidentified paper of around August, 1890. T. P. file, Harv.

[40]The *Clipper* for Aug. 25, 1860, stated: "Frank and William Pastor have been performing for some time past at Gibralter, Spain. Frank is in partnership with Mr. Thomas Price ... William Pastor made his *debut* [in Cardiz] on the 4th of July, and took the Spaniards by surprise, as they had never seen anything like his tumbling before."

CHAPTER TWO

[1]Quoted by Charles Darnton, "Tony Pastor, 39 Years a Manager," *N. Y. Herald*, March 26, 1904. T. P. file, NYPubl.

[2]Tony Pastor, "Life of Tony Pastor," *Tony Pastor's Songs* (N. Y.: Frank Harding, 1891), p. 2.

[3]Harry S. Sanderson, "Reminiscences of Tony Pastor, Vaudeville's Dean," *Variety*, XII (Dec. 12, 1908), 50.

[4]Ad for "American Concert Hall," *Spirit of the Times*, III (Feb. 23, 1861), 400.

[5]Douglas Gilbert, *American Vaudeville* (New ed. of 1940 work; N. Y.: Dover Publications, 1963), p. 107.

[6]"The Concert Saloons," *N. Y. Times*, XI (Jan. 5, 1862), 5.

[7]George C. D. Odell, *Annals of the New York Stage* (15 vols.; N. Y.: Columbia University Press, 1927-1931), VII, 352.

[8]Ad for "American Concert Hall," *Clipper*, IX (April 27, 1861), 14.

[9]George Templeton Strong, *The Diary of George Templeton Strong*, eds. Allan Nevins and Milton H. Thomas (4 vols.; N. Y.: Macmillan Co., 1952), III, 127.

[10]Pastor, "Life of Tony Pastor."

[11]"A Tribute to Tony Pastor," *Elks Antler*, sometime shortly after Pastor's death on Aug. 26, 1908. T. P. file, NYPubl.

[12]Quoted in Odell, VII, 373.

[13]"Music and Drama," *Spirit of the Times*, IV (May 4, 1861), 144.

[14]*Ibid.*, July 6, 1861, p. 288.

[15]Tony Pastor, "Tony Pastor Recounts the Origin of American Vaudeville," *Variety*, V (Dec. 15, 1906), 17.

[16]Ad for "American Concert Hall," *N. Y. Herald*, LXXXVI (June 1, 1862), 7.

[17]Quoted in "Mirror Interviews: Tony Pastor," *Mirror*, XXXIV (July 27, 1895), 2.

[18]"The Union Volunteers," *Tony Pastor's Union Songster* (N. Y.: Dick and Fitzgerald, *ca.* 1862), p. 7. This book bears the earliest date of those Pastor songsters uncovered. Pastor was not the only comic vocalist of his day to have song books on the market. For example: *Will Carleton's Dandy Pat Songster*, *Fattie Stewart's Comic Songster*, and *Joe English's Irish Comic Songster*. Minstrel song books were also numerous.

[19]"Freemen, Rally," *Tony Pastor's Union Songster*, p. 58.

[20]"The New England Boys," *Tony Pastor's Union Songster*, p. 69.

[21]"The Yankee's Escape from Secesh," *Tony Pastor's Union Songster*, p. 10.

[22]Quoted in "Mirror Interviews: Tony Pastor," *Mirror*, July 27, 1895.

[23]"The Draft," *Tony Pastor's "444" Combination Songster* (N. Y.: Dick and Fitzgerald, *ca.* 1864), p. 22.

[24]Gilbert, p. 108.

[25]*Ibid.*

[26]Reprinted in Charles Edward Ellis, *An Authentic History of the Benevo-*

118

lent and Protective Order of Elks (Chicago: Published by the author, 1910), p. 328.

[27]Quoted in "The Bowery Autocrat Interviewed," *Spirit of the Times,* LXXXVII (Feb. 14, 1874), 15.

[28]Quoted in "Mirror Interviews: Tony Pastor," *Mirror,* July 27, 1895.

[29]Ad for "American Concert Hall," *Spirit of the Times,* IX (Dec. 26, 1863), 261.

[30]Nick Norton, " In the Olden Days," *Variety,* II (Dec. 23, 1905), 4.

[31]"Our Dramatic Portrait Gallery: Tony Pastor," *Clipper,* XII (Sept. 17, 1864), 181.

[32]"Theatrical Record: Music Halls," *Clipper,* XII (March 25, 1865), 399.

CHAPTER THREE

[1]"Theatrical Record: City Summary," *Clipper,* XII (March 11, 1865), 882.

[2]"They Talked of Tony Pastor," unidentified N. Y. C. paper sometime soon after Pastor's death on Aug. 26, 1908. T. P. file, Harv.

[3]See the biographical sketch on Fernando Pastor in Charles Edward Ellis, *An Authentic History of the Benevolent and Protective Order of Elks* (Chicago: Published by the author, 1910), pp. 70-71.

[4]See Charles Darnton, "Tony Pastor, 39 Years a Manager," *N. Y. World,* March 26, 1904; "The Famous Tony Pastor," *N. Y. World,* sometime in the mid-1890's; and "Vaudeville in its Infancy," unidentified paper, Feb. 19, 1898. All are to be found in T. P. file, NYPubl.

[5]Program of "Tony Pastor's Combination" for its performance in Newark, N. J. on either March 24 or 25, 1865. Townsend Walsh, NYPubl.

[6]Quoted in "Vaudeville in its Infancy," unidentified newspaper, Feb. 19, 1898.

[7]"Theatrical Record Miscellaneous," *Clipper,* XII (April 1, 1865), 407.

[8]"Theatre and Things Theatrical," *Spirit of the Times,* XII (June 10, 1865), 240.

119

[9]Quoted in "Theatrical Record: Miscellaneous," *Clipper*, XIII (April 29, 1865), 22; "Theatrical Record: Miscellaneous," *ibid.*

[10]"Theatrical Record: Miscellaneous," *Clipper*, XIII (June 17, 1865), 78.

[11]*Ibid.*, July 22, 1865, p. 119.

[12]See ad for "Sam Sharpley's Iron-Clad Minstrels," *Clipper*, XIII (June 3, 1865), 62.

[13]"Dean of Vaudeville Celebrities," *Variety*, II (March 24, 1906), 5.

[14]The building quartered different groups through 1859, then remained unoccupied until converted into a minstrel hall by S. D. Campbell in June, 1864. Richard M. Hooley had become associated with Campbell by January, 1865, and the Hooley and Campbell Minstrels held forth in the building until the end of May, 1865. Its next occupants were the Iron-Clads.

[15]James Dabney McCabe, Jr., *Lights and Shadows of New York Life* (Philadelphia: National Publishing Co., 1872), p. 192.

[16]Edward Winslow Martin, *The Secrets of the Great City* (Philadelphia: Jones Bros. and Co., 1868), p. 51.

[17]"Theatrical Record: City Summary," *Clipper*, XIII (Aug. 12, 1865), 142.

[18]*Ibid.*, XV (April 27, 1867), 21.

[19]*Ibid.*, XVI (March 30, 1869), 898.

[20]Copy of the playbill for Pastor's first week at the Opera House. T. P. file, Hoblitzelle. Also see the list of performers in "Theatrical Record: City Summary," *Clipper*, XIII (Aug. 5, 1865), 134.

[21]For reference to a ballet see William E. Horton, *About Stage Folks* (Detroit: Free Press Printing Co., 1902), p. 11.

[22]"Theatrical Record: City Summary," *Clipper*, XIII (Aug. 12, 1865), 142.

[23]*Ibid.*, Feb. 10, 1865, p. 350. All of the paper's figures on monthly receipts were reputedly drawn from the books of the Assessors of the Fifth and Sixth Internal Revenue Districts of New York City.

[24]*Ibid.*, Sept. 16, 1865, p. 182.

[25]*Ibid.*, Feb. 10, 1866, p. 350.

[26]This amount is calculated from figures in *ibid*, Feb. 10, 1866, p. 350; and in *ibid.*, XIV (Jan. 19, 1867), 326.

[27]*Ibid.*, Aug. 18, 1866, p. 150.

[28]Ad for "Tony Pastor's Combination," *Clipper*, XIV (Nov. 10, 1866), 248.

[29]"Theatrical Record: City Summary," *Clipper*, XIV (July 7, 1866), 102.

[30]*Ibid*, Aug. 11, 1866, p. 142.

[31]"Vaudeville," *Mirror*, L (Dec. 19, 1903), xliv.

[32]"Theatrical Record: City Summary," *Clipper*, XIV (Feb. 9, 1867), 350.

[33]*Ibid.*, March 23, 1867, p. 398.

[34]*Ibid.*, XV (July 27, 1867), 126.

[35]"Tony Pastor's Wife a Hartford Girl," *Hartford Courant*, Aug. 29, 1908. T. P. file, NYPubl.

[36]"Theatrical Record: City Summary," *Clipper*, XV (Nov. 2, 1867), 238; *ibid.*, XVI (Dec. 26, 1868), 302.

[37]*Ibid.*, XV (Jan. 18, 1868), 326; *ibid.*, XVI (Jan. 30, 1869), 342.

[38]*Ibid.*, XVII (Jan. 29, 1870), 342. This was the last time the paper printed receipt figures.

CHAPTER FOUR

[1]"The Bowery Autocrat Interviewed," *Spirit of the Times*, LXXXVII (Feb. 14, 1874), 15.

[2]Parker Morell, *Lillian Russell, the Era of Plush* (N.Y.: Random House, 1940), p. 8.

[3]Lillian Russell, "Lillian Russell's Reminiscences," *Cosmopolitan*, LXXII (Feb., 1922), 18.

[4]Michael Bennet Leavitt, *Fifty Years in Theatrical Management* (N.Y.: Broadway Publishing Co., 1912), p. 194.

[5]Program for "Tony Pastor's Opera House," Aug. 4, 1865. T. P. file, Hoblitzelle.

[6]Ad for "Tony Pastor's Opera House," *Clipper*, XVIII (March 11, 1871), 387.

[7]Edward Bennet Marks, *They All Sang, From Tony Pastor to Rudy Vallee* (N. Y.: Viking Press, 1935), p. 16.

[8]Ad for "Tony Pastor's Opera House," *Clipper*, XVIII (May 7, 1870), 89.

[9]*Ibid.*, XV (March 7, 1868), 383.

[10]"Theatrical Record: City Summary," *Clipper*, XV (April 20, 1867), 14.

[11]Ad for "Tony Pastor's Opera House," *Clipper*, XV (April 20, 1867), 6.

[12]*Ibid.*, Jan. 4, 1868, p. 303.

[13]"Theatrical Record: City Summary," *Clipper*, XV (June 1, 1867), 62.

[14]*Ibid.*, XVI (Dec. 12, 1868), 286.

[15]*Ibid.*, XVII (May 29, 1869), 62.

[16]*Ibid.*, Feb. 19, 1870, p. 366.

[17]*Ibid.*, Feb. 26, 1870, p. 374.

[18]See William E. Horton, *About Stage Folks* (Detroit: Free Press Printing Co., 1902), pp. 101-102.

[19]"Theatrical Record: City Summary," *Clipper*, XIV (March 2, 1867), 374.

[20]*Ibid.*, May 12, 1866, p. 38.

[21]Douglas Gilbert, *American Vaudeville* (New ed. of 1940 work; N. Y.: Dover Publications, 1963), p. 122.

[22]"The Bowery and the Bowery Boy," *Clipper*, XIV (May 12, 1866), 34.

[23]Charles Cochran, *The Secrets of a Showman* (N. Y.: Henry Holt and Co., 1926), p. 11.

[24]"Tony Pastor's Theatre," *Clipper*, XXXII (March 22, 1884), 10.

[25]"Theatrical Record: City Summary," *Clipper*, XXI (Sept. 27, 1873), 206.

[26]"It Very Much Depends Upon the Style in Which It's Done," *Tony Pastor's 201 Bowery Songster* (N. Y.: Dick and Fitzgerald, *ca.* 1867), p. 35.

[27]"Theatrical Record: City Summary," *Clipper*, XV (April 20, 1867), 14.

CHAPTER FIVE

[1]"The Passing of Tony Pastor," *Green Book Album*, I (Jan., 1909), 192.

[2]Douglas Gilbert, *American Vaudeville* (New ed. of 1940 work; N. Y.: Dover Publications, 1963), p. 122.

[3]Tony Pastor, "Tony Pastor Recounts the Origin of American Vaudeville," *Variety*, V (Dec. 15, 1906), 17.

[4]George C. D. Odell, *Annals of the New York Stage* (15 vols.; N. Y.: Columbia University Press, 1927-1931), VII, 599.

[5]Montrose Moses, "Tony Pastor, Father of Vaudeville," *Theatre Guild Magazine*, April, 1931, p. 4. T. P. file, Museum CNY.

[6]Quoted in "Stage Stories Written by the Late Tony Pastor," *St. Louis Star*, Aug. 28, 1908. T. P. file, NYPubl.

[7]Sophie Tucker, *Some of These Days* (Garden City, N. Y.: Doubleday, Doran and Co., 1945), p. 46.

[8]*Ibid.*

[9]Quoted in "The Famous Tony Pastor," *N. Y. World*, sometime in the mid-1890's. T. P. file, NYPubl.

[10]Tony Pastor, "Life of Tony Pastor," *Tony Pastor's Songs* (N. Y.: Frank Harding, 1891), p. 2.

[11]*Ibid.*

[12]Program for "Tony Pastor's Opera House," Aug. 4, 1865. T. P. file, NYPubl.

[13]Quoted in "Tally One More Birthday for 'Tony' Pastor As a Manager," *N. Y. Morning Telegraph*, March 23, 1904. T. P. file, Harv.

[14]Ad for "Tony Pastor's Opera House," *N. Y. Herald*, LXXXIX (Aug. 6, 1865), 7.

[15]*Ibid.*, Aug. 25, 1865, p. 7.

[16]*Ibid.*, Oct. 23, 1865, p. 7.

[17]"Tony Pastor's," *N. Y. Herald*, LXXXIX (Sept. 26, 1865), 1; "Tony Pastor's Opera House," *ibid.*, Oct. 2, 1865, p. 4; *ibid.*, Nov. 8, 1865, p. 6.

[18]"The War Between the Theatrical Managers and the Herald," *N. Y. Times*, XIV (Oct. 1, 1865), 5.

[19]Phineas T. Barnum, *Struggles and Triumphs; or, Forty Years of Recollections* (Buffalo: Warren, Johnson, and Co., 1882), p. 673.

[20]Alvin Harlow, *Old Bowery Days* (N. Y.: D. Appleton and Co., 1931), pp. 380-81.

[21]"Theatrical Record: City Summary," *Clipper*, XV (June 22, 1867), 86.

[22]Program for "Tony Pastor's Opera House," Dec. 2, 1865. T. P. file, Museum CNY.

[23]"Theatrical Record: City Summary," *Clipper*, XIX (April 18, 1871), 6.

[24]Program for "Tony Pastor's Opera House," week of October 14, 1872. Amer. Vaud. file, NYPubl.

[25]Quoted in "Tally One More Birthday for 'Tony' Pastor As a Manager."

[26]Ad for "Tony Pastor's Opera House," *Clipper*, XIII (July 22, 1865), 120.

[27]Program for "Tony Pastor's Opera House," Aug. 4, 1865. T. P. file, NYPubl.

[28]"Dean of Vaudeville Celebrities," *Variety*, II (March 24, 1906), 5.

[29]"Tony Pastor's Opera House," *N. Y. Herald*, LXXXIX (Oct. 2, 1865), 4.

[30]Douglas Gilbert, "Vaudeville," *Oxford Companion to the Theatre*, ed. Phyllis Hartnoll (Oxford: Oxford University Press, 1951), p. 822.

[31]Gilbert, *American Vaudeville*, pp. 112-13.

[32]Lloyd Morris, *Incredible New York* (N. Y.: Random House, 1951), p. 72.

[33]See Edward Winslow Martin, *The Secrets of the Great City* (Philadelphia: Jones Bros. and Co., 1868); Matthew Hale Smith, *Sunshine and Shadow in New*

York (Hartford: J. B. Burr and Co., 1869); James Dabney McCabe, Jr., *Lights and Shadows of New York Life* (Philadelphia: National Publishing Co., 1872).

[34]"Theatrical Record: City Summary," *Clipper*, XVIII (June 11, 1870), 78.

[35]Pastor, "Tony Pastor Recounts the Origin of American Vaudeville."

[36]Ad for "Globe Theatre," *Spirit of the Times*, XXII (Sept. 23, 1871), 96; "Theatrical and Musical," *ibid.*, XXV (Aug. 3, 1872), 400.

[37]"Theatrical Record: City Summary," *Clipper*, XX (Dec. 14, 1872), 294.

[38]Odell, IX, 326.

[39]See Thomas A. Brown, *A History of the New York Stage* (3 vols.; N. Y.: Dodd, Mead, and Austin Publishers, 1903), II, 351.

[40]"Theatrical Record: City Summary," *Clipper*, XIX (Jan. 13, 1872), 326.

[41]Quoted in "Stage Stories Written by the Late Tony Pastor."

[42]Pastor, "Tony Pastor Recounts the Origin of American Vaudeville."

[43]"Theatrical Record: City Summary," *Clipper*, XXI (Oct. 18, 1873), 30.

[44]Ad for "Tony Pastor's Opera House," *Clipper*, XX (Dec. 21, 1872), 298.

[45]Michael Bennett Leavitt, *Fifty Years in Theatrical Management* (N. Y.: Broadway Publishing Co., 1912), p. 400.

[46]"Theatrical Record: City Summary," *Clipper*, XXI (March 7, 1874), 390.

[47]*Ibid.*, XXII (Nov. 28, 1874), 278.

[48]*Ibid.*

[49]*Ibid.*, Dec. 5, 1874, p. 286.

[50]*Ibid.*, Jan. 2, 1875, p. 318.

[51]See *ibid.*, Feb. 13, 1875, p. 363; and *ibid.*, Jan. 30, 1875, p. 350.

[52]*Ibid.*, Feb. 20, 1875, p. 374; and *ibid.*, March 13, 1875, p. 398.

[53]Pastor, "Tony Pastor Recounts the Origin of American Vaudeville."

[54]Quoted in an untitled article by George Morton in an unidentified and undated paper sometime in 1906. T. P. file, NYPubl.

[55]Leavitt, p. 387.

[56]Odell, IX, 603.

[57]"Theatrical Record: City Summary," *Clipper*, XXII (March 27, 1875), 414.

[58]*Ibid.*, Oct. 31, 1874, p. 246.

[59]*Ibid.*, XXIII (July 31, 1875), 142.

[60]Leavitt, p. 397.

[61]See Ruth Crosby Dimmick, *Our Theatres To-day and Yesterday* (N. Y.: The H. K. Fly Co., 1913), p. 55.

CHAPTER SIX

[1]Ad for "Tony Pastor's Metropolitan Theatre," *Clipper*, XXIII (Oct. 9, 1875), 223.

[2]Postbill for "Tony Pastor's New Theatre," Oct. 16, 1876. T. P. file, Princeton.

[3]"The Can Can," *N. Y. Times*, XXIV (Dec. 24, 1874), 5.

[4]"Tony Pastor's Metropolitan Theatre," *Spirit of the Times*, XC (Oct. 9, 1875), 215.

[5]"Theatrical Record: City Summary," *Clipper*, XXIII (Oct. 16, 1875), 230.

[6]See Charles Edward Ellis, *An Authentic History of the Benevolent and Protective Order of Elks* (Chicago: Published by the author, 1910), p. 129.

[7]"Music and Drama," *Spirit of the Times*, XC (Oct. 16, 1875), 238.

[8]"New York City Drama," *Dramatic News*, I (Oct. 23, 1875), 2. The *New York Dramatic News* was founded as a weekly all-theatrical paper by C. A. Byrne on October 2, 1875. Its reputed policy of high-pressure tactics and blackmail to secure advertising earned it the nickname of the "Vulture." For commentary on its shady character see Archie Binns, *Mrs. Fiske and the American Theatre* (N.

Y.: Crown Publishers, 1955), p. 40; and James L. Ford, *Forty-Odd Years in the Literary Shop* (N. Y.: E. P. Dutton and Co., 1921), p. 229. The paper added *and Society Journal* to its title in 1876, but the addition was dropped in 1883. It absorbed the *Dramatic Times* in 1896 and added that title to its own. The paper seems to have become more respectable by the late 1880's. It published until May, 1919.

[9]"Tony Pastor's," *Dramatic News*, I (Nov. 27, 1875), 2.

[10]"Theatrical Record: City Summary," *Clipper*, XXIII (March 4, 1876), 390.

[11]"Domestic Notes," *Dramatic News*, I (March 4, 1876), 2.

[12]"Theatrical Record: City Summary," *Clipper*, XXV (Nov. 3, 1877), 254. There is a photograph of William Pastor in Ellis, p. 299.

[13]Ad for "Theatre Comique," *Clipper*, XXIV (Nov. 4, 1876), 255.

[14]"Pen and Pencil: Tony Pastor's," *Mirror*, VI (Dec. 3, 1881), 3. The *New York Mirror* was a weekly journal devoted entirely to the stage. It began publishing on January 4, 1879, for the express purpose of attacking what its editor, Ernest Harvier, considered the underhanded tactics of the *New York Dramatic News*. (See note 8) The paper resolved to be the honest, prudent, yet aggressive organ of the theatrical profession. It was indeed aggressive. It attacked injustice, narrow-mindedness, and shoddy practices whenever and wherever they appeared in the theatrical environment; it championed numerous causes, including the establishment of an Actors' Fund and an adequate international copyright law; and it supplied a news coverage of professional doings around the country and even abroad. Harrison Grey Fiske became editor in the summer of 1880; the paper changed its name to the *New York Dramatic Mirror* on January 26, 1889, finally dropping the *New York* in 1917. Fisk's editorship ended in 1911, and the paper itself ended in 1922, having just changed to a monthly publication.

[15]Ad for "Tony Pastor's Metropolitan Theatre," *Clipper*, XXIII (Oct. 9, 1875), 223.

[16]Ad for "Tony Pastor's New Theatre," *Clipper*, XXIV (Nov. 4, 1876), 255.

[17]Douglas Gilbert, *American Vaudeville* (New ed. of 1940 work; N. Y.: Dover Publications, 1963), p. 4.

[18]*Ibid.*

[19]Michael Bennett Leavitt, *Fifty Years in Theatrical Management* (N. Y.: Broadway Publishing Co., 1912), p. 189.

[20]Ad for "Tony Pastor's New Theatre," *Clipper*, XXIV (March 17, 1877), 407.

[21]"The Decline of Variety," *Dramatic News*, IV (May 12, 1877), 4.

[22]"Theatrical Record: City Summary," *Clipper*, XXV (Oct. 13, 1877), 230.

[23]Gilbert, p. 112.

[24]Ad for "Tony Pastor's New Theatre," *Dramatic News*, I (Oct. 23, 1875), 1.

[25]Ad for "Tony Pastor's New Theatre," *Clipper*, XXIV (Oct. 14, 1876), 231.

[26]"Theatrical Record: City Summary," *Clipper*, XXIV (Oct. 21, 1876), 238.

[27]"Dramatic Doings," *Dramatic News*, III (Feb. 17, 1877), 2.

[28]Postbill for "Tony Pastor's New Theatre," Oct. 16, 1876. T. P. file, Princeton; ad for "Tony Pastor's New Theatre," *Clipper*, XXVI (Feb. 1, 1879), 3.

[29]"Dramatic Doings," *Dramatic News*, IV (May 19, 1877), 2; "Tony Pastor's," *Mirror*, I (March 15, 1879), 3.

[30]"The Week at the Theatres," *Mirror*, II (Dec. 27, 1879), 5; *ibid.*, III (Jan. 31, 1880), 5.

[31]Quoted in an untitled article by George Morton in an unidentified and undated paper sometime in 1906. T. P. file, NYPubl.

[32]"At the Theatres," *Mirror*, V (Jan. 29, 1881), 7.

[33]All quoted in ad for "Tony Pastor's Troupe," *Clipper*, XXVI (May 18, 1879), 59.

[34]Gilbert, p. 10.

CHAPTER SEVEN

[1]"Theatrical Record: City Summary," *Clipper*, XXVI (April 6, 1878), 14.

[2]George C. D. Odell, *Annals of the New York Stage* (15 vols.; N. Y.: Columbia University Press, 1927-1931), XI, 102.

[3]"Spirit of the Stage," *Spirit of the Times*, C (Jan. 1, 1881), 567.

[4]"Theatrical Record: City Summary," *Clipper*, XXVI (Jan. 11, 1879), 334.

[5]"Tony Pastor 'Raised' Big Family of Stars," *N. Y. Herald*, Sept. 13, 1908, T. P. file, Museum CNY.

[6]"Tony Pastor Looks Far Back," *N. Y. Sun*, no date. Amer. Vaud. file, NYPubl.

[7]"Dramatic Doings," *Dramatic News*, I (Feb. 19, 1876), 2.

[8]Quoted in Charles Darnton, "Tony Pastor, 39 Years a Manager," *N. Y. World*, March 26, 1904. T. P. file, NYPubl.

[9]Nat. C. Goodwin, *Nat Goodwin's Book* (Boston: Richard G. Badger, the Gorham Press, 1914), p. 79.

[10]Quoted in "Stage Stories Written by the Late Tony Pastor," *St. Louis Star*, Aug. 28, 1908. T. P. file, NYPubl.

[11]Goodwin, p. 79.

[12]Douglas Gilbert, *American Vaudeville* (New ed. of 1940 work; N. Y.: Dover Publications, 1963), p. 89.

[13]*Ibid.*, p. 110. Gilbert made the same claim about Nat Goodwin. See *ibid.*

[14]Felix Isman, *Weber and Fields* (N. Y.: Boni and Liveright, 1924), p. 31.

[15]"The Variety Stage," *Harper's Weekly*, XLVI (March 22, 1902), 380.

[16]Quoted in "The Matinee Girl," *Mirror*, LX (Aug. 1, 1908), 2.

[17]*Ibid.*

[18]Odell, X, 283.

[19]Gilbert, p. 92.

[20]Lillian Russell, "Lillian Russell's Reminiscences," *Cosmopolitan*, LXXII (Feb., 1922), 18.

[21]Quoted in "Stage Stories Written by the Late Tony Pastor."

[22]Russell, p. 92.

[23]Quoted in "Stage Stories Written by the Late Tony Pastor."

[24]Russell, p. 92.

[25]Parker Morell, *Lillian Russell, the Era of Plush* (N. Y.: Random House, 1940), p. 11.

[26]"Professional Doings," *Mirror*, V (Jan. 8, 1881), 10.

[27]"Tony Pastor's," *Mirror*, I (Feb. 22, 1879), 3.

[28]"New Year's With the Managers," *Mirror*, V (Jan. 8, 1881), 7.

[29]"Spirit of the Stage: New York," *Spirit of the Times*, C (Jan. 22, 1881), 631.

[30]Morell, p. 27.

[31]"At the Theatres," *Mirror*, V (Feb. 19, 1881), 7.

[32]Gilbert, p. 113.

[33]"At the Theatres," *Mirror*, V (March 12, 1881), 7.

[34]Morell, pp. 29-30.

[35]Odell, XI, 316.

[36]"Tony Pastor's New Theatre," *Mirror*, VI (July 30, 1881), 8.

[37]Thomas A. Brown, *History of the New York Stage* (3 vols.; N. Y.: Dodd, Mead, and Co., 1903), II, 122.

CHAPTER EIGHT

[1]"At the Theatres," *Mirror*, XIV (Oct. 24, 1885), 2.

[2]See "Fire in Tony Pastor's," *Clipper*, XXXVI (June 16, 1888), 217.

[3]"At the Theatres," *Mirror*, XX (Oct. 27, 1888), 2.

[4]*Ibid.*, VI (Oct. 15, 1881), 1.

[5]Ad for "Tony Pastor's New Fourteenth Street Theatre," *Mirror*, VI (Aug. 5, 1881), 12.

[6]"Tony Pastor's New Fourteenth-Street Theatre," *Clipper*, XXIX (Oct. 29, 1881), 522.

[7]"At the Theatres," *Mirror*, VI (Oct. 29, 1881), 2.

[8]Douglas Gilbert, *American Vaudeville* (New ed. of 1940 work; N. Y.: Dover Publications, 1963), p. 113.

[9]Fred Stone, *Rolling Stone* (N. Y.: Whittlesey House, 1945), p. 115. Stone started in variety as half of the comic team of Montgomery and Stone, then went on to become a popular comedian on the legitimate stage.

[10]"Mirror Interviews: Tony Pastor," *Mirror*, XXXIV (July 27, 1895), 2.

[11]Ad for "Tony Pastor's New Fourteenth Street Theatre," *Clipper*, XXIX (Oct. 29, 1881), 526.

[12]Ad for "Tony Pastor's New Fourteenth-Street Theatre," *Mirror*, VI (Sept. 3, 1881), 10.

[13]"At the Theatres," *Mirror*, VII (Jan. 14, 1882), 2.

[14]*Ibid.*, VIII (Nov. 18, 1882), 2.

[15]"Tony Pastor's Theatre," *Clipper*, XXXI (Feb. 23, 1884), 834.

[16]"At the Theatres," *Mirror*, XI (March 8, 1884), 2.

[17]Ad for "Tony Pastor's New Fourteenth-Street Theatre," *Mirror*, LVL (Dec. 18, 1886), 31.

[18]Gilbert, p. 113.

[19]Quoted in "Tony Pastor, Vaudeville Dean, Forty Three Years a Manager," *N. Y. Morning Telegram*, March 21, 1908. T. P. file, NYPubl.

[20]"At the Theatres," *Mirror*, VII (Jan. 28, 1882), 3.

[21]"The Musical Mirror," *Mirror*, VII (March 25, 1882), 2. May Irwin was not in the cast but she did appear in the farce, *Fun at School*, which was part of the accompanying olio.

[22]Parker Morell, *Lillian Russell, the Era of Plush* (N. Y.: Random House, 1940), pp. 44-45.

[23]"Noted Performers of Our Times: Miss Lillian Russell," *Clipper*, XXXI (Jan. 19, 1884), 754.

[24]Ad for "Lillian Russell's Comic Opera Co.," *Clipper*, XXIX (Feb. 25, 1882), 815.

[25]"At the Theatres," *Mirror*, IX (March 3, 1883), 2.

[26]*Ibid.*, March 24, 1883, p. 2.

[27]"Pen and Pencil: Tony Pastor's," *Mirror*, VI (Dec. 3, 1881), 3.

[28]"Professional Doings," *Mirror*, X (July 28, 1883), 3.

[29]"Personal," *Mirror*, XI (Feb. 16, 1884), 6.

[30]"Professional Doings," *Mirror*, XI (March 15, 1884), 3.

[31]*Ibid.*, XIII (Feb. 7, 1885), 7.

[32]*Ibid.*, XV (March 27, 1886), 3.

[33]Quoted in "Tony Pastor, Vaudeville Dean, Forty-Three Years a Manager."

[34]Michael Bennett Leavitt, *Fifty Years in Theatrical Management* (N. Y.: Broadway Publishing Co., 1912), p. 193.

[35]"Obituary Notes," *N. Y. Times*, XXXVI (July 12, 1887), 2. See also "Funeral of Tony Pastor's Mother," *ibid.*, Aug. 4, 1887, p. 2.

[36]Harry Ralph [Little Tich], *Little Tich* (London: John Lane, the Bodley Head, 1927), p. 56.

[37]*Ibid.*, pp. 59-60.

CHAPTER NINE

[1]Untitled item in an untitled and undated paper. T. P. file, NYPubl.

[2]Quoted in an untitled article by George Morton in an unidentified and undated paper sometime in 1906. T. P. file, NYPubl.

[3]Espes W. Sargent, "Fathers of Vaudeville," *Green Book Album*, II (Sept., 1909), 561.

[4]Letter from Tony Pastor to the editor of the *Dramatic News*, dated March 4, 1888. T. P. file, Harv.

[5]Harry S. Sanderson, "Reminiscences of Tony Pastor, Vaudeville's Dean," *Variety*, XII (Dec. 12, 1908), 50.

[6]Lillian Russell, "Lillian Russell's Reminiscences," *Cosmopolitan*, LXXII (Feb., 1922), 18.

[7]*Ibid.*

[8]C. R. Sherlock, "Where the Vaudeville holds the Boards," *Cosmopolitan*, XXXII (Feb., 1902), 414.

[9]"The Mirror and the Season," *Mirror*, IV (Dec. 25, 1880), 8.

[10]Sargent, p. 561.

[11]Douglas Gilbert, *American Vaudeville* (New ed. of 1940 work; N. Y.: Dover Publications, 1963), p. 123.

[12]Parker Morell, *Lillian Russell, the Era of Plush* (N. Y.: Random House, 1940), p. 4.

[13]Gilbert, p. 123.

[14]Edwin A. Goewey, "Tony Pastor, the Starmaker," *Dance Magazine*, XII (Aug., 1929), 13.

[15]Edward Bennet Marks, *They All Sang, from Tony Pastor to Rudy Vallee* (N. Y.: Viking Press, 1935), p. 16.

[16]Quoted in an untitled article by George Morton.

[17]Gilbert, p. 113.

[18]Arthur Roberts, *Fifty Years of Spoof* (London: John Lane, the Bodley Head, 1927), p. 197.

[19]Charles Edward Ellis, *An Authentic History of the Benevolent and Protective Order of Elks* (Chicago: Published by the author, 1910), p. 327.

[20]"Personal," *Mirror*, XI (May, 17, 1884), 6.

[21]Sanderson, p. 81.

[22]Sime Silverman, "Recollections of Pastor's," *Variety*, XII (Dec. 12, 1908), 50.

[23]Quoted in "Tony Pastor's Fortune," *Billboard*, XXII (Oct. 22, 1910), 12.

[24]*Ibid.*

[25]Sargent, p. 560.

[26]Quoted in "In Memoriam," *The Elks Antler*, sometime soon after Pastor's death on Aug. 26, 1908. T. P. file, NYPubl.

[27]Sanderson, pp. 50-51.

[28]"Up a Tree," *Tony Pastor's 201 Bowery Songbook* (N. Y.: Dick and Fitzgerald, *ca.* 1867), p. 40.

[29]Tony Pastor, "Stage Stories Written by the Late Tony Pastor," *St. Louis Star*, Aug. 28, 1908. T. P. file, NYPubl.

[30]Harvey A. Higgins, "Origin of Vaudeville," *Mirror*, LXXX (May 13, 1919), 720.

[31]Morell, p. 10.

[32]Untitled article, *Chicago Record*, Dec. 25, 1906. T. P. file, NYPubl.

[33]"Bread Upon the Waters," *Mirror*, Feb. 8, 1890. T. P. file, NYPubl.

[34]"Tony Pastor," *Clipper*, XXXVIII (March 29, 1890), 2.

[35]*Ibid.*

[36]"Tony Pastor Jubilee," unidentified paper, March 29, 1890. T. P. file, Harv.

[37]*Ibid.*

[38]"Notes," *Mirror*, XIX (Dec. 24, 1887), 25.

CHAPTER TEN

[1]"At the Park," *Mirror*, XXVIII (Sept. 3, 1892), 8.

[2]"Like a Foreign Music Hall," *Mirror*, XXVIII (Oct. 8, 1892), 4.

[3]"The Imperial Music Hall," *Mirror*, XXVIII (Nov. 26, 1892), 2.

[4]"Proctor's," *Mirror*, XXIX (Jan. 14, 1893), 11.

[5]William M. Marston and John H. Feller, *F. F. Proctor, Vaudeville Pioneer* (N. Y.: Richard R. Smith, 1943), p. 50.

[6]Espes W. Sargent, "Fathers of Vaudeville," *Green Book Album*, II (Sept., 1909), 561.

[7]Henry Collins Brown, *In the Golden Nineties* (Hastings-on-Hudson: Valentine's Manual, Inc., 1928), p. 190.

[8]Douglas Gilbert, *American Vaudeville* (New ed. of 1940 work; N. Y.: Dover Publications, 1963), p. 190.

[9]"Mr. Hammerstein is 'in it,'" *Mirror*, XXX (July 29, 1893), 2.

[10]Quoted in "Tony Pastor, Vaudeville Dean, Forth-Three Years a Manager," *N. Y. Evening Telegraph*, March 21, 1908. T. P. file, NYPubl.

[11]"The Usher," *Mirror*, XXII (Dec. 14, 1889), 3.

[12]*Ibid.*, XXIV (Nov. 29, 1890), 3.

[13]"Tony Pastor's," *Mirror*, XXV (Feb. 28, 1891), 2.

[14]Quoted in "Tony Pastor, Vaudeville Dean, Forth-Three Years a Manager."

[15]"Personal," *Mirror*, XXV (March 21, 1891), 4.

[16]Irving Berlin, personal letter, May 23, 1963.

[17]"At the Theatres," *Mirror*, XXX (Aug. 5, 1893), 6.

[18]Gilbert, p. 186.

[19]Benjamin F. Keith, "The Origin of Continuous Vaudeville," in an unidentified issue of the *Mirror* near the end of the 1890's. Robinson Locke, NYPubl.

[20]Gilbert, p. 201.

[21]Robert Grau, *Forty Years of Observations of Music and the Drama* (N. Y.: Broadway Publishing Co., 1909), p. 4.

[22]Quoted in *ibid.*, p. 5.

[23]"Keith's Union Square Theatre," *Mirror*, XXXIII (Dec. 29, 1894), 3.

[24]Sargent, p. 563.

[25]George C. D. Odell, *Annals of the New York Stage* (15 vols.; N. Y.: Columbia University Press, 1927-1931), XV, 687.

[26]Grau, p. 2.

[27]Odell, XV, 689.

[28]Matilda Alice DeFrece [Vesta Tilley], *Recollections of Vesta Tilley* (London: Hutchinson and Co., 1934), p. 183.

[29]"Tony Pastor's," *Mirror*, XXXI (April 21, 1894), 3.

[30]*Ibid.*, May 26, 1894, p. 6.

[31]"At the Theatre," *Mirror*, XXXII (June 30, 1894), 3.

[32]See ad for "Tony Pastor's Fourteenth Street Theatre," *Mirror*, XXXIII (Feb. 16, 1895), 19; *ibid.*, Feb. 23, 1895, p. 15.

[33]*Ibid.*, April 20, 1895, p. 3.

[34]Quoted in "Tony Pastor to Move Uptown," *Mirror*, XXII (Nov. 24, 1894), 2.

[35]Quoted in "Tony Pastor's Plans," *Mirror*, XXXIV (Aug. 10, 1895), 17.

[36]*Ibid.*

[37]Quoted in "Hammerstein Secures Mlle. Guilbert," *Mirror*, XXXIII (March 23, 1895), 2.

[38]Sargent, p. 560.

[39]Quoted in "Tony Pastor, Vaudeville Dean, Forty-Three Years a Manager."

[40]"Pastor's New Departure," *Mirror*, XXV (Jan. 18, 1896), 19.

[41]Ad for "Tony Pastor's Fourteenth Street Theatre," *Mirror*, XXXV *(Jan. 25, 1896), 18.*

[42]Edward Bennet Marks, *They All Sang, From Tony Pastor to Rudy Vallee* (N. Y.: Viking Press, 1935), p. 15.

[43]Joseph Laurie, Jr., *Vaudeville: from the honky-tonks to the Palace* (N. Y.: Holt, 1953), p. 61.

[44]Ad for "Tony Pastor's Fourteenth Street Theatre," *Mirror*, XXXV (Jan. 25, 1896), 18; *ibid.*, Feb. 1, 1896, p. 11.

[45]"Tony Pastor's Surprise," *Mirror*, XXXV (Jan. 25, 1896), 20.

[46]Quoted in "Pastor's New Departure," *Mirror*, XXXV (Jan. 18, 1896), 19.

[47]"Tony Pastor's," *Mirror*, XXXV (Feb. 1, 1896), 19.

[48]*Ibid.*

[49]*Ibid.*, XXXVIII (Nov. 13, 1897), 18.

[50]"Tony Pastor's," *Spirit of the Times*, Sept. 26, 1896. T. P. file, NYPubl.

CHAPTER ELEVEN

[1]"Trend of Vaudeville," *Independent*, LIII (May 9, 1901), 1093.

[2]Bernard Sobel, *A Pictorial History of Vaudeville* (N. Y.: Citadel Press, 1961), p. 65.

[3]"Vaudeville Managers Confer," *Mirror*, XLIII (May 26, 1900), 17.

[4]For information on the merger see "The Vaudeville Situation," *Mirror*, LV (June 9, 1906), 16; and "The Big Merger Completed," *ibid.*, June 23, 1906, p. 16.

[5]Douglas Gilbert, *American Vaudeville* (New ed. of 1940 work; N. Y.: Dover Publications, 1963), p. 238.

[6]Sobel, p. 66.

[7]"Pastor the Last of a Famous Group," *N. Y. World*, Aug. 30, 1908. T. P. file, Harv.

[8]Gilbert, p. 123.

[9]"Trial Turn at Pastor's," *Mirror*, XXXVIII (Dec. 25, 1897), 19.

[10]George M. Cohan, *Twenty Years on Broadway* (N. Y.: Harper and Bros., Publishers, 1924), p. 174.

[11]Gilbert, p. 123.

[12]Quoted in Cohan, p. 172.

[13]"The Passing of Tony Pastor," *Green Book Album*, I (Jan., 1909), 192.

[14]Matilda Alice DeFrece [Vesta Tilley], *Recollections of Vesta Tilley* (London: Hutchinson and Co., 1934), pp. 202-203.

[15]*Ibid.*

[16]Quoted in "Vaudeville in its Infancy," unidentified paper for Feb. 19, 1898. T. P. file, NYPubl.

[17]"Tony Pastor Imports Singer," *Mirror*, LVIII (July 20, 1907), 14.

[18]"The Hammerstein Testimonial," *Mirror*, XXXIX (July 9, 1898), 9.

[19]"The Usher," *Mirror*, LX (Sept. 5, 1908), 5.

[20]Quoted in Charles Darnton, "Tony Pastor, 39 Years a Manager," *N. Y. World*, March 26, 1904. T. P. file, NYPubl.

[21]"Gossip from Gotham," unidentified N. Y. C. paper for March 25, 1900. T. P. file, Harv.

[22]"Tony Pastor's," *Mirror*, XLVI (Aug. 31, 1901), 16.

[23]"$300 Gift for Mr. Tony Pastor," *N. Y. Evening Telegram*, March 23, 1905. T. P. file, NYPubl.

[24]Harry S. Sanderson, "Reminiscences of Tony Pastor, Vaudeville's Dean," *Variety*, XII (Dec. 12, 1908), 81.

[25]"Proctor Abandons the 'Continuous,' " *Mirror*, LIII (April 29, 1905), 18.

[26]Quoted in "Tony Pastor Looks Far Back," *N. Y. Sun*, sometime in late March, 1906. Amer. Vaud. file, NYPubl.

[27]See "The Ten-Cent Theatres in the West," *Mirror*, LIII (June 3, 1905), 16; "Cheap Vaudeville Invades Harlem," *ibid.*; "Five Cent Vaudeville Here," *ibid.*, LV (March 24, 1906), 16.

[28]"Pictures at Union Square," *Mirror*, LIX (Feb. 22, 1908), 13.

[29]This cartoon appeared in the *Mirror*, LVIII (July 20, 1907), 13.

[30]Sime Silverman, "Recollections of 'Pastor's,' " *Variety*, XII (Dec. 12, 1908), 50.

[31]*Ibid.*

[32]"Pastor's," *Variety*, VIII (Oct. 12, 1907), 12; *ibid.*, Feb. 8, 1908, p. 17.

[33]"Pastor's Reduced Admission," *Variety*, IX (Feb. 29, 1908), 2.

[34]"Tony Pastor Celebrates his 43rd Anniv.," *Variety*, X (March 28, 1908), 10.

[35]*Ibid.*

[36]"Pastor's Playing Pictures," *Variety*, XI (June 13, 1908), 7.

[37]*Ibid.*

[38]" 'Tony' Pastor Will Move Uptown," *N. Y. Herald*, June 23, 1908. T. P. file, NYPubl.

[39]Quoted in "Tony Pastor Will Move," *Mirror*, LX (July 11, 1908), 14.

[40]"Pastor in Charge Again," *Variety*, XI (July 18, 1908), 9.

[41]"Tony Pastor Very Ill," *Mirror*, LX (Aug. 22, 1908), 7.

[42]Cited in "Pastor Congratulated," *Variety*, VI (March 30, 1907), 12.

[43]"They Talked of Tony Pastor," unidentified N. Y. C. paper sometime soon after Pastor's death on Aug. 26, 1908. T. P. file, Harv.

[44]"Tony Pastor Seriously Ill," *Variety*, XI (Aug. 15, 1908), 4.

[45]"Tony Pastor Very Ill," *Mirror*.

[46]"Tony Pastor Much Improved," *Variety*, XI (Aug. 22, 1908), 9.

[47]" 'Tony' Pastor Dead in his 77th Year," *N. Y. Times*, LVII (Aug. 27, 1908), 7.

[48]"Tony Pastor," *Billboard*, XX (Sept. 5, 1908), 18.

[49]Cited in "Pastor Funeral Tomorrow," *N. Y. Sun*, Aug. 28, 1908. T. P. file, NYPubl.

[50]"Death of Tony Pastor," *Mirror*, LX (Sept. 5, 1908), 6.

[51]*Ibid.*

[52]See the "Report of the Appraiser, in Matter of Transfer Tax upon Estate

of Antonio Pastor," filed on Oct. 4, 1909; and the "Account of Proceedings, in Matter of the Judicial Settlement of the Account of Josephine M. Pastor as Administratrix with the will annexed, of Antonio Pastor," filed on Jan. 11, 1911. Both documents are in the Hall of Records, Surrogate's Court of the County of New York, N. Y. C.

[53]"Tony Pastor's Fortune," *Billboard*, XXII (Oct. 22, 1910), 12.

[54]Quoted in *ibid.*

[55]Quoted in "Stage Children to See St. Nick," *N. Y. Morning Telegraph*, Dec. 15, 1910. T. P. file, NYPubl.

[56]See Joseph Laurie, Jr., *Vaudeville: from the honky-tonks to the Palace* (N. Y.: Holt, 1953), p. 336.

[57]Marion Spitzer, "Morals in the Two-a-day," *American Mercury*, III (Sept. 1924), 35.

[58]Laurie, pp. 336-37.

Bibliography

BOOKS

"Antonio Pastor," in *National Cyclopedia of American Biography*. 45 vols.; N. Y.: James White and Co., 1918, XVI, 30.

Barnum, Phineas T. *Struggles and Triumphs; or, Forty Years of Recollections*. Buffalo, N. Y.: Warren, Johnson, and Co., 1872.

Binns, Archie. *Mrs. Fiske and the American Theatre*. N. Y.: Crown Publishers, 1955.

Brown, Henry Collins. *In the Golden Nineties*. Hastings-on-Hudson: Valentine's Manual, Inc., 1928.

Brown, Thomas A. *A History of the New York Stage*. 3 vols.; N. Y.: Dodd, Mead, and Austin Publishers, 1903.

Browne, Walter and F. A. Austin (eds.). *Who's Who on the Stage*. N. Y.: Browne and Austin, Publishers, 1906.

Cahn, Julius. *Julius Cahn's Theatrical Guide*. N. Y.: G. P. Putnam's Sons, 1957.

Chindahl, George L. *A History of the Circus in America*. Caldwell, Idaho: Caxton Printers, 1959.

Cochran, Charles B. *The Secrets of a Showman*. N. Y.: Henry Holt and Co., 1926.

Cohan, George M. *Twenty Years on Broadway*. N. Y.: Harper and Bros., Publishers, 1924.

Dana, Ethel Nathalie. *Young in New York, a memoir of a victorian girlhood*. N. Y.: Doubleday and Co., 1963.

DeFrece, Matilda Alice [Vesta Tilley]. *Recollections of Vesta Tilley*. London: Hutchinson and Co., 1934.

Dickens, Charles. *American Notes for General Circulation*. N. Y.: D. Appleton and Co., 1876.

Dimmick, Ruth Crosby. *Our Theatres To-day and Yesterday.* N. Y.: The H. K. Fly Co., Publishers, 1913.

Disher, Maurice Willson. "Music-Hall," in *Oxford Companion to the Theatre.* Edited by Phyllis Hartnoll. Oxford: Oxford University Press, 1951.

Downes, Olin and Elie Siegmeister. *A Treasury of American Songs.* N. Y.: Alfred A Knopf, 1943.

Ellis, Charles Edward. *An Authentic History of the Benevolent and Protective Order of Elks.* Chicago: Published by the author, 1910.

Ford, James L. *Forty-Odd Years in the Literary Shop.* N. Y.: E. P. Dutton and Co., 1921.

Foy, Eddie and Alvin F. Harlow. *Clowning Through Life.* N. Y.: E. P. Dutton and Co., 1928.

Gilbert, Douglas. *American Vaudeville, its Life and Times.* N. Y.: Dover Publications, 1963.

——————. "Vaudeville," in *Oxford Companion to the Theatre.* Edited by Phyllis Hartnoll. Oxford: Oxford University Press, 1951.

Goldberg, Isaac. *Tin Pan Alley.* N. Y.: John Day Co., 1930.

Golden, George Fuller. *My Lady Vaudeville and her White Rats.* N. Y.: Broadway Publishing Co., 1909.

Goodwin, Nat C. *Nat Goodwin's Book.* Boston: Richard G. Badger, The Gorham Press, 1914.

Grau, Robert. *The Business Man in the Amusement World.* N. Y.: Broadway Publishing Co., 1910.

——————. *Forty Years of Observation of Music and the Drama.* N. Y.: Broadway Publishing Co., 1909.

Green, Abel. *Show Biz, from Vaudeville to Video.* N. Y.: Holt, 1951.

Harlow, Alvin. *Old Bowery Days.* N. Y.: D. Appleton and Co., 1931.

Hibbert, Henry G. *Fifty Years of a Londoner's Life.* N. Y.: Dodd, Mead, and Co., 1916.

Horton, William E. *About Stage Folks.* Detroit: Free Press Printing Co., 1902.

I, E. J. R. [Edith J. R. Isaacs]. "Antonio Pastor," in *Dictionary of American Biography.* Edited by Dumas Malone. 21 vols.; N. Y.: Charles Scribner's Sons, 1934, XIV, 290.

Isman, Felix. *Weber and Fields.* N. Y.: Boni and Liveright, 1924.

Hunt, Gaillard. *Life in America One Hundred Years Ago.* N. Y.: Harper and Bros., 1914.

Jenkins, Stephen. *The Greatest Street in the World—Broadway.* N. Y.: G. P. Putnam's Sons, 1911.

Kouwenhoven, John A. *The Columbia Historical Portrait of New York.* Garden City, N. Y.: Doubleday and Co., 1953.

Laurie, Jr., Joseph. *Vaudeville: from the honky-tonks to the Palace.* N. Y.: Holt, 1953.

Leavitt, Michael Bennett. *Fifty Years in Theatrical Management.* N. Y.: Broadway Publishing Co., 1912.

McCabe, James Dabney. *Lights and Shadows of New York Life.* Philadelphia: National Publishing Co., 1872.

Marks, Edward Bennet. *They All Sang, From Tony Pastor to Rudy Vallee.* N. Y.: Viking Press, 1935.

Marston, William M. and John Henry Feller. *F. F. Proctor, Vaudeville Pioneer.* N. Y.: Richard R. Smith, 1943.

Martin, Edward Winslow. *The Secrets of the Great City.* Philadelphia: Jones Bros., and Co., 1868.

May, Earl Chapin. *The Circus from Rome to Ringling.* N. Y.: Duffield and Green, 1932.

Moody, Richard. *America Takes the Stage.* Bloomington, Indiana: Indiana University Press, 1955.

Morehouse, Ward. *Matinee Tomorrow.* N. Y.: McGraw-Hill Book Co., 1949.

Morell, Parker. *Lillian Russell, the Era of Plush.* N. Y.: Random House, 1940.

Morris, Lloyd. *Incredible New York.* N. Y.: Random House, 1951.

Mott, Frank Luther. *A History of American Magazines.* Cambridge: Harvard University Press, 1938.

Nevins, Allan and Milton Halsey Thomas. (eds.). *The Diary of George Templeton Strong.* 4 vols.; N. Y.: Macmillan and Co., 1952.

Odell, George C. D. *Annals of the New York Stage.* 15 vols.; N. Y.: Columbia University Press, 1927-1931.

Page, Brett. *Writing for Vaudeville.* Springfield, Mass.: The Home Correspondence School, 1915.

Pastor, Tony. "Life of Tony Pastor," in *Tony Pastor's Songs.* N. Y.: Frank Harding's Music Store, 1891, p. 2.

Ralph, Harry. [Little Tich]. *Little Tich.* London: John Lane, the Bodley Head, 1927.

Renton, Edward. *The Vaudeville Theatre.* N. Y.: Gotham Press, 1918.

Rice, Edward LeRoy. *Monarchs of Minstrelsy.* N. Y.: Kenny Publishing Co., 1911.

Roberts, Arthur. *Fifty Years of Spoof.* London: John Lane, the Bodley Head, 1927.

Rovere, Richard H. *Howe and Hummel; their True and Scandalous History.* N. Y.: Farrar, Straus, and Co., 1947.

Sheean, Vincent. *Oscar Hammerstein I; the life and exploits of an impresario.* N. Y.: Simon and Schuster, 1956.

Sherwood, Robert Edmund. *Here We Are Again: Recollections of an Old Circus Clown.* Indianapolis: The Bobbs-Merrill Co., 1926.

Short, Ernest Henry. *Fifty Years of Vaudeville.* London: Eyre and Spottiswoode, 1946.

Smith, Matthew Hale. *Sunshine and Shadow in New York.* Hartford: J. B. Burr and Co., 1869.

Sobel, Bernard. *Burleycue.* N. Y.: Farrar and Rinehart, 1931.

——————. *A Pictorial History of Burlesque.* N. Y.: Bonanza Books, 1956.

——————. *A Pictorial History of Vaudeville.* N. Y.: Citadel Press, 1961.

Still, Bayd. *Mirror for Gotham.* N. Y.: New York University Press, 1956.

Stone, Fred. *Rolling Stone.* N. Y.: Whittlesey House, 1945.

Tony Pastor's Book of Six Hundred Comic Songs and Speeches. N. Y.: Dick and Fitzgerald, *ca.* 1867.

Tony Pastor's Complete Budget of Comic Songs. N. Y.: Dick and Fitzgerald, *ca.* 1864.

Tony Pastor's "444" Combination Songster. N. Y.: Dick and Fitzgerald, *ca.* 1864.

Tony Pastor's Irish American Song Book. Glasgow: Cameron and Ferguson, *ca.* 1870.

Tony Pastor's New Union Song Book. N. Y.: Dick and Fitzgerald, *ca.* 1862.

Tony Pastor's Opera-House Songster. N. Y.: Dick and Fitzgerald, *ca.* 1865.

Tony Pastor's "Own" Comic Vocalist. N. Y.: Dick and Fitzgerald, *ca.* 1863.

Tony Pastor's Songs. N. Y.: Frank Harding's Music Store, 1891.

Tony Pastor's Stories and Jokes. N. Y.: W. Small and Co., *ca.* 1872.

Tony Pastor's 201 Bowery Songster. N. Y.: Dick and Fitzgerald, *ca.* 1867.

Tony Pastor's Waterfall Songster. N. Y.: Dick and Fitzgerald, *ca.* 1866.

Tucker, Sophie. *Some of These Days.* Garden City, N. Y.: Doubleday, Doran and Co., 1945.

Wallace, Irving. *The Fabulous Showman.* N. Y.: Alfred A. Knopf, 1959.

Wilson, James Grant. *The Memorial History of the City of New York.* 4 vols.; N. Y.: New York History Co., 1893, III, 564-65.

Wright, Mabel Osgood. *My New York.* N. Y.: Macmillan Co., 1926.

ARTICLES AND PERIODICALS

Albee, Edward. F. "Twenty Years of Vaudeville," *Theatre,* XXXI (May, 1920), 408, 450.

"The Can Can," *New York Times,* XXIV (Dec. 24, 1874), 5.

Canfield, Mary C. "The Great American Art," *New Republic,* XXXII (Nov. 22, 1922), 334-35.

"The Concert Saloon Reform," *New York Times,* XI (April 25, 1862), 5.

"Concert Saloon Reform," *New York Times,* XI (April 26, 1862), 8.

"Decline of Vaudeville," *Harper's Monthly,* CVI (April, 1903), 811-15.

Eaton, Walter Prichard. "The Wizards of Vaudeville," *McClure,* LV (Sept., 1923), 43-49.

"Funeral of Tony Pastor's Mother," *New York Times,* XXXVI (Aug. 4, 1887), 2.

Goewey, Edwin A. "Tony Pastor, the Starmaker," *Dance Magazine,* XII (Aug., 1929), 12-13, 57, 58.

Hartley, M. "Vaudeville," *Dial,* LXVIII (March, 1920), 335-42.

Kingsley, W. J."Reconstruction of Vaudeville," *National Magazine,* XL (May, 1919), 173-75.

Laurie, Jr., Joseph. "Early Days of Vaudeville," *American Mercury,* LXII (Feb., 1946), 232-36.

New York Clipper. 1853-1895, and random issues.

New York (Dramatic) Mirror, 1879-1908.

New York Dramatic News. 1875-1880, and random issues.

New York Herald. 1860-1865, and random issues.

"The Passing of Tony Pastor," *Green Book Album,* I (Jan., 1909), 190-92.

Royle, Edwin. "The Vaudeville Theatre," *Scribner's Magazine,* XXVI (1899), 485-95.

Russell, Lillian. "Lillian Russell's Reminiscences," *Cosmopolitan,* LXXII (Feb., 1922), 560-64.

Sargent, Espes W. "Fathers of Vaudeville," *Green Book Album,* II (Sept., 1909), 560-64.

Sherlock, C. R. "Where the Vaudeville holds the Boards," *Cosmopolitan,* XXXII (Feb., 1902), 411-20.

Spitzer, Marian. "Morals in the Two-a-day," *American Mercury,* III (Sept., 1924), 35-39.

" 'Tony' Pastor Dead in his 77th Year," *New York Times,* LVII (Aug. 27, 1908), 7.

"Tony Pastor, Father of Vaudeville," *Harper's Weekly,* LII (Sept. 5, 1908), 10.

"Tony Pastor's Fortune," *Billboard,* XXII (Oct. 22, 1910), 12.

"Tony Pastor's Funeral," *New York Times,* LVII (Aug. 29, 1908), 9.

Traber, J. Milton. "Pen Sketch of 'Tony' Pastor, the Father of Modern Variety," *Billboard,* XXIII (Feb. 18, 1911), 5, 42.

"Trend of Vaudeville," *Independence,* LII (May 9, 1901), 1092-93.

"The Variety Stage," *Harper's Weekly,* XLVI (March 22, 1902), 380.

"The Variety Stage," *Harper's Weekly,* XLVI (March 29, 1902), 414.

"The Variety Stage," *Harper's Weekly,* XLVI (April 12, 1902), 466.

Variety. 1905-1908.

Wilkes' Spirit of the Times. 1860-1880, and random issues.

MISCELLANEOUS

"Account of Proceedings, in the Matter of the Judicial Settlement of the Account of Josephine M. Pastor as Administratrix with the will annexed, of Antonio Pastor," filed on Jan. 11, 1911, Hall of Records, Surrogate's Court of the County of New York, N. Y. C.

American Vaudeville File, MWEZ n.c. #4547, Theatre Collection at the New York Public Library.

Bristow, Eugene. "Look Out for Saturday Night: A Social History of Professional Variety Theatre in Memphis, Tennessee, 1859-1880." Unpublished Ph.D. dissertation, State University of Iowa, 1956.

Davidson, Frank Costello. "The Rise, Development, Decline, and Influence of the American Minstrel Show." Unpublished Ph. D. dissertation, New York University, 1952.

Letter from Irving Berlin, May 23, 1963.

Letter from Sophie Tucker, May 9, 1963.

New York City Vaudeville File, Theatre Collection at Harvard University.

New York State Legislature. "An Act to Regulate Places of Amusement in the Cities and Incorporated Villages in this State." *Statutes at Large of the State of New York.* Edited by John W. Edmonds. 5 vols.; Albany: Weed, Parsons, and Co., 1869, III, chp. 281, pp. 323-25.

"Report of the Appraiser, in Matter of Transfer Tax Upon Estate of Antonio Pastor," filed on Oct. 4, 1909, Hall of Records, Surrogate's Court of the County of New York, N. Y. C.

Robinson Locke File, Series II, Theatre Collection at the New York Public Library.

Tony Pastor File, Theatre Collection at Harvard University.

Tony Pastor File, the Hoblitzelle Theatre Arts Library, the University of Texas at Austin.

Tony Pastor File, Theatre Collection at the Museum of the City of New York.

Tony Pastor File, MWEZ n.c. #11,143, Theatre Collection at the New York Public Library.

147

TONY PASTOR: DEAN OF THE VAUDEVILLE STAGE

Tony Pastor File, Theatre Collection at the Princeton University Library.

Townsend Walsh File of Miscellaneous Programs, MWEZ n.c. #5181, Theatre Collection at the New York Public Library.

Vaudeville and Variety File, Theatre Collection at Harvard University.

"Will of Antonio Pastor," dated Jan. 21, 1899, and filed on Sept. 3, 1908, Hall of Records, Surrogate's Court of the County of New York, N. Y. C.

INDEX

INDEX

INDEX